ABACUS

THE WAVES

PEN & SWORD MILITARY CLASSICS

We hope you enjoy your Pen and Sword Military Classic. The series is designed to give readers quality military history at affordable prices. Pen and Sword Classics are available from all good bookshops. If you would like to keep in touch with further developments in the series.

Telephone: **01226 734555**
email: **enquiries@pen–and–sword.co.uk**
or visit our website at **www.pen-and-sword.co.uk**

ABOVE US THE WAVES

THE STORY OF MIDGET SUBMARINES AND HUMAN TORPEDOES

by
C.E.T. WARREN & JAMES BENSON

With a Foreword by
Amiral Sir George Creasy
G.C.B. C.B.E. D.S.O. M.V.O.
Commander-in-Chief, Home Fleet

PEN & SWORD MILITARY CLASSICS

We shall see, while above us
The waves roar and whirl,
A ceiling of amber,
A pavement of pearl.

Matthew Arnold,
The Forsaken Merman

First published in Great Britain in 1953 by George G. Harrap & Co. Ltd

Published in this format in 2006 by
Pen & Sword Military Classics
An imprint of
Pen & Sword Books Ltd
47 Church Street
Barnsley
South Yorkshire
S70 2AS

ISBN 1 84415 440 8
ISBN 978 1 84415 440 1

Printed and bound in England
By CPI UK

Pen & Sword Books Ltd incorporates the Imprints of Pen & Sword Aviation,
Pen & Sword Maritime, Pen & Sword Military, Wharncliffe Local history,
Pen & Sword Select, Pen & Sword Military Classics and Leo Cooper.

For a complete list of Pen & Sword titles please contact
PEN & SWORD BOOKS LIMITED
47 Church Street, Barnsley, South Yorkshire, S70 2AS, England
E-mail: enquiries@pen-and-sword.co.uk
Website: www.pen-and-sword.co.uk

Foreword

by

ADMIRAL SIR GEORGE CREASY
G.C.B. C.B.E. D.S.O. M.V.O.
Commander-in-Chief, Home Fleet

I HAD the great honour to command the Submarine Branch of the Royal Navy from September 1944 to October 1946.

Included in my command were the gallant officers and ratings who manned our midget submarines and were our 'charioteers.'

This book tells their story. The reader will note how great were the differences between the work of those who served 'in' the midget submarines and those who sat 'on' and 'outside' the 'chariots.' But I am sure the reader will also note the similarities in the human qualities called for in both types of service. Both demanded great courage, cool wits and determination, and physical endurance of a high standard. He or she will also be able to judge from these pages the splendid response to these demands that came from those whose adventures are here described.

I chanced to be visiting the Twelfth Submarine Flotilla at Port Bannatyne when *X.24* returned from her successful mission to destroy the floating dock at Bergen described on pages 167 to 170. I was present when Lieutenant H. P. Westmacott, who commanded her, came in to make his report and to tell his story. He made the whole business seem entirely matter-of-fact and a purely routine affair. I do not think I was half so successful in concealing the thrill I got out of hearing his description of his exploit or my admiration for the stout-hearted crew who had achieved it.

These thoughts came back to me in reading the proofs of this book. I hope it will be widely read by the public and its readers will find the same difficulty in laying the book down before finishing it which I encountered.

GEORGE CREASY
Admiral

H.M.S. *Vanguard*, PORTSMOUTH
July 21, 1953

Acknowledgments

THE authors wish gratefully to record their indebtedness to the following who, by supplying photographs, information, and advice, have helped in the production of this book. It is emphasized, however, that the authors are solely and jointly responsible for all opinions expressed, for all factual errors contained in the text, and for all shortcomings.

Lieutenant R. Aitken, D.S.O., R.N.V.R.; Captain W. E. Banks, C.B.E., D.S.C., R.N. (retired); C. L. Berey, D.S.M.; Sub-Lieutenant A. K. Bergius, D.S.C., R.N.V.R.; Lady Boynton (especially for her help in matters relating to the late Admiral Sir Max Horton); Lieutenant W. R. Brewster, D.S.C., R.N.V.R.; Sub-Lieutenant J. Britnell, R.N.V.R.; Lieutenant-Commander J. Brooks, D.S.C., R.N.; A. Brown, D.S.M.; S. Buxton; Sub-Lieutenant M. R. Causer, D.S.O., R.N.V.R.; Commissioned Bos'n C. W. Chadwick, R.N. (retired); The Controller, Her Majesty's Stationery Office (for permission to quote extracts from Supplement to *The London Gazette*, Cmd. 38204/993, of February 10, 1948, and from *His Majesty's Submarines*); Lieutenant L. G. Cooper, R.N.V.R.; Rear-Admiral R. B. Darke, C.B., D.S.O.; Sir Robert H. Davis, D. Sc.(Hon.), F.R.S.A. (Chairman of Siebe, Gorman and Co. Ltd); J. W. Eides Forlag, Bergen (for permission to quote extracts from *Shetlands Larsen*, by Frithjof Saelen); Lieutenant R. Elliott, R.N.V.R.; Lieutenant-Commander D. C. Evans, R.N.V.R.; Captain W. R. Fell, C.B.E., D.S.C., R.N. (retired); A. Ferrier, C.G.M.; Lieutenant D. T. J. Grant, R.N.V.R.; Lieutenant R. T. G. Greenland, D.S.O., R.N.V.R.; Sub-Lieutenant G. Harding, R.N.V.R.; Commander P. E. H. Heathfield, R.N. (retired); Commander G. Herbert, R.N. (retired); Lieutenant R. S. Hobson, R.N.V.R.; Lieutenant G. B. Honour, D.S.C., R.N.V.R.; Lieutenant D. C. Howarth, R.N.V.R. (author of *The Shetland Bus*); Lieutenant K. H. Hudspeth, D.S.C., R.A.N.V.R.; Lieutenant R. H. Kendall, D. S. O., R.N.V.R.; A. C. Kirby; Lieutenant G. W. J. Larkin, R.N.V.R.; Leif Larsen, D.S.O., D.S.C., C.G.M., D.S.M.; Lieutenant J. T. Lorimer, D.S.O., R.N.V.R.; Lieutenant-Commander

J. McCarter, S.A.N.F. (V.); Lieutenant W. Morrison, R.N.V.R.; Sub-Lieutenant F. Ogden, M.B.E., R.N.V.R.; Lieutenant-Commander S. G. S. Pawle, R.N.V.R.; Lieutenant P. H. Philip, M.B.E., S.A.N.F. (V.); Commander B. C. G. Place, V.C., D.S.C., R.N.; H. A. Pomeroy, D.S.M.; Commander H. L. Rendell, R.N. (retired); St Catherine Press, Ltd (for permission to quote extracts from *Deep Diving and Submarine Operations*, by Sir Robert H. Davis); Commissioned Gunner W. S. Smith, D.S.M., R.N.; Lieutenant H. L. H. Stevens, R.N.V.R.; Mr E. G. A. Thompson (of the Department of the Chief of Naval Information, Admiralty); Lieutenant-Commander H. E. W. Washington, R.N.V.R.; and Commander H. P. Westmacott, D.S.O., D.S.C., R.N.

The authors also feel that they would like to indicate the division of labour involved in the preparation of this chronicle. First of all, the responsibility for all the human torpedo content was Warren's, while Benson was similarly concerned with all the midget submarine parts of the book. Secondly, Warren undertook the general preparation of rough drafts, the collection of data, and other miscellaneous duties, with the large part of the creative writing and the editing of the contributed matter being the work of Benson. Both authors found it only too easy to develop a keen critical faculty in respect of the *other's* work!

C.E.T.W.
J. B.

Contents

PART IV.   THE COAST OF EUROPE

PART V.   THE FAR EAST

Illustrations

Maps and Diagrams

PART I: HOME WATERS

CHAPTER ONE

Safely in Harbour

Prime Minister to General Ismay for Chiefs of Staff Committee.
January 18, 1942.

Please report what is being done to emulate the exploits of the Italians in Alexandria Harbour and similar methods of this kind.

At the beginning of the War Colonel Jefferis[1] had a number of bright ideas on this subject, which received very little encouragement. Is there any reason why we should be incapable of the same kind of scientific aggressive action that the Italians have shown? One would have thought we should have been in the lead.

Please state the exact position.[2]

M̶R CHURCHILL had realized that the enemy's employment of a manned torpedo was a mode of warfare particularly suited to the capabilities and needs of Britain in the dark days of 1942. Heavy capital units of the German and Italian navies were constituting a serious menace to our lines of communication and compelling large-scale strategic positioning of our own capital ships, merely by remaining safely for months on end in strongly defended anchorages.

The Navy had not been blind to this situation and was already in the process of producing a midget submarine—the *X*-craft—to be manned by three or four men.[3] The development of this weapon was proving to be a lengthy business, so much so that when the Prime Minister's memorandum reached the late Sir Max Horton,[4] then Flag Officer Submarines, the need for an immediate underwater striking-force became apparent. British human torpedoes were accordingly conceived as a stop-gap, awaiting the completion of the midget submarine.

The two weapons were entirely different, although designed to achieve similar objects. The *X*-craft was a complete submarine in

---

[1] See Appendix I.
[2] From Sir Winston Churchill's *The Second World War*, Vol. IV (*The Hinge of Fate*) (published by Cassell and Co., Ltd).
[3] See Appendix I.   [4] Admiral Sir Max K. Horton, G.C.B., D.S.O.

miniature, with internal living-space for its small crew; the human torpedo—or "chariot," as it became known to the Navy—was ridden by a crew of two, who wore self-contained diving-suits and sat astride. In short, one could 'sit in' or 'sit on.'

Two things were therefore necessary for the building of an efficient human-torpedo force: machines and men. The provision of the former was the easier task. An Italian machine had been salvaged by naval divers after an abortive attack at Gibraltar. Based on this, and on a wealth of pre-War British ideas on the subject,[1] the first chariot was soon in course of construction. About the same size as an ordinary torpedo, but driven by electric batteries, it had a joy-stick control for rudder and hydroplanes, together with pump mechanism and compressed-air supplies for emptying and filling its tanks.

'Number One' of the two-man crew had to be responsible for driving and navigating the machine from the for'ard of the two seating positions. His partner assisted him in negotiating the nets and securing the torpedo's detachable warhead to the hull of the target.

A call for volunteers for human torpedoes—or, for that matter, for midget submarines—while certain to have met a ready response, would have meant telling the enemy what the Admiralty was about. Furthermore, the types of person volunteering would have included many with the suicidal, death-or-glory outlook. And this was not what was wanted. The 'one-way-ticket' was never part of the plan, even though there was to be an admittedly large risk of being taken prisoner-of-war.

Recruitment had to be a somewhat roundabout process, and it needs little imagination to understand the enormous responsibilities that rested on the two officers who were appointed to form the 'selection committee.' The two men were submariners of the same rank: Commander G. M. Sladen, D.S.O., D.S.C., R.N.,[2] and Commander W. R. Fell, D.S.C., R.N.[3]

More widely differing characters it would have been impossible to find. Both were moulded in the traditions of the Submarine Service and both were well known for their eagerness to engage the enemy whenever and wherever he could be found. But there the likeness ended.

"Tiny" Fell was the elder. In spite of his nickname he was slight and somewhat short. He was a sympathetic type of man, considerate to a fault in his dealings with other people, proud of his New

---

[1] See Appendix I.   [2] Now Captain Sladen.
[3] Now Captain W. R. Fell, C.B.E., D.S.C., R.N. (retired).

Zealand parentage and equally of his long service in submarines. All
told, it was not surprising that he had the gift of seeming to reduce
the inevitable gap between officer and rating.

At the beginning of the War he had been Captain (S/M) of a submarine flotilla at Portland. In the depot-ship *Alecto* he was the
father of a very happy family. But it was not long before he succeeded in transferring to a more active rôle and became engaged in
cloak-and-dagger operations off the coast of Eire. After this he was
appointed to lead a series of fire- and block-ships against the invasion
ports of France, and later he commanded the Combined Operations
Infantry Assault Ship *Prince Charles*, operating during this appointment in Norwegian waters. He was still holding that command
when, in March 1942, the ship returned to London to refit.

By chance Tiny made his way from London Docks to Northways,
a block of London luxury flats which formed the war-time headquarters of the Submarine Service. His mission was solely one of
seeking news of old friends, and no one could have been more surprised when he was asked if he would consider rejoining 'boats' in an
unusual capacity. His record service of twenty-two years in submarines made the answer obvious, and he was immediately whisked
in to see Sir Max Horton,[1] who told him of the Italian human-
torpedo attack in Alexandria.

"Are you interested in starting something similar?" asked Sir Max.

"I am, sir," was the reply.

"Well, get down to Blockhouse, find Sladen and two or three mad-
men he has collected, and build and train a team of charioteers."

Sladen was a whirlwind. Whereas Fell appealed to a subordinate's
sense of respect through his immense charm and understanding,
Sladen's attraction was through his extraordinary capabilities. He
had the genius of the quick decision, the unlimited energy, the great
physical strength, and the outstanding ability at sport that the
regular-serving naval rating looks for in the ideal officer. Standing
over six feet tall, weighing a good thirteen stone, and with a personality that swept all before it, "Slasher" Sladen was a man who
could not abide inefficiency. He had gained four England Rugger
caps, but this never stopped him from turning out to play in goal for
his submarine's soccer team—even at short notice on a Sunday
afternoon—and cheerfully accepting all the good-natured abuse from
the touch-line whenever he failed to stop the impossible.

Immediately before coming to human torpedoes he had been in
command of the submarine *Trident*, and before that of the *Oswald*.

[1] See Appendix I.

B

His numerous successes had included the torpedoing of the German heavy cruiser *Prinz Eugen*, many surface gun-actions off the coast of Norway, and several patrols from the Russian base at Murmansk.

His energy and Fell's experience were to make them the perfect pair. Both in the selection and in the training of chariot-classes they made few, if any, mistakes. It was a criterion of their success that within ten months of the first man having volunteered for a "hazardous operation" chariots had shown a credit of several thousand tons of enemy shipping.

The first batch of charioteers, completely unaware of their destiny, assembled in Blockhouse early in April 1942, to form the beginning of the Experimental Submarine Flotilla. They had joined by various routes. Some had volunteered for hazardous operations just for the fun of it; others had been dissatisfied with their previous ships or units; one, at least, had asked Sladen for a job, little knowing that this would not mean a posting to submarines proper. For the first few days the ten volunteers were occupied either with rather detailed medical examinations or else with D.S.E.A. (Davis Submarine Escape Apparatus) training in the diving-tank.

While all this was going on, and unknown to every one except Fell and Sladen, "Cassidy" was being constructed. "Cassidy" was a wooden dummy of a chariot, an inert, lifeless monster who was controlled—this was the intention, anyway—by hydroplanes, rudder, ballast-tank, and compressed air. The day finally dawned when he was ready to be ridden underwater, and he was taken to Horsea Loch. This was an ideal site in a deserted corner of Portsmouth Harbour; a sheltered stretch of water, trough-shaped to a depth of thirty feet. "Cassidy" was unloaded from a lorry several sizes too small, but not before this became the first of many occasions on which Sladen's strength of arm and command of vocabulary came to the fore.

Next morning the sun was shining. Canvas screens were spread round the top end of the loch, and everything was set for the great experiment. "Chuck" Bonnell, a Canadian R.N.V.R. lieutenant,[1] and "Jim" Warren, a stoker petty officer from submarines,[2] formed the first team. They struggled inside their light-weight diving-suits, forced on their nose-clips, and gripped tight on their mouthpieces. Then the oxygen-breathing apparatus was fitted. This was an ordinary Submarine Escape set with a second bottle of oxygen. Sloppy boots, with slabs of lead in the sole, completed the outfit, except for a lifeline

[1] The late Lieutenant C. E. Bonnell, D.S.C., R.C.N.V.R.
[2] Now Lieutenant C. E. T. Warren, M.B.E., R.N.V.R.

on which could be given prearranged signals, the most important of which was "Open the second bottle."

"Cassidy," like an untried colt, was secured by a line to the stern of a small motor-dinghy, in which Fell sat and Sladen stood. Bonnell and Warren mounted. If they knew anything about what to expect, it was certainly very little. Their orders were to open the vent in the ballast tank, to put the hydroplanes hard to dive, and to keep just off the bottom.

It all sounded very simple, and it should doubtless have been a dramatic moment, but "Cassidy" refused to dive. Perhaps it was his extreme youth that made him obstinate, or maybe he just saw no reason for leaving the surface. Anyway, he refused to dive. Pounds and pounds of lead were nailed all over him, but for a long time he remained steadfast. However, he had finally to admit that there was a limit to all things, and sank slowly until his riders looked for the first time on what were to become familiar sights—seaweed, rock, and mud.

While the coercing of "Cassidy" was taking place Fell and Sladen must have exchanged a quiet smile. Unknown to any of the charioteers, they had already ridden the machine in a near-by experimental tank, where they had been towed up and down by the overhead gantry. After having trimmed light in the fresh water, they had made no adjustment for the salt water of Horsea. This had caused the long delay in diving. They never said a word.

CHAPTER TWO

An Idea takes Shape

IT would be some little while before the first mechanical human tor-pedo could be delivered, and the initial emphasis was on the prepara-tion of the 'human' element, leaving the 'torpedo' part until later. In a comparatively short time a new entrant could be initiated into the first principles of the necessary diving-techniques, and he soon lost the feeling of being a greenhorn. An essential qualification for a diving-instructor engaged on this type of training must have been supreme patience and a great understanding of human nature. To the apprentice diver, pitchforked for the first time into a strange diving-suit, everything felt cold and clammy and seemed too insecure to be protective.

Not until the moment of total submersion did the situation improve and confidence come rushing back with the realization that everything the instructor had said was dead right. Definitely the best part of diving was being in the water, and the worst part by far was the business of getting dressed. Shoving one's head inside a tight rubber hood could be painful in the extreme. All the pulling and pushing that was necessary did unbelievable damage to one's hair and ears. There was too the unpleasant job of thrusting hands and wrists through the very narrow, strong rubber cuffs of the suit. Equally unnatural were the mouthpiece and tight nose-clip, which were essential for the efficient working of the breathing-apparatus.

The first training-classes could not have had better diving-instructors. Fort Blockhouse had provided perhaps its two finest D.S.E.A. staff for the new venture. Chief Petty Officers Jack Passey[1] and Tom Otway[2] were both well past retiring age and had spent a life-time in submarines. With their personalities and experience it was small wonder that they were soon the most popular couple in Chariots.

Already the new idea had not divided simply into 'Men' and

[1] Now Warrant Bos'n J. G. Passey, R.N. (retired).
[2] Now ex-Chief Petty Officer T. Otway, B.E.M.

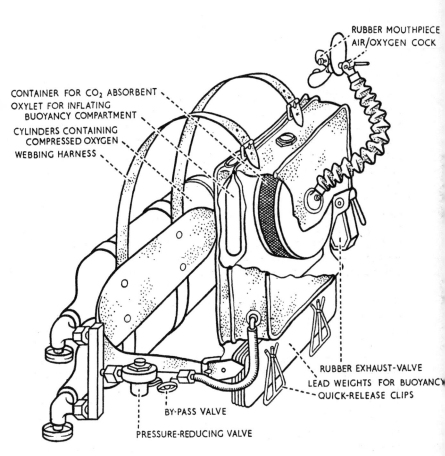

RUBBER MOUTHPIECE
AIR/OXYGEN COCK

CONTAINER FOR CO₂ ABSORBENT
OXYLET FOR INFLATING
    BUOYANCY COMPARTMENT
CYLINDERS CONTAINING
    COMPRESSED OXYGEN
WEBBING HARNESS

RUBBER EXHAUST-VALVE
LEAD WEIGHTS FOR BUOYANCY
QUICK-RELEASE CLIPS

BY-PASS VALVE

PRESSURE-REDUCING VALVE

DIAGRAMMATIC SKETCH OF HUMAN-TORPEDO OXYGEN BREATHING-APPARATUS OF ENDURANCE UP TO NINE HOURS

X-craft divers used the same apparatus modified for shorter endurance.

By Petty Officer Charles Kirby, Royal Fleet Reserve

'Machines.' There was a third element, 'Breathing.' As early as March 1942 Siebe, Gorman and Co., the diving and submarine engineers, were asked to attend a conference. The demand for invisibility in this type of work made any sort of air-diving, with its constant stream of bubbles, completely out of the question. And when the possibility of breathing 'closed-circuit' oxygen at eighty feet was broached Mr Gorman Davis[1] pointed out that this would probably bring about fatal poisoning in a matter of seconds.

The nature of this poisoning—expected in theory to occur in varying degrees as soon as a diver went below thirty feet—was in the form of over-stimulation of the nerve-centres of the brain and also of drastic changes in the metabolism of the body. It was reckoned that divers breathing oxygen could reasonably go to fifty feet for very short periods. Definite symptoms had to be watched for, and these included pronounced twitching of the extremities, the experience of great difficulty in maintaining a tight lip-seal over the mouthpiece, the creation of intense and unjustifiable optimism, and, finally, the usual signs of increasing intoxication until total collapse.

All in all there was a good case for the forming of the Admiralty Experimental Diving Unit,[2] to undertake what was probably the most exhaustive programme of human experiments ever attempted on one aspect of diving.

"Many of the divers"—to quote Sir Robert Davis[3]—

were taken to the point of unconsciousness and convulsions, and the young staff of the Unit showed great courage in submitting themselves cheerfully to these experiments. In spite of the risk and unpleasantnesses of the job, the experimental department was always a scene of cheerful activity.

Meanwhile the charioteers were marking time, some of them not very patiently. In order to keep them busy, and to broaden their underwater experience at the same time, it was decided to give them a course of heavy-suited helmet-diving. Soon they were out in open water in the Solent, where they came under the cheerful care and expressive counsel of Diving Gunner C. W. Chadwick.[4] "Chads" taught them much, not only about diving, but also about the Royal Navy in general. He was a character in a thousand. Red-faced, barrel-shaped, perpetually smiling, he was a man who, when not

[1] Mr R. W. G. Davis, M.A. (Cantab), now Managing Director, Siebe, Gorman and Co., Ltd.
[2] See Appendix I.
[3] Sir Robert H. Davis, D.Sc. (Hon.), F.R.S.A., Chairman, Siebe, Gorman and Co., Ltd, author of *Deep Diving and Submarine Operations*.
[4] Now Commissioned Bos'n C. W. Chadwick, R.N. (retired).

otherwise employed, would endeavour to test his capacity for alcoholic liquid. And he drank, as he worked, extremely capably. When
all other drinkers had retired from the fray he could still be found
emptying his glass and puffing at his enormous pipe, ruminating
about the lack of appreciation of the pleasures of life evidenced by
the modern Navy. The helmet-diving course was something of a
holiday, and it was almost with regret that the classes saw the last of
the diving-boat and of Chads's breezy cheerfulness and returned to
continue training in their light suits in Horsea Loch, breaking the
monotony every now and again with a run on the towed "Cassidy."

Outstanding men are often remembered by small mannerisms or
sayings. So it was with Tom Otway. He will always be known for
his "Are you comfortable?" before he would let a diver go down.
And, although he was inevitably given the affirmative, he would
never relax while a man was in the water. He was unbelievably
painstaking, and in spite of his ability to deliver a reprimand when it
was called for, he was never annoyed by any question, however
simple, nor by any accusation, however outrageous.

Perhaps it may not be easily understood how the instructors could
and did suffer from a day-to-day tension which would persist,
particularly with inexperienced classes. The charioteers were daily
undergoing fresh experiences, some of which were mildly hair-
raising, but all of which could be worrying in the right combination
of circumstances. And then there was the tongue-loosening effect,
so similar to that of alcohol, of oxygen breathed under pressure.
Hard words were spoken occasionally, all from the one side, and it
is to the credit of the two instructors that the remarks were always
accepted in the spirit in which they were usually not offered. They
never retaliated.

A typical bone of contention was a wet shirt. It was most pro-
voking, to say the least, to feel the cold water of Horsea Loch seeping
in round one's middle, and it was the easiest thing in the world to
convince oneself—and to voice that conviction immediately one's
mouth could become active—that the suit was at fault. As the
instructors worked late until every suit was inspected and even the
smallest item of equipment checked, this was tantamount to blaming
them. But they took no offence, and simply pointed out, quite
calmly, that if the 'dresser' had clamped the diver in correctly the
diver would have stayed dry. So one turned one's wrath against
whichever of the others had tightened the belly-clamps. In time
there were enough suits and breathing-sets for each diver to have his
own and to maintain it himself.

The early classes would have been hard put to it to say whom they would have preferred on their diving-ladder—Tom Otway or Jack Passey. The latter's instructional methods were unique. Although he lavished every bit as much care and attention on his charges as did the obviously careful Otway, it appeared to the uninitiated that, so long as he could detect faint signs of life, there was no excuse for coming out of the water before time. In actual fact his exacting demands were invaluable in the difficult task of extending the divers' limits of endurance. His seemingly scornful "No, you stop down" and his boot on a surfacing diver's shoulder were great persuaders. And in off-duty hours he was Chads's only rival.

The weather was good in that early spring, and for the charioteers life was exceedingly pleasant. More and more men were coming in; by the 1st of June there were twenty-four R.N.V.R. officers, two Army officers, and thirty-one ratings (including such trades as cooks, signalmen, and stokers, in addition to the seaman branch), and training was taking a wider and more serious turn. Then, completely out of the blue, the charioteers had their first casualty.

Lieutenant P. C. A. Browning, R.N.V.R., was doing a routine dive when his attendant reported that the lifeline had come free. This did not mean immediate disaster, for it was easy to surface under one's own power. No time was wasted, however. Agreed underwater sound-signals were made, telling Browning to surface. Search-parties explored the bottom of the loch without success. Eventually the horrible truth had to be faced. A team of helmet-divers was sent for, and shortly after six that evening the body was recovered.

Here was an event nobody had foreseen. It came as a shock that death could be lying in comparatively shallow water, in daylight and in perfect diving conditions. There was no doubt that the classes were sobered down, for a time at least. The job was not going to be anything like as easy as it had seemed.

And so, as the first classes packed up at Blockhouse and prepared to leave for Scotland, they were filled with a new spirit of calm determination. They realized that the next stage of the adventure would demand technical efficiency under water, rather than any devil-may-care enthusiasm.

CHAPTER THREE

Scotland and Portsmouth

T HE party travelling north reported on board the newly recommissioned *Titania* (Captain H. R. Conway, R.N.[1]), lying in the Clyde. "Tites"—as she was known throughout the Submarine Service—was a depot-ship of long standing, having brooded over flotillas on the China and Mediterranean stations before the War.

Within a few days she weighed and proceeded for an unknown destination. As she steamed westward down the Clyde estuary the charioteer officers found themselves taking watch-keeping duties, some for the first time. When not on the bridge they joined the others in the profitless business of guessing 'where' and 'when.' This state of affairs continued as "Tites" rounded the Mull of Kintyre and headed north. Rum, Eigg, Skye, and Muck passed abeam, course was laid through the Little Minch, and eventually the islands of the Outer Hebrides were approached close to, and an entry was made into Loch Erisort, not far from Stornoway, in the Island of Lewis. There "Tites" anchored and settled down to stay.

The new base—known as Port D—was really in the wilds. In a position near the head of the loch "Tites" lay abeam of a few scattered houses on the north bank, with the 'village' of several small crofts to the south. The immediate neighbourhood was completed, as far as habitations were concerned, by a large lonely mansion lying roughly due west. The nearest forces of the Crown were a not-far-distant R.A.F. station and a motor-launch and some trawlers operating from Stornoway.

Tiny Fell had travelled north in charge of the charioteers, and he was immediately making plans—and implementing them—for the establishment of an operational training base and the recommencement of training as soon as possible. Emphasis was to be on extending underwater endurance, so that when the machines arrived all that would be needed would be an adaptation to the idea of riding to work. The chapel-cum-schoolhouse, lying down by the water's

[1] Now Captain H. R. Conway, R.N. (retired).

edge, was taken over as a shore workshop, and Tom Otway was installed. Fell decided to operate "Cassidy" in the neighbourhood of the workshop and to prepare another position for the pure diving activities. The latter was sited half a mile away in an excellent spot, sheltered and surrounded by high cliffs. Here "Tites'" shipwrights set to work, with the charioteers' assistance, and soon completed a small landing-stage with a permanent ladder down into the water for the divers. At high tide there was a comfortable twenty feet under the ladder, and as the loch shelved rapidly there was not far to go before a depth of thirty feet was reached. At that time, while results were still being awaited from the A.E.D.U., no diver was supposed to go deeper than thirty feet—so the new site was admirable in every way.

The usual drill with "Cassidy" was for the two divers to get into the water, discover if and where the suits were leaking, and if they did not feel too wet and miserable haul themselves astride. The towing motor-boat would then go ahead, and when the appropriate signal was passed the diver who was riding as Number One would open the main ballast-vent, release the air, and cause the machine to dive. After about fifteen or twenty minutes of being towed under-water, he would bring "Cassidy" to the surface again.

It was at about this time that the diving-apparatus was in the process of changing. The dress itself, which later became known as the Sladen suit[1], remained largely the same, but a visor was incor-porated in place of the individual eyepieces. This window was designed to be wide enough to allow a pair of night binoculars to be used, a great advantage in seeking out targets in dark conditions.

At Erisort during these early weeks there were the first three classes of charioteers, and the fourth was expected to arrive in the near future. Recruitment was continuing, and the interviewing of volunteers was one of the several tasks being performed by Com-mander Sladen, who had stayed south in Portsmouth. His other main occupation was 'chasing' the manufacturers for the first mechanical models and the new diving-gear.

Eventually, and quite suddenly—for Sladen's ideas of security meant putting no one gratuitously "in the picture"—he turned up with the first powered chariot, which immediately became known as the "Real One." "Cassidy," more intimately named, was probably also held closer to the heart in those days. However, the "Real One" had arrived and had to be ridden. For this purpose Sub-Lieutenant Pat Grant and Stoker Petty Officer Warren had been kept behind

[1] Now the Admiralty Pattern Shallow Water Diving Dress.

from the first class, remaining in Portsmouth and helping the instructors until there was new work to be done, or, more accurately, until the new plaything was delivered.

At last, in early June, the great day came. Large packing-cases were joined by a battery, screens were erected at each end of the Blockhouse floating dock, and the monster was assembled. This was done partly by and partly under the watchful eyes of the experts. There were a considerable number of the latter—technical boys, back-room boys, and other very learned boys with titles too difficult to remember—and as soon as the "Real One" was assembled they were tilting her, turning her, examining her, and testing her. What they found out no charioteer ever discovered, which fact caused many good-hearted witticisms, but at the same time no right-minded member of the flotilla was ever unappreciative of the part played by the experts in providing him with a steed that could be relied upon whatever the going.

And so the "Real One" was pronounced ready to be ridden. She was the same size as a normal twenty-one-inch torpedo, with a detachable head containing 600 pounds of explosive. Her battery had an endurance of approximately six hours at 2·9 knots, giving a range of eighteen miles. She had a ballast-tank, as in the wooden model, a compass, an instrument panel with several luminous dials, rather like a car dashboard, and a rudder and hydroplanes aft. There was the same trouble with manhandling her into the water as there had been with "Cassidy," but there the likeness was going to end. It would be easy. One just had to sit astride and drive along— or so every one thought.

Final tests were made. The pumps were run, the hydroplanes and rudder were found to answer, the high-pressure air-bottle was full. In short, she was in perfect working condition. It was at this point that Sladen sprang the surprise of the afternoon.

"Get dressed, Warren. And, Passey, get me into a suit."

So that was how it was to be. Sladen was going to 'have a go,' on the principle of an officer not asking his men to do something he was not prepared to do himself. For Warren this was to be a temporary resumption of the close relationship that had been built up in a submarine's control-room. But there may have been one or two doubtful minds about the wisdom of Sladen's decision, for he had not used the suit or the set more than half a dozen times. However, no one argued with him, and as soon as his huge frame had been forced inside an ordinary-size suit they were ready to start.

With the two divers seated astride—Sladen acting as Number One

—the machine moved off slowly into the middle of the loch. There, after much fiddling with the controls to the accompaniment of many muttered curses, the "Real One" was baptized. Once she reached the bottom Sladen and Warren dismounted and made all the adjustments necessary to give her a perfect 'trim.' This process of trimming a machine on the bottom was to become the most reliable and the most frequently practised method, whenever conditions permitted. In actual fact a pure neutral buoyancy was seldom obtained. It was easier, and most people preferred it, anyway, to have the machine slightly positive and the riders slightly negative.

Soon after this first trimming experiment Sladen and Warren returned to the shore, where Sladen undressed and Grant mounted astern of Warren, who had taken over the controls. Then came an announcement from out of the blue that Flag Officer Submarines and Admiral King, U.S. Navy, would be down on the following morning to see a demonstration. This meant rushing the afternoon's programme, and the two divers were hard put to it to master the little lady's habits as well as rehearse the morrow's show-off. Eventually Sladen was satisfied, and he ordered the machine to be driven on the surface to the other end of the loch, where she could be lifted, split open, and the battery put on charge. It was in the carrying out of this simple instruction that tragedy was only averted by the prompt action of Jack Passey. Warren was still at the chariot's controls when, turning to see who was following in the motor-boat, he knocked open his D.S.E.A. cylinder valve. The full pressure hit him in the lungs, and, unconscious, he rolled off the machine and into the water. In a flash Passey was alongside and had grabbed him before serious harm could be done. This near-tragedy was another reminder that there could be no relaxation at any time while there was a man in the water.

There can be no doubt that the next day was a very happy one for Geoffrey Sladen. He had succeeded in producing some men, some diving-gear, and a real human torpedo within less than three months of the project having been started. And if all went well he and his boys were going to show the American admiral something that was scarcely thought possible. As it turned out Admiral King did not think the whole thing *was* possible. Even after the demonstration he still thought the idea was "crazy"—though a few months later the charioteers were wondering whether he had changed his mind. However, before a large crowd of senior officers Warren and Grant set off. They were in luck's way. The "Real One" behaved perfectly. She dived and surfaced, answered rudder and hydroplanes, all in the

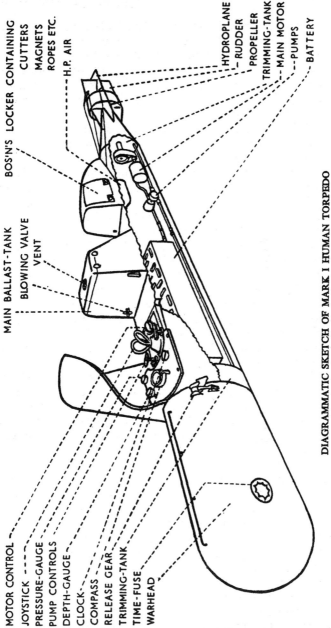

MOTOR CONTROL
JOYSTICK
PRESSURE-GAUGE
PUMP CONTROLS
DEPTH-GAUGE
CLOCK
COMPASS
RELEASE GEAR
TRIMMING-TANK
TIME-FUSE
WARHEAD

MAIN BALLAST-TANK
BLOWING VALVE
VENT

BOS'N'S LOCKER CONTAINING
CUTTERS
MAGNETS
ROPES ETC.
H.P. AIR

HYDROPLANE
RUDDER
PROPELLER
TRIMMING-TANK
MAIN MOTOR
PUMPS
BATTERY

DIAGRAMMATIC SKETCH OF MARK I HUMAN TORPEDO
By Petty Officer Charles Kirby, Royal Fleet Reserve

sweetest temper. Nearly everybody seemed pleased, most people
were impressed, but it was apparent that Admiral King was certainly not among the latter and probably not among the former either.
He had the machine brought alongside, gave it and the gear a
peremptory inspection, and then set off back to London. No doubt
this all led to a number of conferences. But for Grant and Warren it
did at least mean beer for lunch, laid on by Sladen.

The fête-day over, preparations were immediately made for the
"Real One" to be transported to Erisort in company with Grant,
Warren, and the fourth class. Sladen still stayed behind for a while,
and soon had produced another two machines. These went straight
up north, where they were most welcome, for, by the time they
arrived, training had got so far ahead that restlessness was beginning
to set in. The problems of the new machines soon dispelled all such
complaints. And as the men and the weapons were united in Erisort
the time had come to think seriously about the enemy, about where
he could be met and how he could be damaged. It was in this mood
that chariot-training began in earnest.

CHAPTER FOUR

Depot-ship Number One

F ROM June onward the emphasis was almost entirely on Scottish waters, with Portsmouth fading out of the picture. And Scottish waters meant *Titania*. It was in her wardroom and on her mess-decks that the problems brought by the new machines were hammered out. Successful charioteering boiled down to 'technical efficiency underwater,' which was itself composed of 'efficiency in the suit' and 'efficiency on the machine.' The whole business of driving a machine below the surface had to become second nature. Before any hope of operational successes could be entertained the charioteers had to be able to forget all about their suits and sets, and drive along with no thought except for the scenery. And the controls of the machine had to be as familiar to one's hands as those of a car.

All the initial training, approximately three months of it, had been designed to secure the first of these two necessities—familiarity with the diving-gear. The training had been based on the principle that the only way for a diver to forget that he was uncomfortable, cold, miserable, and wet was for him to be in this state so often that he came to realize that it was not as bad as he had thought. And up to a point this principle—and there could be no other in the circumstances—worked satisfactorily. Discomfort, and not danger, was always the bugbear in both chariots and X-craft, and, although one could and did forget in the excitement of charioteering, the unpleasantnesses of the life were never far away from one's mind. With nose tightly clipped for hours, swollen and raw from the previous day's dive, with gums cut and puffed from constant gripping of the mouthpiece, and with hands cold to the point of numbness, cut and torn with each day's diving, forgetting could be difficult. And when one surfaced, and hands thawed out while one undressed, there was the feeling that all hell had broken loose with the returning circulation. Some of the divers were 'naturals,' but for the remainder the unnaturalness probably never disappeared completely. There was always an element of strain.

It was somewhat of a relief when the machines arrived. Compared with the pure-diving training they had been undergoing, the business of driving a chariot under water seemed easy—so long as the machine was in perfect trim and tanks and pumps were not leaking. It was, indeed, comparatively relaxing to ride along about twenty feet below the surface at a comfortable knot-and-a-half, admiring a new world. Few except charioteers have ever seen such splendour of colour and such antics as the fish displayed. A helmet-diver descending soon disturbs the mud; the peace-time frogman, breathing compressed air and not oxygen, is bound to scare with his stream of bubbles. But the gentle turning of the propeller, together with the fact that through months of training never a bubble of surplus oxygen escaped through the divers' exhaust valves, all meant that men and machines became part of the scene. More often than not there was a glorious feeling of being alone in the ocean, but sometimes, by prior arrangement, a few chariots would form line ahead or abreast and gently cruise round, their riders marvelling at how rewarding life could be.

It would be then that, suddenly, without warning or apparent reason, a machine would crash to the bottom. In no time the divers' ears would be paining to the point of madness, their lungs caving in for the want of oxygen. Face squeezed hard against the rigid visor, violent spasms of pain attacking the whole body—but particularly all the joints; wherever, indeed, the sudden increase in pressure had found the folds of the diving-dresses, causing them to nip the flesh—the divers would struggle until control of the machine was regained and a more reasonable depth reached. But all this was no unexpected danger; it was, in fact, nothing more than a patch of fresh water in the salt-water loch. The chariots, having inevitably been trimmed in pure sea-water round *Titania*, were therefore heavy in these too-frequent patches of fresh water, which formed off the mouth of each of the burns that careered down the hillsides to feed the loch.

What was the drill in these cases? As in nearly every patch there was a potential—and often an actual—drop of over a hundred feet, extreme measures were always taken right from the first moment of losing depth. This meant hanging on, opening the bypass valve, gasping in the extra oxygen, and allowing as much as possible to escape round the lips and form a cushion between face and visor. At the same time one swallowed determinedly, twisted one's neck muscles, or blew hard down one's nose against the clip, until the resultant pressure forced its way through the passages of the face and equalized the external pressure on the eardrums. This stopped the pain and left only a dull ache.

As soon as these physical necessities were performed one could attend to the machine. Sometimes a Number One would have to float up to the surface if he could not relieve the pressure, and his partner would then have to clamber forward, take over the controls, bring the chariot to the surface, and commence the search. More often than not, however, both of them would manage to keep their seats. Perhaps a Number One would turn round to be greeted with an undiscernible smile and a very jubilant thumbs up, for a Number Two would occasionally be able to spot a patch by the slight discoloration of the water and "guff up" with extra oxygen in time.

Not the least of the troubles was that of people's losing consciousness at depths below forty feet. It therefore says a lot for the men engaged in this work that, although at least 75 per cent. of them 'passed out' at one time or another, they continued with the job. At one period it was a fairly common thing to see a boat return to the depot-ship with a diver having the most peculiar convulsions. Chariots were lost and then recovered by helmet-diving; men came up to the surface in a semiconscious condition; and the whole thing was treated as a good joke.

In those days, too, human torpedoing was not the more exact science it was later to become. Nobody could know all the answers, nor, indeed, all the questions, for there was no drill-book. Instead, there were discussions aboard "Tites." These were not just discussions between individuals—although these occurred too—but were among the whole company of charioteers with the instructors and the two commanders. Sladen would want to know every detail of what had happened from a mechanical, operational point of view. Fell would ask you how you felt; had you noticed any extra discomfort and so on.

An assortment of nets had been laid, on which and through which training was carried one stage further. The charioteers had to pit their newly gained skill against the years of experience of the Boom Defence Department. Of course, the nets really had no chance, and it was soon apparent that, although they might be able to stop a submarine or a submarine's torpedo, they had absolutely no hope of stopping a diver getting his chariot through or under their meshes.

Indeed, as time went by and as experience was gained and exchanged, the nets became regarded as the diver's home-from-home. For the charioteer who was driving his machine along in the pitch-black water with twenty feet showing on the 'clock' it was very comforting to find their wires; it was very heartening to know that the several navigational guesses had been near enough right. And

C

for the charioteer who was lost and going round hopefully in irregular circles it was a source of great joy to discern or sometimes to hit a net.

Many a Number One left his Number Two to mind the machine while he climbed to the surface to find his bearings. And what a sense of security came with the first grip of the wire strands. One was no longer suspended over 150 feet of water on a queer machine. The way to the stars was purely in one's own hands and arms, and a star-embroidered sky seen from a net's jackstay could be a gloriously safe-looking phenomenon.

The nets were of two varieties, the large-mesh, deep, anti-submarine specimen and the small-mesh, shallower anti-torpedo. Their depth was determined by the weight that their supporting line of buoys and their jackstay could stand. One day Boom Defence produced one covered with interwoven barbed wire—just to make training a little more realistically difficult! In the end the whole chariot party won a bet of "Gins all round" from the Boom Defence Officer by getting through his, according to him, impenetrable nets.

The biggest headache among all the crews, which soon began to take up an increasingly large proportion of all discussion times, was to decide the most satisfactory way of getting under the target to secure the torpedo's warhead. Some favoured pulling themselves down and under by using the securing magnets on the ship's hull. Others decided that the ideal method would be to secure a line to the ship's cable, at a depth equal to the draught of the vessel, and then swing in a circle until the machine hit the hull or until the divers could see the hull just above them. Then a puff of air in the ballast-tank would bring the chariot snugly up and under for as long as anyone could wish. In theory this sounded all very satisfactory, but in practice it proved shocking. Apart from anything else, no one seemed to have considered that it might not be possible to find the cable at night. But, even allowing the premise that the cable could be found, the theory was still unsatisfactory. The first trial ended in utter failure, with Able Seaman "Jock" Brown bringing back Warren, his Number One, completely 'out.' They had been unable to maintain depth and had crashed to the bottom too quickly for Warren to be able to counteract the increased pressure. Chuck Bonnell and Able Seaman Malcolm Causer[1] tried next, but they got foul of the line and had the devil of a job getting clear, and had to abandon the attempt. Meanwhile, the advocates of the 'pull down' method were getting a little success in an impossibly long time.

[1] Now Sub-Lieutenant M. R. Causer, D.S.O., R.N.V.R.

Something was wrong, and, of course, the final answer was simple. Indeed, many realized that they had only been putting off the day when they would have to accept that there was only one completely satisfactory, albeit unpleasant, way of solving the problem. The chariot would have to be dived a long way out and driven along at the depth of the target's draught until it hit, or until it began to pass underneath. In the latter event the machine would have to be stopped quickly and blown up to the hull. Somebody had to be the first, and it turned out to be Bonnell and Causer. They met no snags, suffered no damage apart from a certain initial misgiving, and carried out a perfect attack, the first perfect attack ever made. Within a week all the dislike of the unknown had gone and every one was attacking the 'new' way without the slightest hesitatio n. All the teams were provin g that it was easy, and so another problem had been solved. This was just another stage in the acquisition of 'technical efficiency o n the machine.' First of all the diving, then the machines, and then attacking from the machines—all had been mastered.

Casualties had been suffered—so far no more fatal ones—and some men were beginning to feel the strain. They were the ones— and, indeed, there were few braver—who knew the risks, who disliked the whole idea, but who nevertheless stayed on and fought their nerves. Burst eardrums and varieties of sinus trouble had claimed several, and there were others—only a few—who just failed to make the exacting standard of fitness that the work required. But in spite of this reduction in numbers the fierce determination to press on to the first operation was growing rapidly. It later transpired that it was from about this time that Sladen and Fell began looking and canvassing the powers-that-be for just that very thing, an operation. They too felt that the new weapon was ready to be used, and, in spite of their greater experience of the Service and their greater wisdom, they too were only slightly less impatient than the charioteers that the business of choosing and planning an operation was taking as long as it did.

It was Sladen who was the more concerned in the matter. He was the one who travelled to Northways, to Portsmouth, and finally to a Norwegian base in the Shetlands, interviewing, pleading, suggesting, planning. And it was perhaps wise that Fell should have been the one who stayed at 'home,' for, with his great sympathy for human problems, he was the more suited to placate and care for a group of men for whom life was becoming increasingly too inactive. But for some people things were just the opposite. The D.S.E.A.

staff and the engine-room and electrical mechanics of the maintenance parties had all the work and none of the excitement. In
many ways theirs must have seemed a most unrewarding job.

Training continued, the main objective by this time being the
extension of the charioteers' endurance, though one important new
development had been introduced by Sladen. He had realized that
after a chariot had successfully attacked and deposited its 'Easter
egg' the chances of its returning to its carrier were pretty slim. The
crews would therefore most probably have to make their way ashore.
What then? Escape, of course. Physical fitness had always been an
important item in the curriculum, but this was now a new conception,
and included the idea of 'taking care of oneself ashore.' This was,
indeed, a novel idea, because Sladen's training methods were so
intensive that 'taking care of oneself' was the last thing envisaged.
There were few of the fit young charioteers who could stand up to his
expectations and example.

A typical exercise would start off with a colossal picnic being
prepared and carried off into the wilds on an impossibly long hike.
This soon developed into a splitting up into two parties—attackers
and defenders—one party having to reach a certain objective and the
other trying to prevent them. Weapons were usually confined to
lumps of turf—effective enough when hurled by Sladen at short
range—and there were no rules. Quite a lot of beautiful countryside
round Erisort was explored in this strenuous fashion.

The climax was reached when Sladen persuaded a local Home
Guard officer—who was either completely uninformed or insane—
that it would be a valuable exercise for all concerned if *Titania* took
on the defending forces of the area. This proved to be a night
beyond all forgetting. New weapons were perfected aboard "Tites,"
and it was found that a calcium flare dipped in a tin of water and
passed through a letter-box was most effective. It proved particularly
so when inserted in the letter-box of the local police-station, and the
resultant melee gave the charioteers opportunity to secure several
prisoners, who were immediately relieved of their kilts.

There were some wonderful sights to be seen: rotund, bullnecked
Chads, in a pair of tropical shorts several sizes too large, being pursued through heather and water by an irate Highlander; a charioteer
coolly climbing a telegraph pole to cut away whole lengths of wire;
three or four others working like beavers to transfer a crofter's
whole winter supply of peat out of the yard at the back of the croft
to form a road-block.

In the early hours of the morning the charioteers returned aboard.

They were tired, but convinced that even in matters military they were more than capable of holding their own. They were confirmed in this conviction a few hours later, when some of the "pongoes" came aboard at gin-time to claim the previous night's souvenirs. There may even have been a suggestion that the charioteers had gone a little too far. But to Sladen, with his singleness of mind, such a suggestion would have seemed plainly stupid.

Throughout this period of training only one serious alarm occurred. There had naturally been several incidents—occurring and being sorted out by the charioteers themselves, without outside help, too quickly for an alarm to be raised—but there had been nothing serious enough to concern the whole of the unit. But on this one night everybody was involved. "Jock" Brewster[1] had lost his Number Two, Jock Brown, on the nets. They had been on a practice attack. The machine had not been too well trimmed, and as they dived to go through the nets she careered to the bottom, coming to rest by the foot of a net. Brewster turned to feel for Brown, quickly realized that he had disappeared, found he could not move the chariot, and, the drill bearing fruit, released the marker-buoy and climbed up the net. Once on the surface he could try to find Brown, giving the alarm at the same time.

Dicky Greenland[2] was on net-watch in a dinghy, waiting there for just such an emergency as this. It took him no time at all to understand Brewster's gesticulations, whereupon he fired the statutory alarm signal—one Very light. Sladen was in charge of the exercises that night and he immediately ordered all charioteers to the nets and sent a signal for an M.L. that was stationed at Stornoway. The nets were searched as best they could be in the inky blackness, but no sign of Brown resulted. Hope faded as every mind calculated the time-limit of his oxygen-supply. Hour followed hour until this limit was approached, reached, and passed. Perhaps if it had been daylight, they thought, they might have found him.

As it turned out, it took the daylight to restore Jock Brown to *Titania*. He began by grudgingly admitting that the whole thing was his own fault—for not reporting sick before the exercise commenced. For some hours during the afternoon and evening he had been suffering with toothache. He had almost 'jagged in,' but thought he would wait until the exercise was completed. Things were no better when Brewster had tilted the chariot's nose down for the nets and yet Brown held on for the greater part of the plunge to the bottom. He

---

[1] Now Lieutenant W. R. Brewster, D.S.C., R.N.V.R.
[2] Now Lieutenant R. T. G. Greenland, D.S.O., R.N.V.R.

had held on just too long, as it happened, for he had barely started to climb the net before he passed out. He next remembered being on the surface and hearing Brewster and Greenland starting the alarm. They were less than ten yards away, but he could not attract their attention, and he was being carried away from them. So he set course for the loch-side, pulling himself hand over hand along the jackstay of the net. His head was still buzzing with pain and it was no small wonder that he lost his grip of the wire and, once again, drifted away from a chance of saving his life. But he was still not beaten, and, as game as they come, he started to swim ashore. Only those who had worn this equipment could understand what a terrible task this must have been. This was no light-weight frogman's outfit. The suit was self-contained, but it was heavy for all that, and weighted boots were poor substitutes for flippers.

But Brown made it. Once on dry land he cut off his diving-dress and breathing apparatus and, clad only in a suit of woollen combinations, proceeded to knock up the nearest crofter. Shelter and food were gladly provided—but no clothes. Whether the crofter thought that Brown was the advance-guard of an invading force, as his security measures seemed to indicate, or whether he had a personal score to settle from one of Sladen's shore-side exercises, no one will ever know. But suffice it to say that it was in woollen underclothes that Brown knocked up the crofter; it was in woollen underclothes that he was handed over by the crofter to the police; and it was in woollen underclothes that he was returned by the police aboard *Titania*. He never really lived that down.

This incident had taken place in early August 1942. The three classes of charioteers who had travelled north with "Tites" had by this time been hard at it for over three months. The strain was beginning to tell. Tempers were shortening, the machines were beginning to develop imaginary faults, and the 'snap' was slowly going. One young officer, realizing this, took upon himself the hero's task of telling Sladen that people were getting a bit too much of a good thing and that a spot of leave was needed. Typically, Sladen listened courteously, said nothing in reply, and posted the leave-lists on the notice-board the next day.

The majority of the party were for London and the South, a two-day journey from Erisort, which meant four days' travelling out of fourteen. Definitely this was not good enough. Something better than ship and train was called for, and out of the need arose a meeting on the after-well deck. Some of the leave-party decided to travel the conventional way and hope for the best, but seven of them made up their minds to take a chance on the U.S. Air Force. Just outside Stornoway there was a ferry-base for aircraft crossing the Atlantic. It seemed a possible short cut to Prestwick, if not farther.

And this was exactly how it worked out. From Stornoway they were flown to Prestwick in a transport aircraft, with an escort of Lockheed Lightnings to ensure a safe passage. The Americans also laid on a wonderful meal, a special bus into Glasgow, and sleepers for all on the night train. Within twenty-four hours of leaving Erisort, therefore, they were starting their leave in London. And at noon that day the Tivoli Bar witnessed quite a party.

Meanwhile the A.E.D.U. was experimenting to ascertain divers' reactions to extreme cold. If charioteers were to carry out any attacks in Norwegian waters during the coming autumn this would mean operating in water temperatures of about 45 degrees Fahrenheit. Unfortunately the problem was put before the Unit during a very hot August, and this meant that several tons of ice had to be emptied into one of Siebe, Gorman's training-tanks to reduce the temperature.

"Various combinations of underclothing were tried," writes Sir Robert Davis in the latest edition of his *Diving Manual*,

> it being by no means easy to find warm enough clothing which would go under the suits and not encumber the divers. Electrically heated suits could not be considered, since the divers had to leave the craft during the attack, while chemically heated pads were liable to overheat if the suit leaked and let water on to them. The final choice lay in silk underwear next to the skin and kapok-padded jerkins and trousers under the waterproof suit, with woollens between them.

The only remaining problem were the hands, a perennial difficulty with all cases of diving in cold water, because a sense of touch has always been so essential. The Unit tried many types of gloves, the experiments taking the form of a row of divers sitting with their hands in basins of crushed ice. The problem was never satisfactorily solved, and charioteers had to make their own individual choice in the matter. Usually the decision was for bare hands with a liberal coating of grease.

One other lesson had been learnt in respect of the diving-equipment. The steel oxygen-cylinders then in use were found to have an adverse effect upon the compass of the chariot. This might well have been difficult to overcome. No alloy cylinders were being made in this country at that time, but it was fortunately discovered that German bombers carried their oxygen-supply in a large bank of alu-

minium-alloy cylinders of almost the same size and shape as our own.
Even the screw-thread at the neck would take British cylinder-valves.

Orders were given, therefore, for all shot-down aircraft to have
their oxygen-cylinders collected, and the undamaged ones were then
tested, revalved, and fitted to the breathing-sets. The R.A.F. maintained its toll of the Luftwaffe at a sufficiently high rate to meet the
needs of the chariot scheme and other similar diving-requirements
until the production of suitable cylinders could be started in England.

With the first leave-party on its way back to Erisort, one of the
charioteers had to be taken off the train with acute appendicitis.
A telephone call to Sladen elicited the instruction that two of the
others were to stay alongside the casualty until he came out of the
anæsthetic, in case any secrets were divulged. But the combination
of ether and alcohol was too strong, and security was maintained.

Back at Erisort the routine was as before, but the rhythm was
faster. The 'buzz' had got round that there was definitely an
operation in the offing and that the teams would soon be picked.
The standard improved rapidly. But they were all getting to know
the course too well. The nets were in ribbons. Attacking "Tites"
was just 'money for old rope.' Something more difficult was needed
—a more complicated run-in, a stronger net-defence, and a target
drawing thirty-five feet or more instead of *Titania's* modest twenty-six.

Even the night exercises were no longer any trouble, though the
ordered precautions were occasionally found to have a very real
value. Every team carried a submersible torch, and there were also
calcium flares which would ignite on being exposed to the water and
provide an emergency signal and an invaluable homing beacon for
the rescuers. It was usual to rope the two divers together too, just as
another precaution. But neither night exercises, nor new precautions,
nor 'buzzes,' nor anything but a major development in the training
programme would keep the charioteers happy for long. Sladen and
Fell knew this.

Requests were made to Flag Officer Submarines, and orders came
back that the Erisort base was to be dismantled and that *Titania* was
to weigh and proceed. Only Captain Conway and the two Commanders knew where they were going, and, indeed, the name, Port HHZ,
would have meant nothing. The new home, however, turned out to
be Loch Cairnbawn, on the mainland not far south of Cape Wrath,
and due east of Stornoway. *Titania* had been preceded to this new
base by the subsidiary depot-ship H.M.S. *Alecto* and by the drifter
H.M.S. *Easter Rose*. With these two vessels had gone a small party

of charioteers and staff. Their story, which was that of the first chariot operation, is told later.

Soon after *Titania* had moored she was followed in by H.M.S. *Howe*, at that time pretty well the Navy's latest line in battleships. She anchored close inshore, stern under the coast, and was immediately laced in with a few layers of nets. Hospitality was exchanged, plans were made, bets were arranged. Everything was soon ready for the first attack. *Howe* agreed that she had taken every possible precaution and reckoned she was impregnable. In addition to the nets there had been rigged a series of special hydrophones slung out on booms from the ship's side, and between the inner net and the ship herself there was to be a launch patrolling, equipped with an Aldis signalling lamp for use as a searchlight. Most important of all, and a condition which would almost certainly not prevail in any real attack, the target knew on what night and at approximately what time the attack would be made. Her observers could be at one hundred per cent. efficiency.

The attack began. The seven teams left *Titania* at fifteen-minute intervals, sliding away in to the darkness with the sole orders, "Get your charge under the *Howe* and get away undetected." Sladen and Fell must have been somewhat apprehensive in spite of the confidence they had in the crews. There were so many extra difficulties. The defences were stronger than anything the charioteers had yet faced; none of the loch's freshwater pockets had been identified; *Howe* was drawing more than the toxic depth of oxygen; the approach dive would have to be commenced as much as half a mile from the target; and the background of the shore prevented any well-marked silhouette guiding the attack.

George Goss[1] and Leading Seaman Trevethian were the first to return. Theirs was a complete success. Score, one-nil. Goss had noticed that the nets had not completely reached the land and had therefore gone out to seaward; so he crept in along the shore, dived under the last net, placed the charge under the *Howe's* stern, and returned, unseen, the same way.

Geoff Larkin[2] and Petty Officer C. L. Berey[3] were the next pair back. As soon as they drew alongside their joyful thumbs proclaimed that the score was now two-nil. This had been a straightforward attack; into the nets, through, charge amidships, through the nets on the other side, and home.

[1] The late Sub-Lieutenant G. G. Goss, R.N.V.R.
[2] Lieutenant G. W. J. Larkin, R.N.V.R.
[3] Now ex-Petty Officer Cook C. L. Berey, D.S.M.

Third to return was Chuck Bonnell. This was another success. Three-nil. After Goss's 'Attack with Guile' and Larkin's 'Attack Straightforward,' this had been the 'Attack Navigational.' In his usual fashion Bonnell had obeyed all the text-books; he dived within a hundred yards of *Titania* and did not resurface until he was outside the nets again, with his charge left sticking to the *Howe*.

The next to be seen were Sargent[1] and Ordinary Seaman Anderson. They had had the worst possible luck. As they had penetrated the nets on the inward journey Anderson had ripped his breathing-bag on a jagged piece of wire. The whole set immediately flooded, but Anderson had a remedy. He found that by using the bypass valve (normally for providing extra oxygen at times of extra exertion) he could blow into his lungs a mixture of oxygen and water. The latter he endeavoured to spit out into the headpiece of the suit. He decided not to tell Sargent, and it was not until the attack was well under way that his condition was discovered.

Sargent wisely decided not to complete the exercise, and, forcing a way back out through the nets, brought the machine to the surface. Anderson was in a grim state. Doing all that could be done in the circumstances, Sargent opened his Number Two's visor, brought the machine to maximum buoyancy, and returned to "Tites" at full speed. With a hot bath, some whisky, and a quiet "Good show" from Sladen, a recovery was soon effected. This had been no attack, but the machine had not been spotted, so the score read, three-nil, with one draw.

Shortly after this Al Moreton[2] and Stoker White drew alongside. They had had mechanical trouble right from the beginning, but managed to find the nets, which they penetrated through to the last one. There Moreton left White with the machine and climbed up to get his bearings. He was just in time to duck below the surface as the patrolling launch went past. One more look and he went down to rejoin White. But it was immediately apparent that the chariot was by this time quite uncontrollable under water. Accordingly they blew main ballast and took her in alongside *Howe* on the surface. They were unable to complete the attack by leaving the warhead, but left one of the securing magnets on the battleship's side and departed, manhandling the chariot over the nets, unseen the whole way. Score, three-nil, with two drawn.

Last but one to return were Stretton-Smith[3] and Leading Seaman

[1] The late Sub-Lieutenant J. Sargent, R.N.V.R.
[2] Lieutenant A. Moreton, R.C.N.V.R.
[3] The late Lieutenant S. F. Stretton-Smith, R.N.V.R.

Rickwood. Their compass had failed them soon after the first dive, but they continued by coming to the surface regularly to check their track. To facilitate navigation in these conditions they decided, like Goss, to follow the coast. But before they could reach *Howe* they found a bad freshwater patch, and crashed down to the bottom—some seventy feet. Both of them suffered rather bad ear-trouble in this tumble, and neither felt in very good condition for continuing. Bearing in mind that they were only one member of a team of seven, and remembering the oft-repeated instructions for just such a state of affairs, they reluctantly decided to return to "Tites" on the surface and not to risk giving away the presence of chariots in an anchorage, as would have been the correct drill in an actual operation when the enemy would not have been primed beforehand. Score, three-nil, with three drawn. As a result of the unfortunate crash both these two were laid off all diving for some weeks, to give their strained ears a chance to recover.

The last machine to leave and the last to return was driven by "Jock" Kerr, who five months previously had been a Second Lieutenant in the Highland Light Infantry with no nautical ambitions. He had jumped to the same conclusion as Goss, that *Howe*'s stern was vulnerable from inshore. He could not quite find the landward gap, however, and had to dive under the nets. In so doing he hit the bottom about twenty feet under the battleship's stern. A slight puff of air in the tank and the chariot rose to wedge happily under the rudder. There they secured the charge and started back home, only to break surface on the way out and be spotted by the launch. So with four charges placed, one chariot presumed destroyed, and three 'No attacks,' the score-card for the night read four-one to the chariots.

There could be no doubt as to who had come off best, and Sladen and Fell read in this success the happy message that two more weeks of such mock attacks would make their fitness for operational activity beyond dispute.

The second night followed much the same pattern as the first, except that magnets fitted with pellet buoys were used instead of charges—to help *Howe*'s divers! Four teams attacked, four magnets were left, but two machines were detected as they made their way home. The amusing part of the whole show was provided by "Taffy" Evans[1] and Petty Officer W. S. Smith,[2] who placed their magnet on the underside of the starboard accommodation ladder, under the very eyes of the officer of the watch and the quartermaster.

[1] Lieutenant (now Lieutenant-Commander) D. C. Evans, R.N.V.R.
[2] Now Commissioned Gunner W. S. Smith, D.S.M., R.N.

To increase information about hydrophone effect the third day was spent running a few machines up and down in front of the 'phones. This was plain sailing for all concerned, until one of the charioteers struck a hydrophone with a spanner from the tool-kit— "just to make sure the bloke at the other end was still awake." Luckily the operator's eardrums were not permanently damaged. Sladen warned that skylarking must stop.

The third night was to be *Howe*'s last. Admiralty could ill spare her for as long as they did. And it was on this third night that tragedy and great bravery were to visit the flotilla.

Sub-Lieutenant Jack Grogan, a South African, and his Number Two, Able Seaman "Geordie" Worthy, had made a good run. But they had been forced deep on the way in, and while they were under the target Grogan became unconscious. Worthy acted immediately in a very difficult position. There could be no immediate surfacing— with 35,000 tons of battleship in the way—so he moved forward and took the controls, with his arms round and supporting Grogan. In this precarious position he manœuvred the machine out from under the hull and to the surface. Thence immediately alongside one of the dinghies. But it was too late. Grogan was dead.

Worthy had behaved in the best traditions of the Service. His handling of the machine in circumstances that could easily have seen him crushed between it and the hull, or just as easily plunged swiftly to the bottom, was completely cool, equally as efficient as that of any Number One, and accomplished at great speed.

The loss of Jack Grogan was keenly felt. He had been a great character and a first-class charioteer.

These were worrying days for Commanders Sladen and Fell.

"I remember going off one night with the skiff," wrote Commander Fell some years later,

in drizzling rain and a moderate south-west wind. A big swell was flopping icily over us and making us bail, while the chariot disappeared into the blackness to make for "Tites," six miles away.

Then the endless wait at the entrance for a glimpse of the chariot or for word that she had attacked. . . . Two A.M. and still no sign. . . . Then the search among the islands and along the lee shore, and finally the discovery, in the cold, grey, first light, of the pair of them. . . . The chariot high and dry, and two great blown-up, sinister-looking sea-slugs asleep on the shingle. I thought they were dead.

I remember a sort of furious relief from the anxiety of the night, mingled with the dread of having to force everybody out again after a few brief hours. It was only one of a thousand similar incidents.

CHAPTER FIVE

The First X-craft

U NLIKE the first chariot, the first X-craft was to take a long time to construct, and it was not until Sunday, March 15, 1943, that X.3 was launched on the Hamble river, just off Southampton Water, after having been on the stocks for the best part of three years.[1] Her crew of three, who had arrived from 'big' submarines midway through 1941, were Lieutenant W. G. Meeke, D.S.C., R.N.[2] (in command), Lieutenant Donald Cameron, R.N.R.[3] (First Lieutenant), and Chief Engine Room Artificer Richardson.[4]

The thoughts of this first crew must have been mixed when they saw, partly completed, the vessel they were to man. She was approximately fifty feet long overall, but, as propeller, rudder, and hydroplanes were included in this, the internal living-space length was nearer thirty-five feet, or about half the length of a cricket-pitch. The maximum diameter of the circular pressure-hull was five feet six inches, so that, with the deck-boards cutting off the bottom six inches or so, there was barely five feet of head-room.

The control-room, for'ard, contained the steering and depth-keeping controls, the periscope and various navigational items, and pieces of miscellaneous machinery. Next came the escape compartment, known as the "W and D," or "Wet and Dry." As envisaged by Sir Robert Davis in his original design, this allowed one member of the crew to leave and re-enter the submarine in diving-gear, for the purpose of cutting nets or placing explosive charges. Farther aft came the battery compartment and engine- and motor-spaces.

She was, in fact, a complete submarine in miniature. Pretty well all she lacked were torpedo-tubes, for the armament of the X-craft was to consist of two crescent-shaped explosive charges housed externally one on either side of the pressure-hull. Known as side-cargoes, these

[1] See Appendix I with reference to the whole of this chapter.
[2] Now Commander W. G. Meeke, M.B.E., D.S.C., R.N.
[3] Now Commander D. Cameron, V.C., R.N.
[4] Now Chief Engine Room Artificer Richardson, B.E.M.

each contained two tons of amatol explosive and a time-clock. They were to be left on the bottom, beneath the hull of the target.

Propulsion for the craft, as for any other type of submarine, came from the diesel engine on the surface and from the battery-driven main motor while submerged, giving maximum speeds of approximately $6\frac{1}{2}$ and $4\frac{1}{2}$ knots respectively.

During the autumn and winter of 1941–42 things progressed slowly but steadily. In September H.M. Drifter *Present Help* was attached to act as tender to *X.3*. Her commanding officer, Lieutenant "George" Washington, R.N.V.R.,[1] was a former submariner, setting the pattern for the selection of non-operational officers for the flotilla. In November a number of submarine ratings joined the complement of the drifter. Three weeks later she was lying off Itchenor, in Sussex, where two experimental side-cargoes were exploded, making a satisfactory upheaval. Similar experiments continued during December, and all the time *X.3* was nearing completion. During January 1942 there was a visit from Sir Max Horton; it was so pleasant and informal that it could scarcely be called an inspection; experiments were carried out with a separate "W and D" in the Solent and elsewhere; and Commander T. I. S. Bell, D.S.C., R.N., joined the flotilla. With Commander Cromwell Varley, D.S.O., R.N., the designer of *X.3*, this officer was later commemorated in the naming of the first midget-submarine shore-base, H.M.S. *Varbel*, but from his first arrival in the late winter Commander Bell was in charge of personnel and training.

The "W and D" tests were carried out partly to check the capabilities of the compartment itself, and partly to find the most suitable design of self-contained diving-suit to enable the diver to dress himself in the space available.

Finally came the day of the launch. The ceremony did not take place until the evening, after dark, and it was at 2300 that His Majesty's Midget Submarine *X.3* became water-borne. Under her own power she drew away from the launching cradle and proceeded to secure inside a large, specially constructed catamaran which lay alongside *Present Help*.

The next few weeks saw all the tests of a full-scale working-up gradually being undertaken and concluded. *X.3* was 'wiped' on March 19; on the 20th she commenced surface trials; and on the 24th she started diving, giving her first performance before Rear-Admiral R. B. Darke, who commanded the submarine flotilla at Gosport.

It was some five or six weeks later that the next milestone was

[1] Now Lieutenant-Commander H. E. W. Washington, R.N.V.R.

reached, in the recruitment of the first *X*-craft training-class. One day late in April a class of newly commissioned officers, still at training establishment, were asked if they would like to volunteer for Special Service. They had to be good swimmers, they were told, but apart from that they were given no idea of what the whole thing was about. There were five volunteers, who were interviewed there and then by a submarine staff officer. Three were accepted.

On May 23 they reported to Fort Blockhouse. One of them, John Lorimer,[1] remembers that he felt rather small walking into the wardroom, a newly commissioned Midshipman R.N.V.R. among so many decorated and successful officers. He felt he was regarded, together with his companions, as something of a curiosity. Later the pillars of the wardroom were to become used to these periodic incursions.

After a guarded description of what the job entailed they were given the chance, before they were finally accepted, to return to General Service. This was immediately followed by intensive training and a theoretical course on *X.3*. Then to the Hamble river.

Of this John Lorimer wrote:

> I remember the great day when David Locke and I went down to the yard on the Hamble to see the first, the only *X*-craft, H. M. S/M. *X. 3*. We were shown over by Don Cameron, and I remember thinking how incredibly small everything looked and wondering how such a frail craft was expected to cross the North Sea.
>
> The next day I went out for my first trip. It was just a surface run. We were doing a trial with the Taut Wire Measuring Gear.
>
> During the next three weeks we went over to the Hamble occasionally, but *X. 3* spent most of her time in the big shed where she was built, while various Admiralty experts arrived, trying to sell their various instruments, most of which would not even get inside the craft.

Training continued for the class with a fortnight's submarine course at Blyth, in Northumberland. Then they transferred to the submarine depot-ship H.M.S. *Cyclops*, in Rothesay Bay, for further training in submarines. After *Cyclops* came some leave and a return to Blockhouse, where they were informed that they were to report to Scotland, to a special base. This was to consist of the Hydropathic Hotel at Port Bannatyne, not far from where *Cyclops* lay off Rothesay, together with a shooting-lodge on the mainland at the head of near-by Loch Striven.

In July a second officers' training-class joined, nine strong, followed

[1] Now Lieutenant J. T. Lorimer, D.S.O., R.N.V.R.

in late August by a third class of sixteen. The new recruits included four Australians and two South Africans.

Meanwhile *X.3* was 'pressing on.' In addition to all the trials of human adaptation on the part of the crew, there were a hundred and one trials and tests, ashore and afloat, to be performed by the craft. There were the towing, navigation, and speed trials, surfaced and submerged. There was the gyro-compass test. And there were tests with side-cargoes. Meeke, Cameron, and Richardson wondered whether they were submariners or scientists.

Security was a difficulty. It was easy to impress the danger of careless talk upon those concerned, but it was less easy to prevent *X.3* being seen at work. The catamaran in which she was housed, the use of the dark hours for inshore manœuvring and the avoidance of all contact with the outside world, wherever possible, all helped to keep the secret.

During the month of May the craft carried out a series of mock attacks on Portland Harbour. For the normal routine exercise Meeke would be at the periscope, Cameron at the hydroplanes and pump-controls, and Richardson at the wheel, when he was not superintending the engine. The evening would begin with *Present Help* towing the craft out to the diving-area and then following her in during the course of the attack. A peculiarity of this stage of the experiments, dispensed with later when confidence in the craft had grown, was the "buff"—a small pellet-buoy—which was towed on the surface by *X.3* all the time she was dived, to facilitate *Present Help*'s task of keeping in touch. The buoy and its line would also have guided any team of divers who might, for all anyone knew, have been required in salvage and rescue operations. *X.3* was very much an unknown quantity, and any sort of disaster had to be borne in mind, even if not expected.

The Hamble river part of the story ended on August 26. *X.3* was taken by *Present Help* to Southampton Docks, where she was loaded on to a specially constructed railway-truck, for carriage north to Faslane, on the Clyde Estuary. There she would enter Scottish waters on the hoist of a giant crane. With the training-classes also transferring to Port Bannatyne, the removal to Scotland was complete.

And it was in Scotland, of course, that the charioteers were rapidly completing their working-up. In their north-western stronghold they had begun to suffer, as the summer progressed, from what was to become a regular complaint in the flotilla—lack of aggressive action.

CHAPTER SIX

Attempt upon "Tirpitz"

Iт was in the early autumn that things began to look up for the charioteers. Working-up under Fell and Sladen had reached even greater heights of devilment as the summer came to an end. The charioteers thought that they were as good as ready for whatever they were going to do. Theories became rife; some of them were plausible, some were too fantastic for words. The favourite dog-watch occupation was speculating as to "What?" and "Where?" and "How to get there."

Into all this suddenly came Larsen. A problem in himself, for there was little to be learnt about his past, he was at the same time the solution to so many of the other problems. He was immediately the obvious answer to "How?"; and very soon he became part of the answers to "What?" and "Where?"

Larsen's route to Loch Cairnbawn had not been uneventful. In those days he was just plain Leif Larsen, D.S.M., of the Royal Norwegian Navy's Special Service Unit. Now, by contrast, he is "Shetlands" Larsen, D.S.O., D.S.C., C.G.M., D.S.M., Norwegian National Hero No. 1. As a hero in the making he had served, after escaping from German-occupied Norway, as skipper of one of the Norwegian fishing-vessels operating under British instructions from the Shetlands. The duties of these vessels consisted of reconnaissance voyages to the coast of Norway, sometimes landing or picking up agents, sometimes taking supplies for the Norwegian 'underground.' At the back of his mind, during these voyages, Larsen had long entertained some vague idea about attacking the *Tirpitz*. He had gone on leave to London in the summer of 1942, knowing that the powerful 40,000-ton battleship was lying in Asenfjord—a branch of the great Trondhjemsford, situated beyond Trondhjem itself—confined there, so it was said, by damage received from a Russian torpedo.

During his leave in London, as he pondered on the longer autumn nights that would bring to an end the 'close season' of comparative

D

inactivity that made him hate the summer, he brooded on the *Tirpitz*, but could see no way in which a fishing-vessel could penetrate the battleship's defences and launch a death-blow. By the time he returned to Scalloway he had put the idea from his head—almost. His reply, however, was not unprepared when he was asked if he would command a vessel to carry one or more secret weapons to within striking distance of the *Tirpitz*.

His "Yes" was no sooner spoken than he was asking for details and discussing the possibility of achieving an ambition by means of this co-operation with the British Navy's human torpedoes. Things began to happen quickly. Larsen was flown to London for talks with Intelligence officers: he had to prepare his requirements in the way of stores and equipment; he had to choose his boat from those available in the Shetlands; he had to select his crew. Then the boat had to be modified: a stronger derrick, a secret compartment, bolts and mooring-gear fitted beneath the hull. And security had to be maintained as far as the 'others' in the Shetlands were concerned.

Larsen was immediately liked by every one. He was quiet, he was efficient, and he had a sense of humour. And how he hated and feared ceremony and red tape—almost more than did the charioteers! Soon after his arrival there was an example of this when it was announced that Admiral Sir Claud Barry[1] (Sir Max Horton's successor) was due the next day and would inspect the fishing vessel *Arthur*. This was the only occasion when Larsen was ever seen in a panic. No amount of assurance would persuade him that he was to be visited by one of the friendliest people in the business. The Norwegian flag-of-war was hoisted, the deck was scrubbed, the brasswork was shone. It was arranged that Larsen and two charioteers should fall in on deck to receive the Admiral and pipe him aboard. The crew, to their great relief, were instructed to remain below. Larsen had this all rehearsed hours beforehand, and in good time was changed into his number-one uniform, looking as though he were about to face a court martial. At long last Admiral Barry arrived, stepped cheerily aboard the *Arthur*, and immediately began chatting twenty to the dozen. No one was given any chance to indulge in formalities. After a brief look round the deck the party was adjourned below, and Larsen soon found himself taking part in a homely conversation with a "very pleasant gentleman."

Once Larsen was established the new training programme began in earnest. The first part was concerned entirely with towing. It had originally been planned to tow the chariots astern, but after a few

---

[1] The late Admiral Sir Claud Barry, K.B.E., C.B., D.S.O.

trials it was found better to sling them directly under the hull by short painters. Once this had been sufficiently tested a full-scale attack exercise took place. By this time the final selection of crews had been made: Lieutenant Jock Brewster in command, with Able Seaman Jock Brown as his Number Two; Sergeant Don Craig (Royal Engineers), with Able Seaman Bob Evans; and Able Seamen Malcolm Causer and Bill Tebb as spare crew and dressers.

The first full-scale trial attack was made one day in the middle of October. Eleven people sailed from *Alecto* in the *Arthur*: four crew, six charioteers, and Tiny. The little vessel steamed past Rhu Coigach and eventually into a deserted bay in the Summer Isles. There the chariots were hoisted out on the derrick and secured below the hull. Evans and Brewster had dressed ("just like grotesque modern trolls," still says Larsen) and been over the side to secure the painters. Once the two men were inboard again *Arthur*'s engine was restarted and the tow commenced, back towards the loch where *Alecto* and the target, H.M.S. *Rodney*, lay. It was dead on midnight when the engines were finally stopped. *Arthur* had reached the agreed place for loosing the chariots, several miles away from the anchorage. Immediately the four divers completed their dressing, and Tiny gave them a last look over. Larsen has since written of how excited he felt at this moment:

Nevertheless, the serious background of the first trial attack created a restless expectation. A little splash was heard as the four men of the deep let themselves glide down into the coal-black sea to disappear from sight. It was quiet on board while the fellows worked under the bottom of the vessel and unshackled the chariots. It was exciting even though it was not in earnest. The only thing that could be seen was the phosphorescence and the ripples which rose up. Then one machine bobbed up a little way from the side of the vessel. Evans and Craig were holding on to the sides of it and had to strive to mount. Then the other machine appeared.

The electric motors began to hum, the machines drew in alongside the boat and the crews made a sign that all was in order. Fell waved them off and they glided quietly away from *Arthur* and disappeared in the dark. The attack was on.[1]

For the record, this practice attack was a complete success. Both machines cut through two of the three layers of nets that surrounded the battleship, went under the third, and, in spite of the duty-watch on deck, who had been informed of the attack, secured their warheads and made their way out unobserved. Had this not been a mock attack, *Rodney* would have been deep in a Scottish loch.

[1] *Shetlands Larsen*, by Frithjof Saelen (J. W. Eides Forlag, Bergen).

All the charioteers were naturally very pleased at this success, but, of course, Tiny Fell was not completely satisfied. After all it was his job—and very graciously did he go about it—never to be completely satisfied! Other trial attacks were carried out under different weather conditions. Flaws in method and training were rigorously sought. On one occasion only did the battleship's observers spot a machine, which had inadvertently broken surface on a night which, although cloudy, was cursed with occasional shafts of moonlight through openings in the clouds. By this time the training was more intense than it had ever been in the past—"Plain, solid, hard work," as one Number Two described it. But it did not last long. Within three weeks of *Arthur*'s arrival Fell professed himself happy, and one day in the latter half of October he announced that training for the *Tirpitz* was finally concluded—at least, as far as Loch Cairnbawn was concerned. "I thought so," was one comment. "That blighter will never be satisfied." But this came with a laugh and a deep contentment at the thought that if they were really good enough for Tiny almost to say "Yes," then they really were getting somewhere.

In actual fact the selected crews were moving up to the Shetlands, Larsen's old home-from-home, for a final short spell of training. The skerries in the Shetlands were even more like what the crews would encounter in Norway, so they were to have a little more time on underwater-navigation exercises.

While these exercises were going on identification and other papers were being prepared for the *Arthur*. This had been left to the last moment to make sure that the German signatures forged were not those of people who had been reappointed elsewhere! As part of the briefing two Norwegians were flown over from Sweden. One was a Norwegian Secret Service agent, the other from the Norwegian consulate in Sweden. It was essential that after the operation the charioteers and the crew of *Arthur*, which was not planned to return to the Shetlands, should get back to England as soon as possible, as their reports would be invaluable. This meant avoiding internment.

On her false papers *Arthur* was described as a cargo vessel, previously a fishing-boat. She carried a cargo of peat for camouflage, which she was scheduled to deliver in Trondhjem. The papers also contained details of previous cargoes carried, ports of origin and destination, consignors and consignees, times, dates, and German control stampings.

The remainder of the plan consisted of the scuttling of the *Arthur*, the achieving of a rendezvous ashore between the two halves of the party and some representatives of the 'underground,' the provision of some transport, and plenty of instructions to reach the frontier and then back to London.

On October 25 Larsen, Fell, and Brewster felt they could sit back, drink a beer, and say that everything was ready. Sailing orders stood at 9 A.M. the following morning. But the sit-back did not materialize. A message arrived from German-occupied Trondhjem via goodness knew where. Complete changes were needed in the cargo-manifest if the story were to ring true. This meant, for Larsen, sitting up until four in the morning to rewrite the whole of the document, which had to be in his own handwriting. The others helped and stayed up too. They checked to see whether the new departure and arrival times would have been feasible, bearing in mind the tidal and weather conditions which had prevailed. They checked the stores and equipment embarked in the fishing-vessel. They fed to Larsen information about the various parts of the Norwegian coast that they knew, to help him check and recheck his new entries. They kept him company and they cheered him up. Eventually they all turned in for less than four hours' sleep.

Finally the time came. It was 0900 on October 26, 1942. "Let go for'ard; let go aft." A short, embarrassed nod came from Tiny Fell as he saw them off from the pier, and from him too came the last words to speed them on their way: "Good Luck!"

As soon as the *Arthur* pulled away from Lunna Voe it was apparent that the weather was going to be roughish. Indeed, conditions soon became such as to cause Brewster concern about the safety of the chariots, which were lashed down on the upper deck. Larsen and he gave the lashings a good going-over amid the cold spray, and then felt better. The sea would have to get a lot worse before the lashings parted. Thus began a pretty uncomfortable, though otherwise un-eventful, passage across the North Sea.

As the crossing continued the wind came even more strongly out of the north-east, and the swell increased. The chariots, under the layers of tarpaulins and nets that covered them, were regularly inspected by one or more of the charioteers. The warheads were hidden well away beneath the peat in the hold. The weather was far from what they had been promised, and even though the sail was rigged to give stability as well as adding speed, the onset of a strong north-going current made the sea even more unpleasant. Once speed had to be reduced in the face of the weather and the smack pitched even more. It was an unusual motion for the charioteers, and Bill Tebb was the first, though not the only one, to succumb.

By the evening of the first day the weather was going down a little, although it was still rough. Watches on the wheel were shared between Larsen, Brewster, and one of the Norwegians, although Brewster had patches of seasickness. The morning of Tuesday the 27th sustained the overnight promise of slightly improved conditions, but the little boat was still too lively for comfort.

Suddenly but not unexpectedly, at about midday on Wednesday, the 28th, a landfall was made, which Larsen soon identified as a mountain peak behind the small town of Bud, south of Kristiansund. A few minutes after this first bearing had been taken came the first of the troubles that were to try the ten men in *Arthur*. "We were about twenty miles from the coast when the engine broke down," wrote Brewster after his eventual return to England.

We lay for three hours in sight of land, completely helpless. This was, of course, rather worrying in broad daylight, but no one came near us. We got under way again about three o'clock, just as the early Northern darkness was closing in. The Norwegians were quite excited, naturally, at seeing their native land; but my feelings, and those of the others, were hardly affected, which was perhaps surprising.

This breakdown meant that Larsen could not get the cross-bearing he required for fixing the boat's position, but this was soon remedied by the surprising profusion of identifiable shore lights which came into sight as *Arthur* drew closer in to the land. Course was set northward along the coast, passing to the westward of the Griphölen channel and up to the island of Smöla. As the smack neared the little port of Edøy, on the southern shore of Smöla, she became a cargo vessel on passage from Edøy to Trondhjem and ceased to be a fishing-vessel. Most of the nets were accordingly stowed between decks.

The night of the 28th had smoothed the sea to mill-pond consistency and Larsen found conditions during his longish watch well-nigh perfect. There was no moon, and *Arthur* had bobbed along with scarcely a touch of the wheel, her stem breaking the wavelets with a strange, eerie phosphorescence.

First light was near enough eight o'clock, and Causer (an Englishman born and reared in Brazil) was marvelling at the white-blanketed hills, his first sight of snow, as another fishing-vessel passed about half a cable's length abeam. There was no reaction from the stranger, and soon *Arthur*'s anchor was plumbing her native waters in the appointed mooring-place in a sound among the Høg islands not far from Edøy, at the entrance to the great Trondhjemsfjord estuary. A quick breakfast of ham and eggs was organized, and the dishes were barely cleared away before one of the Norwegians gave the alarm.

It was a German plane which seemed to be flying aimlessly backward and forward about a mile away over the mouth of the fjord. *Arthur* should have looked quite innocent from any distance greater than two or three yards, providing no one was interfering with the machines, but to look as natural as possible those on deck busied themselves with odd jobs, and one individual even managed to relieve himself over the side just to give the picture natural colour. But the whole episode nearly ended in disaster. Just before making for home the plane swooped low over the smack, to have a good look at her. She was low enough for the machine-guns in her wings to be clearly seen. One of the Norwegians gave her a casual wave, and then, with the plane at its nearest, up dashed one of the charioteers from below, going straight for *Arthur*'s machine-gun in its concealed mounting.

"What to hell—you bloody fool!" roared Larsen in English that in the excitement was less perfect than usual. Anyway, the sound of his voice, or his fierce facial expression, had the necessary effect, for the offender froze in the hatchway, his face becoming a picture of ashamed sheepishness in a matter of seconds. And the 'bottle' that Larsen served out was such a beauty that Brewster felt he need not add a single word.

CHAPTER SEVEN

Progress of "Arthur"

W<small>E</small> found it very difficult to realize that here we were in German-occupied Norway on a beautiful, if cold, autumn morning," wrote Brewster in his account of the operation.

> Our first concern, after the plane had gone, was to get the chariots overboard and secure them in the towing position. It was easy enough getting them into the water, but there was a bit of a chop on the surface, and it was soon apparent that the actual securing would cause a lot of bother. It should, of course, have been about an hour's job—but it took a devil of a lot longer. Both machines were in the water and I was over the side in the small rowing boat when we realized that the smack was dragging her anchor. So she had to be got under way—the machines and the rowing boat on tow astern—and steamed towards the shore. After much cursing and mucking about we eventually got her made fast to the beach. The rocky bottom was such a poor holding ground that the anchor had to be dragged ashore and secured in a cleft in the rock, with the stern rope also being rowed ashore. By nightfall we still hadn't managed to secure the machines, so, as it was blowing a bit, we decided to pack up trying and leave it for the morrow.

A guard-mounting rota was arranged, with two sentries on duty all night. Mercifully the night hours passed quietly, and at 5 A.M. on the 30th Brewster and Evans were over the side again and in a very short time had the chariots secured in position with little or no trouble.

"Thank the Lord!" said Bill Tebb, as Brewster and Evans climbed inboard, and then immediately followed up with another invocation of the deity: "Oh, Gawd!" It certainly was a case of no rest for the wicked, for, with one difficulty just surmounted, another, in the shape of a little rowing boat, was taking its place. Quickly the Britons disappeared below, while the boat made its way across the sound towards *Arthur*. Now the onus was on Larsen and his crew, and all the charioteers could do was to sit tight and hope that they had not come across some Quislings.

Larsen and Bjørnøy, the engineer, were on deck as their visitor

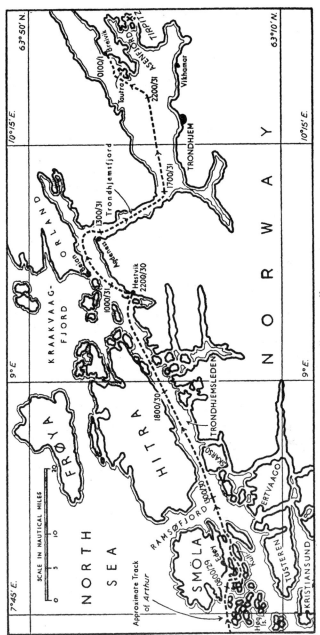

ATTEMPTED ATTACK ON "TIRPITZ" BY HUMAN TORPEDOES

paddled alongside and flung his painter over the rail. He was an old man with several weeks' growth of beard on his wrinkled face, and his dungarees were very patched and oily. One's first impression of him was that he was the inquisitive type; one's second that he was talkative. Both impressions were only too right!

"What kind of people are you who have tied up in here?" he asked, settling himself down on the thwart for a good long yarn.

"Fishermen, with engine trouble."

"I suppose those are your nets," the greybeard surmised, casting what seemed a suspicious eye on the chariots' coverings.

"Of course."

"What fish do you try for?" came the question. But Larsen's cautious and worried answer was never heeded. The old fisherman shot bolt upright and nearly capsized to peer under the smack's hull. The sunlight shining through the clear, shallow water had revealed to him one of the steel-wire hawsers securing the machines.

"And what sort of a device is this?" He still allowed no time for an answer to his awkward question, but, instead, so contorted himself, with his face in and out of the water, that he managed to perceive the machines as they lay long, slim, horizontal, just below the hull.

"How miraculous! And what are they?"

"They are something we use to explode mines with." Larsen had made up his mind what his course of action was going to be.

"You fellows go about for the Germans perhaps?"

"Yes, we do that."

"You must have some experiences." No comment from either Larsen or Bjørnøy.

"Perhaps the Germans are on board?" the old man persisted.

"They are below, asleep," replied Bjørnøy.

At all costs the old fellow had to be put off from asking himself aboard, for the point-blank refusal that would be necessary would surely excite his suspicions still further, and he had given no indication as to the direction in which his sympathies lay.

As Larsen and Bjørnøy wondered how much damage had been done already, and how they could avoid doing any more, the old man stood up, still chewing slowly the quid which must have been stuck away at the back of his mouth during the whole of the conversation. He was obviously meditating what to say next. This would be the turning-point, Larsen felt. And so it was.

"Butter is terribly scarce now, boys." He was nervous about the very plain invitation he had just made; in contrast, Larsen could hardly stop himself laughing with relief. A nod and Bjørnøy went below to return with a very handsome slab.

"Thanks, thanks, many thanks! This is far too much. I had not meant so much."

The old man made to loose his painter from *Arthur*'s rail, but this time it was Larsen who continued the conversation. He asked the old man's name, where he lived, whether he was alone. He learned of the old man's daughter, of the daughter's husband, of where they lived. The poor old fellow was just beginning to enjoy himself when Larsen changed.

"Now listen, old man! If you tell a soul what you have seen this morning you will not have many hours left to live, neither you nor your daughter. You have blabbed all your whereabouts to us, and we shall certainly find you if you blab anything to anyone else. Remember that, and now clear out as fast as you can." Larsen's words, and the roaring German manner in which he had delivered them, certainly seemed to have the frightening effect he had planned. The old man let go his painter and grabbed his oars in complete confusion. In a few moments he had pulled away from *Arthur*, and in a few minutes he had disappeared out of the sound.

Aboard the smack the immediate reaction was one of relief, to be followed by congratulations being showered on Larsen and Bjørnøy for their cool handling of the situation, and to be completed with a unanimous relapse into laughter. Even the fact that the old man had spotted the hawsers and the machines could not damp the hilarity. Anyway, in deeper waters the likelihood of a repetition of this discovery would be nil.

By now it was about the middle of the forenoon, but so much time had been lost that they could not get within striking distance of *Tirpitz* that night. There was no hurry therefore, and the anchor was not weighed—unhooked from the shore, rather—until just after noon. It was another lovely day, and the entrance to the fjord displayed some fascinating scenery. But there was little opportunity for sightseeing. The plans for the operation demanded a thorough check-up of *Arthur* at this point. The wireless transmitter and all its fittings had to be stripped and sunk in deep water. It had been supplied in case any emergency had arisen during the passage across from the Shetlands to the coast. Then any papers and rubbish of British origin—cigarette packets, etc.—had to be cleared up and ditched in a weighted bag. No risk could be taken of anything identifiable floating on the surface. The machine-gun was struck down into the secret recess and stowed alongside the diving-gear.

The course lay between Rostvoll and Kull islands and was such that it could easily have been that of a vessel on passage from Edøy. The water was calm and there was only an occasional breath of wind. People could be seen on the autumn landscape, walking, working, gossiping. Things seemed to be going according to plan. Most of the time the charioteers stayed below in the cabin, although Brewster occasionally took a spell on the wheel. Several Norwegian and German ships were passed during the afternoon, some of them very close to. This excitement was soon interrupted by Bjørnøy. Late in the afternoon he poked his head up through the hatchway and called to Larsen. He had some bad news about the engine. It was misfiring occasionally and labouring badly. He could not tell whether it was a major fault or just something small. Soon after he had gone below again the engine began to smoke and speed fell away to half. It was first assumed that water was getting into the cylinder from the cooling jacket, but as the engine continued turning, albeit slowly, this was soon disproved. Next Bjørnøy thought it might be a cracked piston, and came up for another discussion with Larsen. Calmly the skipper announced his intention to proceed inshore and anchor and then seek assistance from the nearest village. Actually Larsen had hopes of making an anchorage fairly near the fishing-jetty at Hestvik. In the final briefing before they left the Shetlands he had been told of an agent living in Hestvik, by name Olavsen.

Slowly the smack made its way along the coast, the engine spluttering at intervals, but nevertheless keeping some way on the vessel. At 10 P.M. the throttle was finally closed and the anchor dropped within sight of the jetty. Leaving Bjørnøy and the others stripping the engine, Larsen and Strand, the young Norwegian telegraphist, rowed ashore.

As luck would have it, among the first crowd of youths in the street from whom Larsen asked the way was the agent's son. This was a good start, and Larsen was soon in the shop explaining that he required some provisions for his boat. He waited until the several loaves and the bag of flour were being packed before voicing the first part of the code-message he had been given.

"Have you any use for peats?" he asked, and waited for the expected answer, which should have been: "No, I have plenty."

Instead Olavsen quickly turned from wrapping up the provisions and eagerly replied, "Peats! Yes, you can bet your life I have use for peats. I will take what you have."

Larsen was shaken. He quickly discounted the theory that there could be two tradesmen of the same name in the village. The

Intelligence people would have warned him of that. He therefore concluded that the code-message and the reply had for some reason not reached Olavsen. He had to be careful, and accordingly ventured. "Yes, I have a little all right, but it is—well—really Carlstroem who owns the cargo," giving the name of the agent who had briefed him in the Shetlands.

"I presume it is Erik Carlstroem of Arkanger you mean?" countered Olavsen still cautiously.

"No, it was Niels Carlstroem in Trondhjem it concerned."

This did the trick, and the true position was soon explained. To see what was really required Olavsen and his son returned with Larsen and Strand to *Arthur*. They found Bjørnøy with the engine stripped down. As he had supposed, the piston was badly cracked, so that the exhaust would have been blowing through and down into the crank-case. It was wonderful that the engine had gone at all with this defect.

The only solution, Olavsen affirmed, was for them to go ashore and contact the local blacksmith immediately, in spite of the lateness of the hour. And so he and his son and Bjørnøy rowed ashore. "We took the road to the smith's," Bjørnøy told the others afterwards. "Many people lived in the same house, and we did not want to risk knocking. Olavsen's son knew where the smith slept, and he took a fistful of gravel and threw at the window. We could hear people snoring inside. They were evidently in their best sleep.

"The boy had to try throwing twice more, and with heavier shots, before the window went up and a sleepy voice was heard. It was the blacksmith. 'Who is there?' he asked.

" 'You must come down.'

"The smith knew Olavsen's voice, and realized he was not being wakened up in the middle of the night for nothing. He quietly closed the window and came down to join us. I told him the drill I needed, and he asked no more. We went with him to the smithy and he sorted out the correct size. We left him there tidying up, and rushed back here."

The completion of the repair was comparatively plain sailing. In another two hours Bjørnøy had drilled sufficient holes and fitted sufficient bolts to hold for a short time at least. It was just as well that it had been planned to scuttle *Arthur* off Asenfjord, because to effect a permanent repair to a piston-head in these circumstances would have been too much to ask.

By seven o'clock everything was finished and cleared away. A two-hour break for a sleep was agreed upon before the voyage was resumed. "Our fingers were crossed when we started the engine," wrote Brewster. "She was O.K. Surely nothing else could happen."

From Hestvik course was set at reduced speed—just to be on the safe side—for Agdeness. There, they knew, was the main German control position, at the beginning of the body of Trondhjemsfjord proper. There too, presumably, lay the greatest danger. Before they reached Agdeness they had to alter course again to avoid a minefield. It was on this tack that it was expected to encounter the patrol vessel, and the charioteers had already gone down into the secret compartment. They were only to show themselves if they heard any shooting. The machine-gun was in with them, and each of the Norwegians had a revolver under his jersey.

Once more the Norwegian crew were on their own. As *Arthur* and the control vessel closed the wind dropped. Suddenly there was a complete calm. Before the two vessels could come alongside each other there was not a single ripple on the water. There could not have been a more unfortunate occurrence. Larsen prayed for some unobservant Germans.

As the smack drew near to the trawler Larsen decided to draw attention to himself to lessen the chance of a bored Hun glancing casually at the water. He gave a crisp salute and bawled a lusty "Guten Morgen." The German officer on deck looked up at him, but no more. With the two boats still ten yards apart, both propellers were stopped, and they were gliding together over a transparent sheet of water. Eight yards, seven yards, six yards—would the gap never close? For'ard in *Arthur* as this eternity was being endured stood Seaman Johannes Kalve with the mooring-rope coiled in his right hand. Waiting for the rope was his German opposite number, next to whom stood a boy of no more than sixteen or seventeen. Suddenly the boy's face took on an astonished expression. He stared down at the sea, up again at the *Arthur*, and then turned to speak to his companion. Not sure whether he was seeing an optical illusion and not wishing to make a fool of himself, he looked down once more before he spoke. Kalve had noticed his reactions and moved like lightning. Just as he looked back at the sea for the second time, Kalve flung the rope. It shot through the air and coiled round the boy's neck. The situation was saved—for the moment at least.

Solidly *Arthur* eased alongside the German's fenders amid the roars of laughter with which the German crew were greeting the boy's misfortune. Shamefaced and blushing, he extricated himself from the rope and dashed below. Certainly he would not now risk making a double fool of himself.

The German boarding-officer came heavy-footed aboard. Down below in the secret compartment ears were keyed, all except Brewster's, for he was sleeping. He had had almost forty-eight hours solidly on his feet and was impervious to anything. The Hun struck Larsen as possessing the customary arrogance, but somehow lacking personality. Anyway—and rightly, as it seemed—Larsen felt no fear of detection from this quarter.

Down in the cabin the German went through all the papers with great thoroughness, making an occasional note. Finishing his examination of all the documents, he looked up at Larsen. "So you have been in Kristiansund lately?" The examination had ceased, and the tone was now conversational. Did Larsen know Captain Ormann, the German harbour-master in Kristiansund? They came from the same town in Germany. Had Ormann mentioned him? No? Well, mention this meeting to him. It was a pity that it was necessary for Germans to protect Norway against English aggression. Thus the conversation continued, and to those on deck it seemed an age before Larsen and the lieutenant reappeared, laughing and joking together. The hatches were off the hold and one or two of the peat sacks were open ready for inspection. But they were considered worth only a perfunctory glance, as was the engine-room companionway. The examination had really concluded a quarter of an hour previously with the first mention of Captain Ormann.

When they were well clear, and the darkness had come down, the charioteers came up on deck. Brewster had been wakened, and felt the better for his nap. "The weather was quite fine," he wrote subsequently,

and there were many friendly looking lights flickering ashore. There certainly didn't seem to be very much concern about black-out. And so we continued peacefully.

Just before Trondhjem itself, about fifty to sixty miles up from the entrance, the fjord bends left-handed. We had been keeping a more or less south-easterly course, but had to alter to almost due east. As we made this alteration we were faced with a stiffish easterly breeze, but it wasn't enough to cause any worry in its existing strength. The other two had finished their preliminary dressing when Brown and I went below to put on our gear. Almost immediately the weather worsened. Other conditions were still good. There was no moon, so our chances of being seen were small, and the lights of Trondhjem, now lying to starboard, would help our navigation.

We hadn't got very far with our dressing when we began to hear a succession of sharp bumps. The chariots were being swung up against the keel. The weather was deteriorating rapidly. It was already a first-

class storm. Speed had to be reduced, but it was out of the question to
wait another twenty-four hours so near to a busy port. We could maintain a speed that would get us there in time to do the attack before daybreak. "Press on regardless" was the only advice we could give ourselves. There was too the hope that the full force of the north-easter
would blow itself out in the remaining hour or two before we reached
the Asenfjord anti-submarine net and started off on our own. Apparently such fierce storms often ended suddenly on that mountainous
coast. Down below again, therefore, we continued dressing.

I was still below when it happened. It was just after ten o'clock when
we heard a loud, grinding, tearing noise. The vessel jerked and shud-
dered. Something pretty substantial had fouled the propeller. We all
guessed what it had been—one of the chariots. There should still be at
least one serviceable, so we made for the sheltered waters to have a look.
Bob Evans was the most completely dressed, so I ordered him down to
see what was what. He came up and reported nothing there at all.

We were dismayed. The chariots were gone and the attempt was off.
I don't think anyone has ever been so disappointed as we were that
night. We were ten miles from the pride of the German Navy; all our
obstacles were behind us; and we might as well have been at the North
Pole. Looking back, I don't remember one single curse. We were all
too unhappy for that.

CHAPTER EIGHT

"We walked across Norway"

Larsen was heartbroken, and could not even be cheered by Evans's assertions that in each case it had been the bolts on the machines that had sheared and that the hawsers were still firmly secured to the fastenings on the keel. In other words, it had been the British workmanship that had not been strong enough, not the Norwegian.

Brewster brought the discussion to a business footing immediately. Somebody suggested returning the way they had come. No attack would mean no state of alarm. But this plan was soon turned down as they would have no papers to certify them for the outward journey and no receipt for the peat. Anyway, the engine was on its last legs, not to speak of the damaged propeller.

It was Larsen's recommendation that was eventually adopted. They set course in towards the sheltered northern shore of a small island. The sooner they could get ashore the better. *Arthur* could be scuttled, and they could land in two parties and make their way direct to Sweden.

During these last few miles the complement busied themselves with ditching some of the sacks of peat from the hold, to give the smack a better chance of sinking fast. Provisions were collected and packed in rucksacks, together with some ammunition. Meanwhile, the storm was going down as fast as it had come up. It was just as Larsen had prophesied. If the machines had only hung on for less than another hour *Tirpitz* would probably have been destroyed. It was just the luck of the game.

The water was so calm as they came up to the island that it was decided to go farther in, to Breivik, on the mainland. Soon, in the lee of the land, they were floating on a mill-pond. If only this stillness could have come sooner. Bjørnøy stopped the engine about a hundred yards off the beach, and the first five went ashore. As they rowed off Larsen and Brewster began opening the sea-cocks while the others sorted the rucksacks out on deck and bored holes in the hull to help the inflowing water. Kalve was soon back for them.

Water was pouring in fast, but there was no sign of *Arthur* sinking.
She was a wooden ship, and she did not seem to be settling much.
Perhaps the remaining peat had something to do with this. Anyway,
they rowed away and left her. Water was still rushing in, but they
had their doubts as to whether she would sink. Not that they could
do anything if she wouldn't.

The two parties met on the beach. It was 1 A.M. on Sunday morning, November 1, 1942. All the carefully concocted plans which had
been made for them were worthless, although some of the instructions would still be valuable if ever they got as far as Sweden, which
the map showed as fifty to sixty difficult miles away. The immediate
need was for a new plan, and, on the principle that the simplest
devices are almost always the most successful, it was decided simply
to head eastward and to divide into two parties at daylight. No rest
could be looked for until later that day.

The beginning of the journey lay along a narrow path that led up
from the beach. The ten men went in single file, Larsen in the lead.
Soon they reached a secondary road which wound through a countryside that seemed, in the darkness, to be a bleaker counterpart of the
western Scottish isles where the charioteers had spent so many happy
months. There was a light covering of snow on the ground, which
Malcolm Causer could not resist handling.

The road passed a few hundred yards away from an aerodrome.
Several planes were heard landing and taking off, and a tall, red
signal beacon could be seen flashing. One of the Norwegians went
on ahead to see whether they were following a road which would lead
on to the 'drome. Luckily it did not, and progress continued at
normal walking pace, without incidents, until—just before dawn—
it was decided to stop and split up the parties.

Larsen and Brewster had been chatting as they walked, and all
the details of the division of forces had been agreed by this time.
Larsen was to command the first party, with Craig as second-in-
command, and Bob Evans, Bill Tebb, and Roald Strand to make up
the five. The other three British, Brewster, Brown, and Causer,
were to go with Bjørnøy and Kalve. Each man had an escape-
pack—two tins of corned beef, three tins of sardines, and some
biscuits—and each leader had a map and a compass. Every one
was armed.

Farewells were brief and even Tebb seemed cheerless. Larsen and
his party started off first, leaving the road and gaining the rock-
strewn fields as they turned off to the right. Brewster followed the
road a while before finding a likely looking track that bore left.

Larsen's way lay more immediately inland for the moment; Brewster's would keep to the coast for a mile or two.

The two parties were in sight of each other until their diverging courses placed a small hill between them. Brewster stopped for a moment as the last member of Larsen's party disappeared behind the curve of the hillock. Now they were on their own with a vengeance! The guidance and experience of Larsen had possibly not been fully appreciated, even by the most thinking member of the party, until that moment when he vanished out of sight. Kalve voiced the feelings of them all as, in not very confident English, he muttered, "A good man, the Captain."

They stopped for a meal half-way through the forenoon. To their 'rationed' food they added some bilberries and some turnips which they found growing near a little crofter's farm. The bilberries were delicious, being ready frozen, but it could not be said that the turnips benefited from the frost and snow in similar manner. The countryside seemed deserted, and after a short smoke the party was soon on its feet again. They plodded on at a steady pace until midday brought them to the top of a commanding hill.

The view was wonderful—white hills all round giving way to black rock slopes at the edge of the fjords, too steep for snow to lie. The grey-blue water was enlivened by occasional white frothy wave-caps, the whole effect being one of great beauty. But Brewster and company had little time for the scenery. More correctly, they had time for only one little fragment of it, the *Admiral Scheer*. The pocket-battleship was lying in a little bay some seven to eight hundred yards away from where they were standing. Everything seemed very quiet and even the sound of an aircraft somewhere above them, followed by the noise of a German anti-aircraft battery not far from the *Scheer*, caused no burst of activity on deck. Presumably it was a practice shoot, and not 'one of ours' over on reconnaissance, as they had first thought. The whole thing was very galling.

"We had to leave the *Scheer* lying there peacefully and carry on eastwards," wrote Brewster.

In the afternoon we saw three German sailors strolling along a footpath a short distance below us. They were obviously enjoying a spell of leave. I suppose we were, too, come to that. We were keeping well in among the more wooded parts of the landscape and the Jerries didn't see us. We carried on through the rest of the afternoon and the evening, not allowing ourselves any organized breaks for food.

That night we forced a fishing-hut and had some much needed sleep. We were all pretty weary and I suppose we took very few precautions.

The nature of the whole business was such that it would have been impossible not to leave something to chance. We preferred to put speed before everything else, even at the cost of running some rather unwise risks during the daylight hours.

We set off early the following morning and had a completely uneventful day. The weather was grand—had been ever since the storm had gone down less than an hour after we had lost the machines. Malcolm Causer was beginning to feel the cold, but he never complained. We had a certain amount of warm clothing—sweaters, etc.—but we could really have done with more. I expect that coats would have been supplied by the underground people we should have met at Vikhamar. By nightfall we reckoned we were half-way across Norway. This meant we had covered twenty to thirty miles in the two days. We had little sleep this second night as the blokes agreed to keep going. Just before dawn we snatched a couple of hours in a barn at the back of a clean little farmhouse. I don't know how long we would have slept—for we didn't mount sentries—if we hadn't been wakened by a Norwegian voice, presumably that of the farmer, nattering at a horse-team in the field outside the barn. When the coast was clear we slipped away unseen.

Coming on for dark we skirted a village. There was no sign of the enemy, so we decided to approach one of the outlying farms for bed and breakfast. We felt we deserved a comfortable bed and hot meal. Anyway, it was worth a try, we thought. We kept a likely looking farm under observation until nightfall. Then I sent Bjørnøy and Kalve down to see what they could find out. We had our rucksacks at the ready and our route planned in case we had to do a quick bunk. But fortunately there was no need. Kalve came to find us and led us down. We had a wonderful meal of soup, eggs, and potatoes, and then we were taken up to the loft. The hay was divinely comfortable and we slept soundly with some one else to do the worrying for us. Our hosts—father, mother, and two grown-up sons—were just grand. 'Entertaining' us would have meant facing a firing-squad if a German patrol had chanced to find us there. But they didn't seem to be worried.

About three o'clock in the morning we were called and came down from the loft to another meal. And by the time we set off, with the two sons coming to put us on the right road for the frontier, there were sandwiches and ersatz coffee prepared ready for us to take. The boys were still with us at midday, when we stopped for a meal in a little hut on the side of one of the hills dominating the valley. Soon after we restarted we got to the top of this range, and they showed us a jagged line of mountain peaks which marked the Norwegian-Swedish border. This done they turned, gave us a brief good-bye, and set off back down into the valley. They left themselves precious little time to get back to the farm before dark. I have no idea who these people were, but the physical and mental help they were to us enabled us to carry on with our trek, feeling on top of the world.

The five men started off downhill. From the top of the range they had just climbed their path descended only a few hundred feet before levelling out and eventually starting a long, slow ascent towards the border. The snow was beginning to get troublesome. Bjørnøy and Kalve, without actually glorying in it, were certainly very little inconvenienced. But the charioteers, especially Causer, found it somewhat tiring. The cold was sufficiently intense to sap their stamina, and the thick covering—it was about six inches deep on average—made walking difficult. But, from a visual point of view, the weather was marvellous. The setting sun cast their shadows long in front of them, and as they looked back at the way they had come the snow had turned a deep pink.

By nightfall they reckoned they were seven miles off the mountain peaks, seven miles off the frontier. They were wondering where they would find shelter, for in the higher altitude the night would have been too severe to spend out of doors just for the sake of saving half a day. Then the indistinct shape of a building showed among a clump of trees. From the look of the place they decided it was a shooting-lodge, and there were no signs of its being occupied. Jock Brown forced the door and in they went. They were all feeling the cold to a greater or lesser degree, so they risked lighting a fire. Kalve and Causer busied themselves at this while the others explored the house. Bjørnøy found the kitchen, where there was some butter and some flour. This seemed most amazing, but there it was all the same. In no time they were sitting in front of a roaring wood fire eating rather 'gooey' but very acceptable flapjacks which Brewster had concocted from the butter and flour plus some condensed milk from the tubes in the escape-packs.

In the morning they made another meal and tidied the place up, hoping the owner would not begrudge them the liberties they had taken. Brewster noticed that they all sounded excited, as they set their faces eastward. For the first time the wind was troubling them, and they had to be wary of the occasional soft drifts that were being whipped up.

By early afternoon they had reached their last barrier, the mountain range proper. The map told them that they would have to reach 6000 feet in the climb, and then they could go down into Sweden. It was certain that they would be climbing the whole of the night, for it would take several hours to reach the other side, and there was no hope of any shelter. Escaping through uninhabited country was far from being an unmixed blessing.

The night was plain hell for all of them. They were insufficiently clothed, they had no experience of mountains, and the fierce wind which worried their eyes as they strove to pick their way through the darkness would induce a feeling of complete impotence as it blew up into gusts that were stronger than a man, stronger than his legs, arms, heart, and guts, all pushing and straining together. But they carried on. They could do that without thought—stopping would have meant talking, planning, thinking, and they were too tired for anything like that. If only the confounded wind would let up!

They reached the top and passed over into Sweden in the early hours, still going like machines. Over the other side of the ridge the weather was entirely different—no wind, and a feeling of dampness in the air, which, with the starting dawn, proved to be an extensive mountain mist. They slowed up once they were on neutral territory, and before long the mist had thinned, but what was left of it combined with the glare of the snow to form most difficult visibility. It was often impossible to make out the contours of the ground a few yards ahead.

It was in these conditions that Brewster fell over a rock face and down through about ten feet into a drift of soft powdery snow. No damage was done and Jock Brown began laughing his head off at his Number One's surprised shout and sudden disappearance. He was still laughing as he himself fell over the same edge into the same drift. The other three were more careful and, in spite of the deceptive light, managed to come down the conventional way and pull Brewster and Brown out.

All they had left in the way of food were the little bottles of benzedrine tablets. Occasional ones had been used here and there, principally on the night the *Arthur* had lain off Hestvik, but the bottles were almost full. Now they were really necessary. Most of the five men had had one or two tablets to keep themselves awake during the night, and before they started on the last stage of the descent—down the lower slopes and the foothills—every one stoked up again.

They were very weary when at last they got down into a valley and saw a small village lying against the wooded slopes. "It was between ten and eleven in the morning," wrote Brewster,

and we were glad to give ourselves up. We were dishevelled, hungry, and wearing ten days' growth of beard, but, apart from Causer, we were otherwise all right. Malcolm was in a bad way. He had been in pretty bad pain for the last couple of days, but had said nothing about it. It was frost-bite, of course. He was obviously the most susceptible, coming from Brazil, but it was a wonder that Brown and I weren't troubled too.

The local police were very friendly, and before any sort of interview could get under way we asked them to send for a doctor to look at Malcolm's feet. The 'doc' arrived and was most concerned. Not long after this Malcolm was separated from us and, as we learned when he eventually rejoined us in Scotland, was packed off to a Swedish hospital, where he spent a very pleasant month.

The police chief did not seem very concerned about them.

"Who are you?" he asked.

"British and Norwegian Servicemen."

"How did you get here?"

"We walked across Norway."

Then they were told that some other Britishers had arrived earlier that morning. They were taken to see them, and although they had a pretty good idea who the others must be, they were still surprised and delighted to see Larsen's party. There was no sign of Bob Evans.

Larsen and his party had been stopped by a patrol of two German police, one black-uniformed and one in civilian clothes, in a mountain township only a few hundred yards on the Norwegian side of the frontier. In halting Norwegian the Germans had asked them why they had not recognized the police uniform, demanded identity papers, and, although satisfied with the forged documents, told Larsen that all five of them had better come along to the police station for further interrogation. And so off they marched, Britons and Norwegians in front, Germans behind. It was more than unfortunate that most of the party's revolvers had been left with some Norwegians who had helped them earlier in their escape. But Bill Tebb still had his.

"I'm having a go at these square-heads," he muttered, as they bunched together.

"Good idea!" whispered Larsen.

"As soon as we turn this next corner all of you go flat on your faces." This corner-of-a-building trick had been part of their escape training. It gave you just the odd fraction of a second to draw a gun.

As they turned the corner Tebb drew his revolver and fired. His first shot went wide, and the retaliatory volley from the automatic Lugers hit Evans in the stomach. Tebb fired twice more and the Germans dropped. Both of them were dead. Larsen and Craig rushed to where Evans was lying. They tried to lift the body, with the intention of carrying him with them in their dash over the frontier. They would probably have a few minutes' grace before the sound of the shooting brought reinforcements along to the town outskirts. But Bob Evans went a good fourteen stone. He wasn't transportable. Anyway, he was dead. No doubt about it. They all had a good look at him. No doubt about it. He was dead.

"We'll have to leave him," said Craig. "I'll see his identification discs are on him. The Red Cross will want them. And now we'd better beat it."

And so it was that Larsen, Craig, Tebb, and Strand arrived at the little Swedish village and gave themselves up. This story, sorrowfully told to Brewster by Larsen and Craig, dried up conversation. They had all liked Bob Evans very much indeed. They found they didn't know what to say.

Much later in the day they reckoned that the two parties must have crossed the frontier within a mile and an hour of each other. This was somewhat remarkable, for they had been four days and four nights apart.

For the next forty-eight hours they were kept locked up in a private house in the village. The Swedes treated them very well, and they had plenty to chat about once they could put the thought of Evans's death out of their minds for a few minutes. What had happened in the fjord was the subject of much of the conversation. Larsen was glad to see Brewster again. They had become firm friends in the weeks since *Arthur* had first steamed into Loch Cairnbawn. Some of their talk was of return to England. Larsen was already thinking of another crack at the Germans. He wondered what Tiny Fell would say about this idea, what the Admiralty would do about that.

On the morning of the third day transport arrived to take them to an internment camp nearer Stockholm. Ten days later they were taken to Stockholm itself. There was little sign of the difficulties they had been warned to expect in Sweden. Air-passages home were booked, and accommodation was provided until flying weather improved. Brewster found himself in a very modern hotel. Some new civilian clothes had been bought for him, and he was living in a holiday atmosphere. He saw the Royal Palace, Parliament buildings, and the Opera House. He walked and talked, wined and dined. He was almost sorry to leave. But leave he did in the end—as did the others at different times—and it was at ten in the evening of Friday, November 17, that his plane touched down at Leuchars, in his own native Scotland. He had been away just over a month.

He and Larsen were the principal recipients of awards for this gallant attempt. Brewster received the D.S.C., and Larsen the C.G.M., the highest possible decoration, other than the Victoria Cross, that can be given to any rating. This award had an especial significance in that Larsen was the first non-British national ever to receive it.

It was in January 1943 that the rumour reached the flotilla that Evans was still alive. Craig and Tebb went down to Submarine Headquarters in London. The rumour had been correct.

And then, in February, there came another rumour—that Evans had been shot. Again the rumour proved true.

The full story was not learnt until after the War. The Germans came upon Evans's body, but he had not been quite dead. He was rushed to hospital, operated on, and saved. Once fit he was interrogated and, finally, shot as a spy. This was by the express orders of General Keitel.

And it was on the evidence of Bill Tebb, among scores of others, that Keitel was indicted at Nuremberg, found guilty, and hanged.

PART II: THE MEDITERRANEAN

CHAPTER NINE

To Malta

A few days after Brewster's return a chariot party of eleven officers and fifteen ratings left England for Malta. Their last few days in *Titania* had been marred by the loss of Jack Grogan. His death was a very great shock, and it is not difficult to imagine the effect of such a happening on a group of people living closely together and working hard on just the very process that had caused the casualty. Naturally, the atmosphere was tense for a few days. But there were no breakdowns and no resignations.

The party for Malta was under Commander Sladen, with Sub-Lieutenant Pat Grant, by this time disqualified from diving on medical grounds, acting as Staff Officer.

They sailed from the Clyde on November 26 and had an uneventful trip all the way to Gibraltar, where they disembarked, to be flown the rest of the way.

The first thing that is universally remembered about their arrival is the tremendous party that ensued; the second, the accommodation which was provided for the ratings. All non-commissioned personnel were billeted on the top floor of a warehouse on Manoel Island. The roof leaked badly and the usual conveniences were sadly lacking. Even the food situation was not good, although this was easily understandable. By this time Malta had got over the worst period of the blockade forced upon her by enemy air-activity, but existing supplies still seemed inadequate and lacking in variety to people newly out from England. The Services did much better than the civilians in the island in this respect, but submarine crews were always only too glad to go out on patrol and get a decent meal.

Within a very short time Sladen had all the men down to work. For administrative purposes the charioteers formed part of the Tenth Submarine Flotilla (Captain G. W. G. Simpson, C.B.E., R.N.[1]), from which three submarines were detached to operate with

[1] Now Rear-Admiral G. W. G. Simpson, C.B., C.B.E. (Flag Officer Submarines).

and under Sladen. *Thunderbolt*, *Trooper*, and *P.311*[1] were fitted with external containers to carry the chariots to the target area. This was the new method of transport. A few weeks' training saw the three of them ready for the part they had to play.

To operate with chariots—or, subsequently, with X-craft—can have been no submarine commander's dream of heaven. The Submarine Service normally expects, for the pains and risks it must endure, frequent opportunities of engaging the enemy. To become a ferry-boat for some one else who is probably going to be presented by you with the chance of a lifetime, and to be told into the bargain that no potential targets below the rating of capital ships may be engaged until after the operation, can only be the sort of assignment that one wishes for one's colleague. Furthermore, it entailed incurring the greatest of all submarine risks, that of proceeding close inshore into water too shallow for a successful evasive-dive. It is to the great credit of the men concerned, therefore, that in no instance was their undoubted dislike of the work ever manifest in the presence of charioteers or X-craft personnel. Co-operation was always of the highest standard. It was bettered only by the hospitality.

As soon as possible all the chariot crews were started on night-runs. Several of these had to be undertaken before Sladen admitted to being more or less satisfied that an operation could be finally arranged. In actual fact the complete plans for more than one attack were ready to the final detail and were only awaiting the preparedness of the chariots.

Of the domestic side of these December weeks in Malta much must remain untold. The story of life in the Island during the War years is well enough known. Suffice it to say that these young men, keyed to a high pitch, fully trained, impatient, found that their leisure hours had to be filled with any entertainment that offered. Steam had to be let off, adventure sought. Architectural beauties, sunsets, and yellow sandstone soon palled. Opportunities for games were limited. Relaxation was a problem.

The party formed a very private navy. They worked and played as a compact unit—almost a 'gang'—and as such they landed themselves in all the trouble imaginable. It was on Christmas morning that Captain S/M 10 nearly lost his tame rabbit. It would not have been the same as turkey, but still . . .

Hard work was the best antidote and Sladen the man to enforce it.

---

[1] Lieutenant-Commander C. B. Crouch, D.S.O., R.N., Lieutenant J. S. Wraith, D.S.O., D.S.C., R.N., and Lieutenant-Commander R. D. Cayley, D.S.O., R.N., respectively in command.

But his job was nearly complete. He had brought human torpedoes from a hazy idea to a fully developed striking force, and he was already looking for an active appointment where he could pursue his determination to 'engage the enemy more closely.' Later, as commander of the cruiser *Sheffield*, he was to have his wish.

Finally, there was 'the operation.' Sladen selected the teams and gave them their detailed briefing. He saw the three submarines sail from Malta during the two days of December 28 and 29. After that he could only wait.

The story was continuing, but not in Malta. The scene had been transferred to three submarines sailing into a hostile sea. Unfortunately the hostility of the sea was physical as well as political. The weather, indeed, blew up so rough that it was necessary to postpone all operational instructions by twenty-four hours. It was so inclement that dressing up in awkward diving-suits was obviously not going to be anybody's idea of fun, especially as seasickness was claiming its toll. One of the submarines even provided an open-topped five-gallon oil-drum. This would save fishing for buckets, it was explained, and would also allow more people to 'play' at once!

CHAPTER TEN

First Blood

By 9 p.m. on January 3 two of the submarines were in position a few miles to seaward of the North Sicilian port of Palermo. Operation "Principle" had well and truly begun. They had been proceeding on the surface ever since the early winter night had given them a cloak of darkness. In fact, the night in question was one of those of the most intense blackness that are only to be found at sea before a new moon shows.

The third submarine was missing from her billet off Maddalena in Northern Sardinia. *P.311* failed to return from this patrol and must have been lost before reaching the target-area. With her gallant crew died ten charioteers—three teams and four dressers. Aboard the other two 'boats' there were five teams in all. *Trooper* carried three and *Thunderbolt* two.

The final orders from Sladen had been to enter Palermo; to attack targets in the harbour as specifically allocated; to return, if possible, to an agreed position, where their parent submarine would wait for them until 0430 the following morning; and to conduct themselves in any unforseen circumstances as they would think fit and without prejudice to good order and naval discipline. The only difference was that the two teams in *Thunderbolt* had been briefed for an attack on the South Sardinian harbour of Cagliari, plans having been changed while they were at sea.

It was about 10 p.m. when Lieutenant Richard Greenland, R.N.V.R., was completing the arduous business of dressing and was getting his course to reach the harbour entrance from *Thunderbolt*'s navigator. The behaviour of the submarine—he remembered that she was the salvaged *Thetis*—had told him that it was an unpleasant night, The conditions were so bad that they had been rolling noticeably at thirty feet.

The wind was about Force 4, coming directly off shore, as inimical a set of circumstances as could be imagined for an operation of this kind. Water was breaking over the casing with each wave that

pounded against the pressure-hull, and Greenland and Leading
Signalman Alec Ferrier made their way cautiously for'ard from the
gun-mounting and conning-tower to where the two machines were
housed abreast of each other.

Observing the well-worn tradition of "one hand for yourself and
one for the King," they had to struggle hard to keep a grip on the
container while they released the for'ard door. The drill to which
they had become accustomed in training continued. *Thunderbolt*
flooded down in the water and as casing and containers came awash
the machines rose off the chocks and were hauled clear. Their riders
scrambled or were flung astride. From that moment neither Greenland nor Ferrier saw *Thunderbolt* or the other machines again. One
parting gesture was accorded them, however. A second after they and
the machine had been washed off the plunging casing the submarine's
jumping-wire whistled past their shoulders, descending at a rate that
would surely have wrecked their chances right from the start had it
been inches nearer. According to plan, they circled the submarine to
catch sight of Petty Officer Miln and Able Seaman Simpson, the
other crew, but there was no sign of anything anywhere.

So this was what all the training had been for. There they were
—on the surface, alone in the black night. No trim dive to check
the machine's buoyancy in waters that might contain unusually
heavy or light layers, no sight of their companion machines, no
farewell from *Thunderbolt*—in fact, as they thought to themselves,
no damn all! A minute or two after they had been so rudely started
on their journey, Greenland headed his machine round to the compass-bearing and commenced to close the harbour. Soon they were
able to pick out the light which *Thunderbolt*'s Navigating Officer had
pointed out as marking the entrance.

Keeping to the surface, they were badly buffeted by the heavy sea,
and were glad when conditions became easier closer inshore. But,
although the sea was calmer as they neared the land, the weather was
far from ideal throughout the attack. Nearer the harbour entrance
Greenland reached behind him until he found Ferrier's hand. With a
few short words tapped out in Morse code—Ferrier, being a signalman, had taught him this method of communication—he intimated
his intention of stopping to get the long-overdue trim. Down they
went, therefore, and in a few minutes surfaced with a trim caught and
their ears cleared.

They were quite close inshore before they discovered that the
harbour-light was only a street-lamp. However, they followed the
land until they came to a breakwater, where Greenland judged the

entrance must lie. He was right. So the run-in had finished and the
serious business of the night had begun.

Then they found the nets, supported on a row of buoys fitted with
sharp spikes. Some sort of net was only to be expected, Greenland
supposed, but he cursed them all the same. If only the powers-that-
be hadn't changed the target-area things would have been a lot easier.

We had a devil of a job getting through the A/S net. It was several
sizes too big and was lying on the bottom in folds. We tried to lift it,
but couldn't. Eventually we got the nose of the machine under a fold
and blew ourselves, plus the net, to the surface. I was surprised our
buoyancy was capable of this. As we neared the surface I slid round and
underneath the machine to avoid getting spiked. Completely forgot to
give Ferrier the tip to do the same.

Fortune favours the brave—or the devil looks after signalmen!—
for Ferrier escaped contact with buoy, spike, or anything else
unpleasant. But he does recall surprise at suddenly seeing Greenland
slide sideways and temporarily disappear from view.

The A/S net continued as an obstacle even after they were through
it. For some reason it had a definite adverse effect upon the compass,
for from the time of passing under the net Greenland had to treat all
compass-readings with great caution and was forced to act more like
a surface vessel than a submersible.

The off-shore wind, its full force partially screened by the buildings
of the town and the dockyard, was still raising an unpleasant sea
inside the net when Greenland broke surface again. But there was
no time to curse the weather, no time to experience relief at one
hazard overcome, for they were straightway confronted with another
line of buoys, which meant another net. Greenland guessed that,
following the orthodox pattern of harbour defences, the second net
would be the anti-torpedo baffle round the major war vessels'
anchorage.

A signal to Ferrier and the machine dived—slowly, evenly, no
snags. The bottom of the A/T net passed quietly over their heads,
helped by their hands. It was very light, seemed like aluminium, but
was for all that no deeper than the usual steel type, fifty feet. Under,
therefore, and up again.

The big moment had almost arrived. Greenland kept the machine
on the surface, partly due to doubts about the compass, partly
because it is good submarine theory and practice never to submerge
merely for the fun of it, and the darkness and lack of activity in
Palermo harbour that night seemed to guarantee immunity from
discovery. But in spite of the darkness he had no difficulty in finding

his way about. At between 3 and 4 A.M. there could have been none
of the light that precedes dawn, so it could only have been a manifes-
tation of what the doctors had called 'night adaptation.' Anyway, it
was a good thing; and it was a much, much better thing to discern
darkly but quite unmistakably the outline of their target, the 5·3-
inch-gun cruiser of the Duce's Italian Navy, the *Ulpio Traiano*. She
was new from the fitting-out yards, her commissioning crew were
aboard, she had not yet finished her trials, she was there . . . there . . .
there, looming out of the darkness. It was all coming true.

If Ferrier had any objections to his Number One's straightforward
method of approach he never voiced them either at the time, by
Morse, or later, by word of mouth. In a moment they were alongside, right alongside, hull to hull, and then they were both forcing the
machine down below the surface, right underneath the cruiser. By
mutual consent they stopped, and then proceeded to secure the warhead. There then remained one final task to perform before the
attack was complete, and Greenland smiled contentedly as he set the
time-clock on the explosive charge for 'two hours.' By his reckoning
it would then be about dawn.

But it was not "Good-bye, Palermo"—not for the moment anyway. For the night's escapade each team had taken four 5-pound
magnetic charges, which had been stowed in the 'bos'n's locker,'
abaft of Number Two's seat. These they viewed as their own 'perks,'
although they had been told to look for four submarine-chasers.
They had already fixed one charge for the Navy, so now they would
fix a few more, free lance, for their own satisfaction. The unknowing
recipients of their attentions were three of the chasers and one
merchantman, the largest they could see. While withdrawing, on the
surface, from between the second and third chaser the chariot's
hydroplane fouled an anchor-cable, causing the screw to come out of
the water and race violently. Some one aboard the chaser, presumably the quartermaster, walked for'ard and looked over the side,
but luckily did not see them. The two charioteers were feeling
exhilarated by this time. Their last four calls had necessitated a lot of
careering about in a supposedly alert naval harbour, all of it on the
surface. They had just about done enough, thought Greenland, so:
Head to seaward, stern to wind, following sea and full speed ahead!
I didn't know we could go so fast. . . . Over the top of a net, that
was unorthodox. . . . No damage done. And then came: Crash!
Bang! Bump! There were noisy reverberations and a hideous and
frightening loud repetition of metal thumping against metal. The
darkness must have got blacker, or perhaps Greenland had relaxed

his concentration for a moment, for they had collided with a merchantman at a rate of knots. Seemingly they sustained no serious damage from the collision, but the noise they had made in the magnifying silence would have woken even a stokers' mess!

After this shock they both had a good look round, and with the visual equivalent of second wind they immediately managed to get their bearings. It was soon apparent that they were going round in circles. The collision must have accentuated whatever had gone wrong with the compass earlier. Bang had gone any remaining chance of making the rendezvous! *Thunderbolt* and *Trooper* were not waiting after 0430, and both men knew that it could not be very far off that already, if the hour were not indeed even more advanced.

They found themselves near a naval dockyard. Greenland drove the chariot alongside a small motor-launch, which was secured to some steps. He was out of oxygen, so he climbed aboard the launch while Ferrier took the machine back out into the middle of the small basin. There she was soon dispatched to the bottom, and Ferrier, having watched her go, started his short swim back to the steps. Soon he was being helped by Greenland to undress. This they did the easy way, cutting off the breathing-gear and the diving-dresses, which they then tied to the lead-soled diving-boots and ditched into the dark water.

Dockyard steps gave way to quayside, whither two of the Royal Navy's more scruffy-looking units made their way in search of somewhere comfortable to sit. They felt peckish. One of them produced some chocolate, and they munched quietly for a few minutes before deciding in what direction to move off. Perhaps the big bang would not be long.

There had been five human torpedoes launched by *Trooper* and *Thunderbolt* on the night of January 3. Miln and Simpson, the other team in *Thunderbolt*, got away quite happily in spite of the heavy weather, but were out of the running before they reached the harbour entrance. During the run-in they had a battery explosion. The flooding of buoyant compartments caused the machine to dive rapidly. Simpson must have been foul in some way, for he failed to bail out. Miln tried repeatedly to disentangle him, but, with the depth-gauge showing ninety-five feet, he himself was suffering from oxygen poisoning and had to surface to save his own life. Once on the surface he soon recovered, eventually swam ashore, and was taken prisoner. Simpson was presumed drowned.

Sub-Lieutenant R. G. Dove, R.N.V.R., and Leading Seaman Freel

F

were one of the teams to leave *Trooper*. Like Greenland and Ferrier, they succeeded in reaching and attacking their target, the s.s. *Viminale*, an 8500-ton passenger-cargo vessel being used as a troop-transport, on which they secured the explosive head. They also made their way ashore and were taken prisoner.

The machine manned by Sub-Lieutenant H. L. H. Stevens, R.N.V.R., was not blessed with the best of luck. After he was launched from *Trooper* he tried for five hours to find the entrance to the harbour. Some defect showed itself in the breathing-apparatus of his Number Two, Leading Seaman Carter, with the result that the latter had soon run out of oxygen. Stevens immediately decided to leave him on a buoy, where he could be easily picked up, and continue the operation alone. Unfortunately, he was still not able to find the harbour, and as time was getting short decided that the wisest thing to do was to pick up Carter and return to his parent submarine, if he could find it. But they could see no sign of *Trooper*. Indeed, by the time they had been almost six hours in the water, with Stevens still doing what he could for his partner, they were beginning to give up hope of ever being contacted, when suddenly in the darkness they saw what turned out to be the outline of a British U-class submarine. And, what was more important, they in their turn were seen by the U-boat's look-outs. The submarine was the *P.46*,[1] which had been detailed to patrol the inshore area for the express purpose of picking up stray chariot crews.

Able Seaman Worthy was Number Two of the remaining chariot. He was a man who had already distinguished himself below water in the affair with Jack Grogan under the *Howe*. Little did he think that the Scottish episode would be repeated, in part, that night in the waters of the Mediterranean.

Worthy's Number One, Lieutenant H. F. Cook, R.N.V.R., was an able charioteer in all circumstances. They left *Trooper* and found the state of the sea as great an obstacle to the efficient handling of the machine as all the other teams had done. But the seeds of tragedy had already been sown, for Cook had been very ill with seasickness during the last hours of the trip in *Trooper*. Had wisdom been able to silence enthusiasm he would never have embarked on the run-in. However, the feeling of nausea within him mounted, and in no time he was unable to handle the machine. With Worthy now the guiding force, the chariot was run up to some rocks at the harbour entrance. Cook dismounted and clambered ashore to be relieved of the exhaustion, suffocation, and agony that were consuming him.

---

[1] Lieutenant J. S. Stevens, D.S.O., D.S.C., R.N., in command.

It had been Worthy's intention to carry on with the attack and complete the operation on his own. But the mounting seas made the machine increasingly difficult to control, and lack of time prevented his taking Cook back to the rendezvous. He therefore took the remaining course of action and manœuvred the machine some distance away from the rocks into deeper water. There he dismounted and set the chariot off, heavy and diving fast to the bottom. This completed, he turned to swim back. It took him the best part of twenty minutes to reach the rocks. Swimming any distance in a Sladen suit was extremely tiring. But eventually he climbed ashore. Cook was not to be found. He was never seen again. The only deducible theory is that he opened up his visor before he was far enough up the rocks, was washed off into the sea in a non-watertight state, and drowned.

When Worthy was forced to abandon the search for his partner, he made his way inland, to finish up, like five others of his colleagues, as a prisoner-of-war.

There had been quite a large number of Italian ships moored in Palermo harbour that night. Six of the original total had been attacked: the *Ulpio Traiano* (sunk) and three submarine-chasers and a merchantman (possibly damaged), to the account of Greenland and Ferrier; and the merchantman *Viminale* (badly damaged), to the account of Dove and Freel.

It had been worth it.

CHAPTER ELEVEN

"*Great Guys in Rome*"

On the quayside Greenland and Ferrier were chatting about the night's events. It was almost 0600, and Greenland reckoned that the two hours he had set on the time-clock must be about up. Still, they couldn't sit about any longer. It would be a good idea to get moving while it was still dark. Two Italian sailors had already passed along the jetty during 'breakfast,' but the charioteers had apparently not been seen.

They were hardly on their feet before the cruiser went up. "It was a very nice bang—lots of flames. And then the Eyeties opened up with ack-ack." Greenland's description was perhaps a trifle brief and modest, for the explosion, by all accounts, split the night air of Palermo into a vivid inferno of biting flames and shattering noise. Anyway, the Duce was now minus one cruiser.

Within a few minutes of the explosion the first streaks of dawn began to light the untidy skyline, and as jubilant officer and rating moved through the deserted dockyard they began to distinguish enough landmarks to give them a sense of direction. They were two very happy people, for they were the first British charioteers to have drawn blood. Walking away from the scene of their successful operation, they felt like two schoolboys out on a half-holiday.

The lay-out of the dockyard was somewhat confusing, and it was almost half-past seven before they found a gate leading out into the town. It was almost unbelievable, but none the less true, that during the best part of an hour-and-a-half's wandering through a naval dockyard immediately after the sinking of a cruiser with loss of life the only people they saw were a group of indolent-looking Carabinieri at the gate. To these Greenland gave "Good morning" in what he imagined to be a German accent (he had neither German nor Italian), adding a confident 'en' to each word. For his part Ferrier muttered something that was very English and very naval. Owing, presumably, to one or both of these pronouncements, the Carabinieri neither asked for documents nor tried to conduct a conversation. Perhaps they had not heard the bang! Anyway, they contented themselves with a gesture and a word or two in answer before returning to their lounging and chatting. The treatment they had probably received from German naval personnel in the area had possibly made them loath to interrogate any foreigners.

So hurdle number one was passed, either in spite of or because of Greenland's and Ferrier's complete ignorance of any satisfactory language, combined with their peculiar attire. Greenland was wearing a naval-issue boiler-suit, on which were the two regulation buttons required by the Geneva Convention if an escaping officer or rating is to prove himself to be in uniform. The rest of his outfit consisted of a very striking black and white Fair Isle sweater—which screamed for identification—and a pair of Italian cycling-shoes. He was also wearing a full beard—Ferrier described it as a "monstrosity"—which Intelligence in Malta had said would cause no comment in Sardinia! Ferrier was dressed much the same, but without the two horrors of beard and sweater. Their issue of escape-equipment comprised identification papers, 'compass' buttons, hacksawblades, a map, some cigarettes and matches of Italian make, five thousand lire, thirty American dollars, and one gold sovereign apiece—the latter being carried for luck!

The dockyard area of Palermo seemed very poverty-stricken, and even when their wandering led them into the town proper there were few buildings that impressed them. For the capital of the island Palermo's houses seemed poor, badly constructed, whitish stone hovels, with plenty of evidence of primitive sanitation. Once they lost their way among some narrow, winding streets, and had to retrace their steps. Eventually they succeeded in getting clear of the town and kept to a road that led them through four or five miles of 'suburbs,' consisting of occasional, better-built houses scattered at intervals.

They had still not heard any smaller bangs, although another main charge had definitely gone up, which made them wonder whether a later Italian story of the five-pounders having been removed and found to be lacking the vital acid in the fuses had any truth in it.

During the time it had taken them to make their way out of Palermo there had been hardly any people about, and they had been spoken to by no one, unless one counted the Carabinieri. But it would be unwise to assume, they knew, that this good luck would continue, so they decided to turn off the road and gain a vantage-point by climbing a low hill. The countryside was continuously undulating, with vegetation distributed bleakly in the shape of scraggy bushes and stunted trees set among dirty yellowy soil and whitish rock. Fresh water seemed to be a scarce commodity, and they were lucky to find a small stream running down the side of the hill. As they filled their rubber water-bottles they were thinking and talking of their chances of complete escape. The plan they had formulated was to cross Sicily from north to south—a distance of fifty miles or more—and then obtain a boat and sail back to Malta. For Greenland this would have recalled shades of Ipswich's Orwell yacht club.

At this moment a figure came into sight, walking along the path that ran beside the stream. With no possibility of finding any shelter in which to escape detection, Greenland and Ferrier sat where they were and waited. The two Englishmen rose and gave the passer-by a judicious imitation of the Fascist salute. Ferrier muttered the same greeting that he had vouchsafed at the dockyard gate, but the Italian walked on, uncommunicative. As he reached the road three Carabinieri were passing on bicycles, with rifles slung over their shoulders. Greenland and Ferrier saw the man wave to them; they dismounted and a conversation ensued.

Escape was impossible, the only hope being that the Carabinieri would pooh-pooh whatever suspicions the civilian was voicing, in the knowledge that German Service elements were becoming more numerous in the island with every week that passed. However, this hope was in vain, for the Carabinieri were soon leaving their bicycles by the roadside and advancing up the path. To start the encounter off on an amicable footing Greenland and Ferrier offered round their Italian cigarettes. This hospitality the Carabinieri accepted, without its preventing their getting down to sterner stuff.

The demand appeared to be for papers, and there seemed to be no point in not producing them. They were ostensibly German naval service identification papers, but either they or their bearers seemed a bit too much of a good thing, for the Italians were visibly dissatisfied. From the demand for the papers the interrogation, such as it was, became reminiscent of a musical comedy. The voluble Carabinieri were speaking rapid Italian and were being answered—without understanding any of their questions—by Greenland in his home-made German.

"Guten morning. What you wanten? Pop goes der cruiser."

This the Italians failed to understand, which was hardly surprising, and so there was only one thing that could happen. "We were taken to the local police station," said Greenland afterwards, "back among the straggling houses. No force was used, perhaps because we considered it wise to go along quietly. When we arrived we were given oranges and bread, but not before we made signs demanding food."

Things seemed all very friendly until one of the Carabinieri, in spite of Greenland's protest, cut off the naval buttons from his overall suit. This could have appeared malicious, but was probably just an advanced case of souvenir-hunting. But it might have proved awkward in the long run. From the buttons attention was turned to the Fair Isle sweater.

"That'll teach you not to wear stupid clothes," joked Ferrier, glad not to be the centre of attraction himself.

Greenland smiled and tried to ignore the curious Italian, until, by signs, the total strength of the police-station indicated that they wanted to know the reason for the lanyard they could see round his neck. What was on the end that disappeared underneath the neck of the sweater? Greenland was getting somewhat fed up with the strong smell of garlic by this time, and he quickly whipped up the lanyard and produced an open sheath-knife at the end of it. There was immediate panic, all very voluble, among the constabulary, and they seemed very much happier when he made no trouble about surrendering the weapon peacefully.

The atmosphere quietened down after this, and a little while later Ferrier turned to Greenland.

"What about a tot, Dick?" he asked.

Greenland's eyes bulged as out of the hip-pocket appeared a small bottle containing a beautiful couple of measures apiece of genuine Navy rum.

"Good health, Curly!"

"Cheers, Dick!"

They both agreed that "Up, Spirits" had never in the history of the Navy been piped at a more opportune moment. The happy ritual had been watched by the Carabinieri, and the Englishmen's stomachs were still glowing when they were taken and locked away, to be left on their own for the first time since their capture. Time passed slowly, until at midday a car drew up outside and a uniformed Italian, who spoke tolerable American, came in to ask them if they were parachutists. They gave him no reply. For a few moments there was a rapid interchange between the Carabinieri and the newcomer, after which the latter asked Greenland and Ferrier if they were British naval personnel. To this they gave a perfunctory "Yes." Seemingly satisfied, the little man left.

After that everything was peace and quiet. The day was quite

warm. Indeed, with all their woollens, both the charioteers were
feeling distinctly hot.

Suddenly there was a roaring and bumping outside, and they were
hustled into the open and bundled into the back of a lorry. The
driver and escort were collecting all the charioteers from various
outlying guard-posts. All six surviving members had been captured.
This rounding-up gave them an opportunity for exchanging news.
Greenland and Dove had a particularly interesting chat, comparing
notes about their two successful 'jobs.' Everything would have been
completely light-hearted if Worthy and Miln had not had to tell of
the deaths of Cook and Simpson.

The Italians were certainly taking all possible precautions. Once
all the six were collected the lorry sped into Palermo, and then proceeded to drop its load, one at a time, at different Carabinieri stations
in the town. They presumably reckoned that one unarmed prisoner
on his own was a manageable proposition for a group of armed
military police. However, they ran out of Carabinieri stations before
the delivery was complete, so Ferrier and Freel had different cells in
the same station.

Greenland's cell measured exactly eleven paces from corner to
corner. It was lit by a small barred window high up in the wall, and
for furniture had a narrow wooden platform to serve as a bed. No
blankets were provided, even though the nights were cold, but Greenland soon jerked the Carabinieri into supplying some, although not
without a long argument about P.O.W. privileges ensuing between
him and an English-speaking guard. Then he settled down for his
first sleep since leaving *Thunderbolt*.

For the next week he saw no one but his guards. They were very
enlightened captors, sending out and paying for *vino* and oranges to
supplement the prison diet, and in small ways helping to break the
loneliness. It may well have been that they were glad of a job behind
the lines and did not wish to run the risk of being drafted to an active
unit on account of disturbances among their charges. It may just
have been that they felt charitably disposed towards the English.

Eventually the boredom was relieved by the news that he was to be
taken to the Palermo Naval Headquarters for interrogation. Greenland found Ferrier there too, but they were allowed no opportunity
for conversation. The first to be questioned was Greenland. Sitting
facing him in the little office to which he was taken were an Italian
naval captain in uniform, another Italian in civilian clothes, who
claimed to be in charge of Italian chariots, and an Italian army
captain in uniform. The two uniformed members of the 'board'

spoke very good English, and started off by wanting to know the number of Greenland's machine. This was by no means an easy question, for he had ridden the front half of 22 and the rear half of 13. After much thought and not a little prompting from his examiners he agreed that it had been 22. Later in the morning Ferrier was to admit to riding 13, all of which no doubt considerably upset the Italian Navy's estimate of the number of machines that had carried out the attack. Ferrier's replies must have been very successfully confusing, for he was finally told by the army captain, "Signalmen in your Royal Navy must be very dumb." In this he whole-heartedly concurred.

Further questions were addressed to the assembled group of charioteers. They were shown an eye-piece spanner and asked what it was. With straight faces they all denied ever having seen such a thing before. The next exhibit was an excellent large-scale chart of the port of Palermo. Greenland remarked that he wished he had been able to see something comparable before the operation, and the Italians, not knowing that the attack had been originally planned for Cagliari and only altered at sea, were first of all very disbelieving. He managed to convince them, however, purely by the most genuine of innocent protestations, and they stopped being disbelieving to become very, very puzzled. One of them said that he was completely unable to understand how the efficient Royal Navy could carry out such an attack without charts. Then the interview was at an end, and the prisoners were dismissed by the army captain. With a generous smile and a very loud voice he informed them: "You are going to Rome. They are great guys in Rome. I come from Rome."

Their departure did not come for a few days, during which all the guards were changed. For Greenland at least—they were still quartered separately—this meant the stopping of *vino* and oranges. Violent complaints soon worked the oracle again, and life was back to normal. Then there were the individual visits to the barber. Greenland was compelled to allow part of his beautiful beard to be mutilated and was left with the most Italian of goatees, which seemed very incongruous on his strong, full face. Eventually the day came for his and Dove's departure, the ratings having already left. They crossed to the mainland via the Messina ferry, then by train along the foot of Italy and northward to Rome. The Italians were continually offering them cigarettes, but would never accept any of the prisoners' allocation. There was no doubt that Italians in general seemed to be very well disposed towards them.

They arrived at Rome, having been on the move for the best part

of twenty-four hours. At the station they were handed over to some
civilian guards. The naval escort shook hands before leaving and
wished them all the best of luck. Then the two charioteers were
separated again, and in next to no time Greenland was 'signing in'
and being asked how much money he had. He was in the Forte
Boccea and was sharing it with five to six hundred Italian political
prisoners as well as with his fellow-charioteer. He was greeted with
the news that he was to spend one month in solitary confinement.
Conditions were tolerable, inasmuch as sheets and blankets were
supplied, the former being the first since Malta. After three days he
discovered Dove's whereabouts by the simple expedient of bursting
into song every time he was escorted to the lavatory. His repertoire
varied little from "Is there anybody here from the Navy?" but by
this means he managed to locate the whole of the party in time, for
all the ratings were there too.

In addition to hearing Greenland's voice, Ferrier also found his
name written with charred wood under a roll of toilet-paper. By this
time he had been in the detention barracks some few days. He had
travelled north with an escort of two sailors and one Carabiniere, the
four charioteer ratings all having been moved separately.

"We had a reserved first-class compartment," Ferrier told the
others afterwards,

and soon after we had settled in all three of the escort went fast asleep.
Unfortunately I woke one of the sailors as I opened the door, and I
should think his yell must have wakened the whole train. The panic
didn't actually decrease when the carabiniere on guard discovered the
loss of his revolver. After this one sailor was always on guard outside
the compartment, while inside I occupied one whole seat and the two
Italians shared the other. There was quite a bit of argument, incidentally, before the accommodation problem was sorted out to my satisfaction.

In the morning there was no food, so I sent for the Captain in charge
of the train, who managed to organize some bread and cheese. Then, at
the next stop, one of the sailors was sent out to buy whatever was available. The train started pulling out before he had returned, but he managed
to scramble into the last compartment. He had brought some goat's-milk
cheese, which was sadly lacking in salt. After I had consumed this the
Train Captain called me into the corridor and pointed out all the places
of interest we were passing. He had a great deal to say about the Fascists. In Naples there was much evidence of a recent visit from the
R.A.F. bomber-boys, and then, before we got to Rome, the Captain
quietly asked me not to mention our earlier conversation. I felt very
magnanimous as I agreed.

When we got to the barracks, here, the sentry at the gate was asleep, but no one seemed to worry. One of my compass buttons was cut off by a guard as a souvenir, but he hadn't the slightest idea of its use. I still have the other seven, plus a hacksaw-blade and a map of Italy, so I haven't done so badly.

When the month of solitary confinement was completed the charioteers were moved to other parts of the camp. Greenland and Dove found themselves sharing a room in the Officers' Block. The four ratings also were quartered together. The interpreter in the Officers' Block was a cheery soul and produced a whole pile of copies of the *Illustrated London News*. When reading began to pall Dove set out to sketch the Dulwich College crest on the wall of the room as a record of his stay. The Italians seemed to have no wish to prevent this and would often stand and watch. Red Cross parcels started to arrive, but were all badly pilfered. After several weeks of this their liberty was extended to include daily games of football and cricket with a tennis-ball in the fort's quadrangle. This was at least a good way of getting tired enough to sleep. The food was not too bad. There was always breakfast of coffee and rolls and a reasonably substantial meal at midday and in the evening. Clothing was supplied: pants made of wood, socks of paper, excellent Italian naval boots, and an Italian matelot's jumper. It was not until reaching England some years later that it was realized that these were charged for, so that it was perhaps just as well that the uniforms for which most of them were measured never appeared. The collapse of Italy seemed to affect the camp tailoring arrangements.

Throughout their stay at the Forte Boccea they were told at regular intervals that they would soon be going before a tribunal, and once, when they saw the Camp Commandant to protest about the Red Cross parcels, they were told that it was only through Italian naval insistence that they were still being regarded as saboteurs and not as spies, and that they owed their lives to the Italian Navy. Later they were told that their correct status had officially been recognized and that they would soon be transferred to a proper P.O.W. Camp.

The ratings were the first to leave. They went to a camp near Genoa, and then up to Germany, to spend the rest of the War near Luneberg. Several days later Greenland and Dove were told to be ready to go at short notice. When they were fallen in before an army captain, with their few belongings stacked up beside them, they felt they were at last on the move. But, in a scene which displayed the Latin temperament at its most volatile level, they almost had their hopes dashed. It all began with the Warrant Quartermaster of the camp spotting one of his sheets in the shape of Greenland's home-made kit-bag. There followed a voluble accusation and a hot denial, Greenland trying to look as though the suggestion of such vandalism was the worst kind of insult. He further suggested that the Quarter-master should go and count his stocks before making such an outrageous charge. The little man stalked out of the room, to return a few minutes later looking very crestfallen. He had to admit, he said, that there were the right number of sheets in the store (Greenland had cut one sheet in half and returned the unused piece so folded as to look complete), but at the same time he still would not let the kit-bag leave the camp. Even if he could not prove anything he was fairly certain in his suspicions.

The captain had taken no part in this cafuffle, but he at last inter-vened to indicate that Greenland should leave without the kit-bag. This Greenland refused to do, and then played his trump-card by suggesting that in the British Services it would be considered most unusual for a captain to take orders from a warrant officer. The Captain was successfully stung by this, and rapped out some instruc-tions to the W.O., punctuating all his remarks with jerky arm-movements. The W.O.'s reply sounded as though it were highly insubordinate, and the discussion about who would give orders to whom continued for a full couple of minutes. But might had to be right in the end, and the little quartermaster was last seen stumping sulkily away.

The move was to Campo 35, at Padula. They were back south again, in the 'ankle' of Italy. The inmates of the camp were drawn from all three Services and were nearly all officers.

Greenland's foremost memory of his stay at Padula is of the fer-vent optimism throughout the camp that they would all be freed when the Italians signed the armistice that every one knew was in the air. Suddenly, however, half the camp was moved north, and it was realized that their captivity was by no means at an end. The remain-der of them made devious plans to delay any further departure. Indeed, on one occasion, when three hundred officers were being assembled to await transport, it took the Italians twelve hours to complete the roll-call.

First of all they were huddled together in one large room—the refectory of the pre-War monastery that had become a camp—with all their belongings.

"Abbott, Allan, Ashworth, Attingall."

These four men took an extraordinary lot of finding.

"Ayres, Baker, Baynes, Baynton."

Another few minutes before these could assemble their kit.

"Bennett, Charles, Cook, Craker."

And so it went on. It took close on half an hour for the first twenty-four names to be called and for their owners to be paraded outside. All might have gone reasonably well had not an Italian officer decided it would be a good idea to have a check-count. The number of men outside had shrunk to twenty. Recheck and recheck again, but there were still only twenty. No good! Have to start the whole thing again right from the beginning. March them inside.

"Abbott, Allan, Ashworth, Attingal."

With the repetition of such delaying actions the counting was prolonged for twelve hours—from 6 P.M. to 6 A.M.—a rate of twenty-five men an hour. And even after they had all been checked there was another delay, this time of Italian origin, which lasted for three more days. They lived in hopes that they would not be moved in time, but eventually were entrained. Recent and heavy R.A.F. bombing made their journey a long and weary one, but, in the circumstances, they exulted every time the train jerked to a halt. Finally, they reached their next 'home'—a barracks in the Northern Italian town of Bologna, in the province of Emilia, some hundred miles south-west of Venice.

The night of their arrival all Italian units in the area were relieved by German troops. In their case the newcomers were men of the Adolf Hitler Panzer Regiment. There was no change in the good treatment afforded to all the prisoners, though there were strong rumours of purges being carried out among the local populations and the Italian military during the first few days of the new régime.

Thence, after a short stay, they moved to Germany, where they were accommodated in a permanent Marlag for the rest of the War. There they learned that they had been gazetted to the D.S.O., and that Ferrier and Freel had been awarded the C.G.M.

Unbeknown to them they were being credited with mere General Service pay for the whole of their prison career. This still remains a mystery. Submariners, flying personnel, X-craft crews, and other 'special' personnel were paid the increased 'spare crew' rates of pay applicable to their branch of the Service during their period of imprisonment—but not the charioteers. Nor were post-War protests able to rectify this.

CHAPTER TWELVE

Tripoli

WITH the return of the submarines on completion of Operation "Principle" the chariot party in Malta numbered only three officers and five ratings, which small total was soon further reduced by the voluntary departure to rejoin General Service of one of the ratings. Training continued with the two remaining machines.

In North Africa the Eighth Army was fast approaching Tripoli, and the Navy was asked to immobilize the blockships which the Germans were known to be preparing for the harbour entrance. This would have a considerable bearing on the situation when the Army arrived, as, if no supplies could be brought in by sea, the range of further military operations would be severely limited. It was, therefore, decided to attack the blockships with the two chariots on the night of January 18–19, and the machines were accordingly loaded aboard *Thunderbolt* with the remaining members of the party.

On the night in question the R.A.F. co-operated by staging a raid over the town and by dropping red flares over the harbour entrance. Launching had been planned for half-past ten. Unfortunately, and on account of navigational difficulties and lack of star-sights, *Thunderbolt* was a little farther from the shore than had been intended when she surfaced at ten. Lieutenant-Commander Crouch decided to run in on the surface for as long as he could. Soon after surfacing, and while the chariots and their crews were still being prepared, an enemy *E*-boat was sighted at close range. The *E*-boat's crew must have been asleep, for they failed to see *Thunderbolt*'s silhouette during the whole of the thirty minutes that the submarine continued on the surface in sight of the enemy vessel. It was not, indeed, until everything was quite ready that *Thunderbolt* eventually trimmed down and withdrew. This devotion to duty, in the face of considerable risk, enabled the two machines to get away to a first-rate start.

The crews for this operation were Lieutenant Geoff Larkin, with Petty Officer Conrad Berey, and Sub-Lieutenant H. L. H. Stevens, on his second operation, with Chief E. R. A. Stanley Buxton. The latter was really a Number One, but volunteered to make the trip sitting astern of Stevens, rather than miss the operation altogether. As there was a shortage of Number Two's his offer was eagerly accepted.

From the moment that *Thunderbolt* withdrew Larkin lost sight of Stevens. This immediate separation was becoming a feature of chariot attacks. Larkin trimmed his machine down and proceeded on the surface at maximum possible speed. By this means he hoped to avoid being spotted by the *E*-boat and yet to reach sighting distance of the harbour entrance before the flares ceased, at the planned time of eleven o'clock. Within half an hour he was passing a small convoy consisting of another *E*-boat, a trawler, and a barge. Their presence made him decide to dive, and it was only then he discovered that his machine's hydroplanes had been so damaged at the time of launching as to be completely useless. However, he managed to get under the water by judicious use of the pumps.

He continued on the surface for a further hour, during which he tried every possible means of manœuvring the machine with the hydroplanes in their damaged state. But all he succeeded in doing was to convince himself that the chariot was manageable only on the surface. With the known defences of the harbour a surface attack was completely out of the question, and would only endanger the chances of the other team, which consideration had been drilled into all charioteers as being of the utmost importance. Larkin, therefore, turned south, closed the shore, and beached the machine in heavy surf and right under the noses of some Italian sentries just west of Tripoli. The time was approximately 2.30 A.M. As soon as he and Berey had their feet on the ground they sent the chariot out to sea with the pumps open and the charge set to explode later that morning. She dived about a cable's length from the beach.

The charioteers cut off their suits and sank them, together with all other incriminating evidence. This done, they made their way through the outskirts of Tripoli, having decided to spend the day as far as possible from the sea. They passed several sentries without apparently being seen and, having managed to fill their water-bottles en route, bedded down for the day just before seven o'clock in a small trench that lay alongside a road which was being used to take the damaged armour out of, and supplies into, the town.

For almost twelve hours they rested in this rather vulnerable position, leaving the trench at 6 P.M. on the 19th, and striking inland across country. However, they soon found that the going was so heavy in the sand, and the water so scarce, that they were obliged to continue via the principal road. By doing this they hoped also to be able to collect an unattended car or lorry. During the early hours of the night they came across several vehicles, but all of them were heavily guarded. Apart from divers' knives they carried no weapons, and could not therefore hope to prevail against armed troops. The knives, however, proved to be immensely useful in cutting all the telephone and other cables that ran alongside the road. Perhaps this slight effort would help the Allied attack in some small way, they thought.

Following upon a rather severe air-raid, during which they hoped hard not to be destroyed by British bombs, they found a suitable copse in which to spend the following day. This again passed without incident, and nightfall saw them continuing their journey along the road, cutting wires and cables when they could find them and slouching along like Arabs whenever any mechanized transport was passing. Food was largely restricted to malted-milk tablets and water, which seemed to be a satisfactory diet. The moon was bright and visibility good, which conditions favoured the charioteers, in that they could see sentries a good distance away and take the necessary avoiding action. At about ten o'clock three figures crossed the road just ahead of them. Although it was difficult to see for certain, these looked like two Europeans and an Arab. Owing to their furtive actions they were thought possibly to be the other chariot-crew escaping. To try and identify themselves Larkin whistled *God save the King* as softly as he could. But he got no reply, and the three figures disappeared into the darkness. An hour or two later Larkin and Berey entered the heavily defended area of Castel Benito airport. They were just passing a bombed water-tower when two German soldiers walked up to them. As the leading German came nearer he saw only two blue-uniformed backs turned towards him. These appeared to belong to two persons performing a most necessary and personal function. Apologizing for disturbing them, he turned away from within arm's length and made off.

The mumbled German apology was still causing Larkin and Berey considerable elation as they walked away from the water-tower and passed within fifty feet of at least half a dozen separate sentries. The remainder of the night was to be less uneventful than its predecessor had been. The two charioteers made their way past a village, an enemy-occupied farm, some Italian sentries, and an anti-tank ditch. It was while making a detour round a wider part of this last obstacle that they discovered a half-sucked lemon lying on the ground. This they divided and consumed, skin and all. A few kilometres farther on some chickens were heard to one side of the road. Berey went off to acquire one or two of these, and after a masterpiece of stalking, and just as he was about to enter a broken-down chicken-house, an Arab came out of the adjoining hovel and caused the charioteer to fade silently away. Returning to the road, he was just in time to help Larkin drive away a large and very unpleasant dog.

By this time both Larkin and Berey had realized, to their great disappointment, that their pet scheme was not going to be possible. They had intended to tie some heavy telephone cables across the road at about chest height and thus unseat a motor cyclist, preferably at a corner, where he would be going sufficiently slowly for the machine not to be disastrously damaged. But all trees and telegraph poles seemed to be situated only on straight, fast stretches of road, and the idea could not be put into practice.

For the next day's residence they chose a small bush in a hollow in the middle of a deserted vehicle-park. They were sleeping peacefully when Berey was woken by guests arriving in the guise of an armoured column, and he derived much pleasure from waking the snoring Larkin and telling him not to look now, but he thought they were being surrounded. Their immunity lasted only until the Germans started gathering brushwood for fires, when they were discovered lying motionless face downward. A German kicked the nearer body and continued to do so until, after about the third kick, Larkin stood up.

"Good afternoon," he ventured.

"Ha, Tommy," replied the soldier as several of his comrades came running up.

"No, Navy," he was corrected, but, whether the correction was understood or not, the two charioteers were relieved of their knives and packs of concentrated food and led into the centre of the camp. It was immediately decided that they were parachutists, and they were given a billy-can of thick soup-cum-stew apiece.

While they were still at luncheon some American Kittyhawks started a strafe. Within a few moments the only visible human beings were two very hungry Englishmen, rapidly filling themselves, and two very uncomfortable-looking German guards.

As soon as the park had come back to normal they were loaded into a lorry with an officer, a sergeant, and the two guards. Larkin and Berey were not a little worried about the foreign currency, Italian cigarettes, and German identification papers which they were carrying. They would have attempted, had they been taken by Italian troops, to pass themselves off as good Germans, but now all

G

their German impedimenta were a considerable source of embarrassment. Luckily both men were pipe-smokers, and under the guise of getting out, knocking clean, filling, and lighting their pipes they were able to dispose of all the papers, etc., over the side of the lorry. Glancing over the side later on, Larkin was horrified to see that a large portion of his scattered papers had fallen into a tin hat that hung outboard. So he had to go through all the pipe-motions again. Miraculously, he was still not observed.

They stopped for the night at an Italian settlement. The sergeant in charge of the escort was an Austrian, and the treatment which the prisoners received from him was very good indeed. They were given water to wash in and soap—very hard and coarse. Later they sat down to a meal of what tasted like tinned Spam, eaten with coarse, black bread. This they swilled down with some coffee, the sergeant apologizing profusely for the fact of its being about 60 per cent. ersatz. He evidently took his sense of hospitality seriously. It was a most successful repast, and during it conversation was carried on by sign-language, eked out with words of French, German, and English. The prisoners asked what was happening in Tripoli, and were told that the Germans were blowing it up and leaving. "*Kaput*" seemed to be the operative expression. Larkin then sang the chorus of a German drinking-song, which his hosts professed to recognize, singing in return a very near version of *Pack up your Troubles*.

The sergeant produced his wallet and some fifteen to twenty photos of girls. These he described as "*gut*" or "O.K.," and told where all of them lived. He had been in the Afrika Korps twenty-one months, and seemed quite satisfied with life. By the time they all turned in he and the three members of the escort were quite convinced that the prisoners were friendly types.

Shortly after retiring for the night, therefore, the two Englishmen were able to collect some bread, some water, and their clothes, and steal away silently over the tail-board of the lorry, leaving the sergeant and a corporal asleep in the vehicle and the two sentries talking near the bonnet.

Until dawn and for the early part of the following night they headed for Tripoli, spending the intervening day under another bush. By nine in the evening of what was the sixth day after leaving the submarine Larkin and Berey were picking oranges in an orchard on the outskirts of Tripoli. Suddenly a shadowy figure pointed a gun at Berey and said something in Arabic.

Thinking that the stranger was an Arab, Larkin shouted, "Ingleezi, Ingleezi!"

"English?" replied the figure, "I, Italiano."

Hands were shaken all round.

Within a few minutes the Italian had led them into a small building, had given them some wine and the wherewithal to wash and feed, and was talking twenty to the dozen. His one great fear was that the troops advancing with the Eighth Army might be Australians! The charioteers had been fortunate with this encounter and, after their most comfortable night since leaving Malta, strolled round the small farm. Later in the morning of Day 7 they were taken by the Italian to be introduced to two neighbouring farmers, by whom they were pressed to take coffee and liqueurs. Then their first acquaintance changed into his best suit, harnessed his horse and trap, and drove them into town.

The first troops they met were a body of men in charge of a tall captain. Larkin got down from the trap, went across to him and said, "Good morning." Being asked what he and Berey were doing there, he replied, tactlessly but truthfully, "Waiting for you fellows."

Soon they found themselves in front of a brigadier who took notes of what German arms and dispositions they had seen on their travels, and then the Naval authorities were contacted. Their Italian host had promised to kill a chicken for lunch if his guests returned, so leave was sought and obtained—"To collect my kit, sir"—and a very tasty lunch partaken, even though the amount of spaghetti was rather frightening at first sight.

The following day they were flown from Castel Benito to Cairo. After five rather hectic days they joined another plane, for Malta, whence they returned to England in one of His Majesty's submarines.

Meanwhile much had been happening to Stevens and Buxton. By 3.30 A.M. they had reached the lighthouse on the harbour-wall, having been in the water for approximately five hours. As they turned into the main basin the sea-wall of the inner harbour could be clearly seen, as well as the silhouette of Larkin's main target. But the inner entrance was not visible, and a remembered course had to be set.

Buxton was certainly not enjoying the ride. His suit had been torn on *Thunderbolt*'s jumping-wire, and during the deeper dives water was forcing itself inside his layers of woollens. He felt chilled through. Indeed, the effect of the cold water was such that he was experiencing great difficulty in holding his mouthpiece in position, and he was forced to tap Stevens on the shoulder and ask him to stay on the surface. No sooner had he done this than two almost simultaneous explosions took place directly ahead of them, and in the light of the flashes it could be seen that they came from the fore and after holds of a ship lying dead ahead. This vessel was only 150 yards away and seemed to continue the silhouette of the harbour-wall. Stevens then realized that they had arrived too late to prevent the entrance being blocked.

They accordingly attacked the small, deserted merchantman that was their subsidiary target and started looking for a suitable place to land. Within a few minutes they touched bottom just under a section of the sea-wall and dismounted. They were in water up to their necks when Stevens sent the chariot seaward in a sinking condition. It was obvious that the wall, rising sheer to a height of six feet above the water, would be difficult to scale. However, Stevens removed Buxton's breathing-apparatus and tried to help him up to the top. But Buxton was exhausted by his ordeal and found he could not manage the struggle. He dropped back into the water and they set off walking in search of somewhere easier. Unfortunately the depth increased steeply on both sides of them. Buxton was without breathing-apparatus and could not hope to venture deeper. It was almost an impasse. They decided that Stevens should continue the search on his own while Buxton stayed close under the wall, holding on to a small crevice to prevent himself being washed away. At times the waves broke over his head and he swallowed a considerable amount of salt water. He was feeling extremely cold and tired, and knew he could not hold on much longer. Standing up to his neck in water, complete in diving-suit and heavy boots but without breathing-apparatus, he felt that no diver could ever have been in a more frustrating position. His only hope lay in an early return on the part of Stevens, which did indeed materialize before the last of Buxton's strength had gone.

Soon Buxton was free of his suit and boots, and the two of them were making their way, one swimming and the other walking beneath the surface, to a shallower patch a little farther along the wall. A few minutes later they had both gained the top, although not before Buxton had slipped and fallen backward, striking his head on a stone some six feet below on the landward side.

In the half-dawn they left the wall and climbed through some barbed wire, only to find, as the light improved, that they were inside an Italian army camp. Thinking the boldest course to be the best, they began walking towards the main gate. They had not gone far before a large explosion occurred, which seemed to come from a petrol dump behind them. This evidently woke all the sentries, who came running up, apparently convinced that the two charioteers were the perpetrators of the sabotage. It was easy for them to harbour suspicions as Buxton was wet through and, with a badly bleeding temple from where he had fallen off the wall, presented a very bedraggled sight. Stevens commenced an argument in German, and the two of them produced their German papers, but as the sergeant of the guard spoke more German than Stevens this masquerade did not last very long.

From this point their travels followed a routine prisoner-of-war pattern. They were rushed from fort to fort, from authority to authority. They were searched, subjected to the 'stooge-prisoner' trick, and practically starved. One night was spent in the sand, the two of them being chained together by the ankles and given only ground-sheets, in spite of the considerable cold. This was the coldest night either of them had ever spent, and with the chains biting into their ankles every time they moved they felt pretty miserable.

By February 4, sixteen days after having been launched from *Thunderbolt*, they had reached Tunis Docks. In company with eighty other British prisoners and 250 members of the French Foreign Legion, they were crowded into the for'ard hold of a cargo-vessel. Two days later began a nightmare journey. Sanitary conditions were appallingly bad, there being only two fifty-gallon oil-drums, which were emptied by bucket and rope. Then there was the thought that the prison-ship might be attacked by one of our own submarines. With only one hatchway leading from the hold to the upper deck, there would have been sheer chaos.

They arrived at Palermo early the following morning, but the hold was not opened up until 4 P.M., when the whole 330 were lined up on the dock-side and counted and recounted at least a dozen times. Thence Stevens and Buxton were sent direct to Campo 66, at Capua. They were both quartered in the Officers' Compound, which was luxuriously comfortable. There were camp-beds and sheets for all, and hot showers were available at intervals. Unfortunately, it was not long before a routine check on ranks and official numbers revealed that Buxton was in the wrong place. This meant his being transferred to the Warrant Officers' section of the camp and his separation from Stevens.

The latter was soon mixed up in a complicated escape-plan, but just as the arrangements were approaching maturity he was ordered to transfer to Campo 35 at Padula. He was the only prisoner so transferring, but, as he had a guard who refused to leave his side on any pretext, train-jumping was out of the question. Padula Camp was an ex-monastery in a lovely valley of the Appenines, 2000 feet

above sea-level, with towering giants on either side. Its prisoner
population consisted of approximately 500 officers and 150 ratings
and other ranks. It had a field attached, on which the 'inmates'
were able to play soccer, cricket, or baseball.

Early in May Greenland and Dove arrived. Once they were able
to join Stevens a grand reunion party was held. They were allowed
to mix freely without being under observation as Stevens was still
regarded by the enemy authorities as a Commando. He had by this
time already joined forces with two other Naval officers for escaping
purposes. They had together dug a tunnel, complete with electric
lighting, railway, and air-conditioning, to join a disused sewer
leading to a point a hundred yards outside the outermost circle of
wall and barbed wire. The three of them were ready to go, and
planned to make a dash for the coast, twenty miles away, steal a boat,
and sail for North Africa. But the Senior British Officer thought
they should wait a while for outside events to develop after the fall
of Tunis. While they were waiting the Italians discovered the tunnel
and filled it in with concrete. Another was started two days later.

Within a week of this discovery orders came for Stevens to proceed to Campo 50. This he knew to be the interrogation camp in
Rome, where it was customary for all N.O.'s to spend ten days
during the early stages of their imprisonment. The first person he
met there was Buxton. They had little chance for communication,
and were soon separated completely for the next ten or eleven weeks
of what Stevens had expected to be a ten days' stay.

Before this transfer Buxton had led a boring existence at Capua.
Owing to a shortage of firewood it had soon become difficult to make
a brew of tea or coffee in his compound, so he had set to work to
make an electric heater. After a considerable amount of scrounging
he began experimenting, only to receive a number of shocks from
the home-made apparatus. In time, however, he completed a
heater out of a milk-tin and a tin which had contained beef-roll. One
tin was put inside the other and insulated with strips of wood. The
two electric leads were secured one to each tin and the whole con-
traption was immersed in a larger tin holding three-quarters of a
gallon of water. The current passing from one tin to another through
the water created enough heat to boil the three-quarters of a gallon
in nine minutes. All the time the apparatus had to be both made and
used in complete secrecy. It proved eminently successful.

When Mussolini fell from power the atmosphere in the detention
barracks improved considerably. Large numbers of German tanks
began moving into the city, and all the Italian soldiers were disarmed.

This left the prisoners still in the barracks, guarded by unarmed Italians who were in their turn guarded by armed Germans. Within a day or two the Italians received orders to return to their homes, and in the ensuing confusion Stevens and Buxton managed to acquire an Italian uniform apiece and escape into the city.

One of the guards had given them information about roads to take and local customs to observe. Stevens still had some currency left from his escape activities at Padula, so they were able to board a trolley-bus marked "San Pietro." It was only one fare for the whole journey, so there was no need for them to open their mouths. The terminus was St Peter's Church, theoretically part of the Vatican City, but open to the public and with no normal communication into Papal territory. The two charioteers walked in as Italian soldiers, and passed the guards at the entrance, trying to look as though they were going in to pray.

They knelt until their knees got sore, thinking how to enter the Vatican proper and so claim the protection of the Pope. The only way seemed to be to gate-crash, but the Swiss Guards were everywhere. They remained in the church for such a long time that some police officials became suspicious, ordered them out, and started using force when they refused to leave. This resulted in a tremendous scuffle and free-for-all up and down the aisles of the largest church in Christendom, with Stevens and Buxton shouting at the tops of their voices and appealing to every priest they could see. But weight of numbers prevailed, and they were eventually deposited outside the church within sight of a German patrol. All seemed lost, but for some reason the Germans did not come over to see what all the rumpus was about. The Italians were just about to exercise their own authority and take the two suspects away for questioning when a British diplomatic representative arrived.

He immediately entered into a rapid interchange with the police, the content of which seemed to be that he was protecting the two Englishmen with his person—whereupon he took each of them ceremonially by the arm—until permission should be obtained by the British Minister for them to enter the city.

Seven hours later they were admitted, on September 14, 1943. From that date until their return to England, in July 1944, they remained in the Vatican, enjoying all the amenities of a civilized life, awaiting the arrival of the Fifth Army and watching through the window of their room the Germans passing by on the opposite side of the street.

CHAPTER THIRTEEN

Sicily

Of the original party of twenty-six charioteers who had left Scotland for Malta there were eight remaining after Larkin and Berey had returned from their escapade. It was decided to disestablish the unit, and the three officers and five ratings were sent home to the United Kingdom. The total loss on operations, including killed, missing, and prisoners-of-war, was eight officers and ten ratings.

In January 1943 a fresh class of eighteen commenced instruction at Gosport under the jovial Mr Chadwick. After their initial training they were transferred to join *Titania* in Loch Corrie, where they continued to gain experience under Lieutenant-Commander David Shaw, R.N.V.R., who had first entered the flotilla in the original *X*-craft class. Later, in the deeper water of Cairnbawn, the programme followed very much the same pattern as that of the previous year. The same things happened. Chariots were lost, charioteers 'passed out,' and the wardroom was periodically wrecked. Seven officers and six ratings completed the course—a matter of 72 per cent.

On April 16 a party numbering four officers and ten ratings was selected to proceed to Malta. In command of Party "Ted" was Lieutenant-Commander John McCarter, S.A.N.F.(V), a former charioteer who had been forced to give up diving for medical reasons. It was at about this time too that *Titania* went for a refit. Tiny Fell had been appointed to command her, the only possible contender for the honour in the absence of Commander Sladen, who by this time was no longer with the flotilla, much to every one's regret.

When the charioteers arrived in Malta they were accommodated, as the previous party had been, in Manoel Island. As soon as the machines were delivered practice-runs started in Ghain-Tuffieha Bay. Weather and water conditions were magnificent, and the only complaint was that dressing in the control-room of a small *U*-class submarine proved extremely hot and uncomfortable.

Unknown to the rest of the party, McCarter was busily searching for operations. He had been told before leaving Scotland that everything was ready for them in Malta and that they were urgently required. In actual fact the first thing that Captain S/M 10 (Captain G. C. Phillips, D.S.O., G.M., R.N.) knew about the charioteers was their arrival. It therefore says much for McCarter that despite his comparative inexperience in Naval matters—especially in an administrative capacity—he was soon able to find a worth-while occupation for his charges.

The invasion of Sicily was the next move in the Allied offensive, and a detailed and reliable reconnaissance of the proposed landing-beaches was of the highest priority. Initial visits had already been paid by canoeists, but these had proved rather expensive, and it was decided to use chariots for any further work. The technique was worked out and practised in a matter of a few days. By May 19 in fact—only one week after commencing training in earnest—several teams were able to demonstrate a release from U-class submarines before the Governor of Malta, Field-Marshal Lord Gort, in Sliema Creek.

The first successful reconnaissance was made on May 31 by Lieutenant Taffy Evans, and Petty Officer W. S. Smith, operating from the submarine Unseen (Lieutenant M. L. C. Crawford, D.S.C., R.N.). The chariot was carried on the after-casing in special chocks. The principle was for it to be released about three miles offshore and be led to within half a mile of the beach by a collapsible canoe. The latter also carried the infra-red gear for making the subsequent rendezvous. On nearing the beach Evans dived to fifteen feet and proceeded inshore until the machine struck bottom. Then he dismounted, attached the end of a wire to his belt, and commenced wading up the slope until his head broke surface. He had a good look round before signalling to Smith on the wire that he was about to return.

Inboard on the chariot Smith read off the distance his Number One had travelled and watched carefully for the solder-blobs, with which the wire was marked at every five yards. As each of these came in he signalled to Evans, who then recorded the depth shown on his portable pressure-gauge, marking it on a bone-pad beautifully arranged in a fascinating pattern of squares. Thus there was a reading of the depth for each five yards of distance along the sea-bed.

Evans and Smith were able to pay subsequent visits to the beaches, and similar reconnaissances were also made by some of the other teams, among whom Lieutenant W. Jakeman, R.N.V.R., and Petty

Officer, A. C. Kirby and Sub-Lieutenant V. J. Mills, R.N.Z.N.V.R., and Cook D. Cruickshank put up particularly fine performances.

By the second week of June there were no further reconnaissances or other operations on the board, and plans were made to find the charioteers other jobs. Members of the highly trained party accordingly found themselves employed in such varied capacities as staff at a survivors' receiving centre, labourers at the preparation of an L.C.T. slipway, M.T.B. crews, berthing parties, etc. Two fortunates —Petty Officers Smith and Warren—went to the island's D.S.E.A. tank to instruct submarine crews.

As soon as the invasion commenced, frequent and urgent demands began pouring in for shallow-water divers to clear the propellers of landing-craft and perform other such duties. Out of this need was created the Mobile Diving Unit, to consist of Smith, Warren, and Petty Officer Kirby, along with Chief Petty Officer "Ginger" Warr, the D.S.E.A. Coxswain of Malta. The transport by which the mobility was ensured was a rather ancient Hillman Minx, acquired by somewhat dubious means, and a powerful motor-cycle. Most of the diving was undertaken half-naked in appalling conditions, among bilge-oil and other filth, and often meant crawling under an L.S.T. in the middle of the night to see if a "small length of heaving line" could be cleared, only to find that what was round the propeller was a 4½-inch wire hawser.

While these duties were being operated on a 'night-on, night-off' basis Kirby and Warren worked out an idea that would mean getting back to charioteering. They suggested that some useful purpose could be achieved by using the machines as underwater minelayers. Details were checked with the appropriate authorities, and it was discovered that a chariot with only one rider could comfortably take four mines. The charioteers had their eyes on the Corinth Canal as the first area of operation. This seemed to be a pleasant and convenient place to drop eight mines and then walk to a prearranged rendezvous. Semi-official preparations were put in hand and included training for the all-important walk. The scheme was submitted to Captain S/M 10, and then sent home for final approval. But it must have been too ambitious, for nothing more was ever heard.

Towards the end of June an additional six teams arrived. To the older inhabitants this seemed sheer folly, as there was so much unemployment already. Apparently the newcomers had heard wild stories about the success of Party "Ted" and were eager to join in the fun and the operations. Somebody seemed to have slipped.

Eventually a major operation was planned to take place at the end of August and to consist of an attack on the battleships of the Italian fleet in Taranto. H.M. S/M's *Unrivalled* and *Ultor* were each to carry one chariot, and the teams were selected after a full-scale dress rehearsal against our own battle-fleet in Grand Harbour, in which the *Rodney* was well and truly accounted for. The final choice fell upon Jock Brewster and Jock Brown, who had so nearly reached the *Tirpitz*, and Sub-Lieutenant H. Hargreaves, R.N.V.R., and Steward Brown.[1] They were given full escape-programmes before they left, catering for a crossing to Albania and then a period of hiding before the invasion of that country materialized. When the time came for going they went off in high spirits.

"I was most impressed with the enthusiasm and keenness of both submarines and of the four charioteers in this hazardous undertaking," wrote Captain S/M 10, "particularly when the submarine *Traveller* had been lost without explanation in the same area."

Two days prior to the actual attack the operation was cancelled by the Commander-in-Chief, Mediterranean, and the submarines returned to Malta. This was naturally a profound disappointment, but the reason for the decision became clear later when one of the targets arrived off Malta to surrender.

Soon after this Brewster visited Taranto to collect details of an interview between Commander Sladen and Capitano Ernesto Forza, the commanding officer of the Italian human torpedo flotilla—the Decima Flottiglia Mas—at Spezia. Forza had been the officer in civilian clothes who had helped to interrogate Greenland and company at Palermo. He told Sladen that in addition to the damage inflicted directly by the chariots on that occasion, Dove's target, the merchantman *Viminale*, had been subsequently torpedoed when on tow out of the harbour.

Previous to this attack the Italians had had no idea that we were using human torpedoes and thought it unlikely that we should do so after three years of war. There were also some interesting details to be learnt about Italian human torpedo organization. The main base was at Spezia, in Northern Italy, and the flotilla constituted a complete and self-contained branch of the Naval Service. It had three submarines permanently attached, was equipped with the most luxurious workshops, and, in the person of Forza, had a free hand in almost everything it did. The machines were manned by engineer officers and rating divers. Each officer chose his own partner and stuck to him throughout. Before an operation the conditions of the

[1] Now ex-Steward A. Brown, D.S.M.

target were reproduced as nearly as possible at Spezia, and dummy runs were done in great detail. An attack on Scapa Flow was being contemplated, and the initial working-up was in progress when the Armistice came.

Ten to twelve degrees centigrade (about fifty degrees Fahrenheit) was considered the coldest water temperature in which they could operate and eighty feet the greatest depth to which they could go. On each of these counts the British teams could rate themselves superior.

At Algeciras, in Spain, just across the bay from Gibraltar, the Italians had established a depot-ship out of an ordinary merchant vessel ostensibly stuck there for want of spares. Workshops had been built in her and a hole cut in the hull below the water line for launching the machines. However, the nets at Gibraltar proved to be beyond their resources and they achieved little from this rather novel piece of planning.

It was with reference to this vessel that Captain S/M 10 wrote in a covering letter: "It is a matter for regret that this information was not available earlier, as the destruction of the ship by British chariots operating from Gibraltar would have been an interesting operation, and one to which the Spaniards could have hardly objected."

After the surrender of the Italian fleet it was decided that the main future for chariots lay in the Far East, and all personnel were sent back to Scotland, arriving in ones and twos during December 1943. They were glad to be back. What had started as a venture likely to be packed full of excitement and worth-while offensive activity had ended up as several months of acute inaction and frustration. Surely, most people felt, *something* better could have been made of their services?

PART III: NORWAY

CHAPTER FOURTEEN

The Shore-bases

It was on August 20, 1942, that John Lorimer—one of the first X-craft training-class—reported at the Kyles of Bute Hydropathic Hotel. There he met Commander David Ingram, D.S.C., R.N.,[1] a former submarine commander who had been appointed to form a Scottish shore-base from which midget-submarine training could begin in earnest. From Ingram came the initial drive and sense of urgency which put this part of the flotilla on its feet as what it essentially was, a body of men who had to be very highly trained to undertake an unusual job.

The Hydro was a long, three-storied building, with only an entrance porch to break its straight line. Of a rough-faced grey, local rock, it probably dated from the years just before the First World War. Its basements held a fascinating collection of baths, but whatever its hydropathic and residential merits in earlier days it never rated as the friendliest of the flotilla's several homes-from-home.

Situated high on the side of a hill, it overlooked the little fishing-village of Port Bannatyne. From its windows one could see the anchorage that was to form part of the base. Two roads rose up slowly from the pier to the gates at the entrance to the Hydro's drive. One road went direct, the other past the Royal Hotel. The latter was the more patronized, for the beer was good and Peter, the landlord, fast became the flotilla's friend. A more prominent first impression for Lorimer, however, was possibly the steepness of the hotel's long drive. It was to tax many a pair of legs after weary days at sea.

On the last day of the month H.M.S. *Alecto* met *X.3* at the railhead at Faslane. The small submarine was lowered into the water on the jib of a giant crane and proceeded on her engine and under *Alecto*'s escort down the Clyde, passing abeam of Port Bannatyne to enter Loch Striven.

The loch was already reserved as a submarine exercise area and was

[1] Now Captain D. C. Ingram, C.B.E., D.S.C., R.N.

closed to normal surface traffic not under the control of the Hydro. An early bend hid the rest of the loch from view, but once this was rounded a long, narrow fjord-like waterway was revealed. The steep rock walls, scarcely relieved with any vegetation, cast shadows across the water at all hours of the day, giving an impression of mystery and, on some occasions, of evil. But at the head of the loch could be seen a green, lush patch of lowland, giving on to a long winding valley, which was in its turn backed by a dip in the line of encircling hills.

Ardtaraig House, the shooting-lodge at the head of the loch which had been commandeered to form the flotilla's advanced base, lay abeam when *Alecto* anchored that last evening in August. A few days later *Present Help* arrived to relieve her, and with the move into Ardtaraig *Alecto* was able to return to her other duties.

The Hydro having been commissioned H.M.S. *Varbel* four days previously, the shooting-lodge automatically became *Varbel II.* Soon its rooms were full of crews-in-the-making. From Gosport came the second and third training-classes, with many interesting personalities among them, including a shortish, fair-haired South African reserve lieutenant, Peter Philip. Before the War he had been known to thousands of South Africans as Uncle Peter of the radio children's hour programme. It was by the same name that he was to be known to all who served with him.

During October Willy Meeke left for Vickers-Armstrongs at Barrow-in-Furness to advise on the later stages of the construction of the six operational craft that were being built. Without its senior seagoing member the little unit felt very bare, even though his place in command of *X.3* was ably filled by his ex-First Lieutenant, Don Cameron. John Lorimer was appointed as Cameron's Number One.

Training continued fairly smoothly, with occasional excitements to keep people on their toes. Cameron and Lorimer took classes out in the craft forenoon and afternoon, with the odd day off for maintenance. The most exciting occurrence during these early weeks came early in November. Lorimer was taking out Sub-Lieutenants Gay and Laites in the afternoon, when the induction trunk-valve (the trunking was similar to its successor the Snort, or Schnorkel) jammed open on diving and somebody dropped into the bilges the only wheel-spanner, without which it was impossible to blow main ballast-tanks. Water was pouring into the control-room, and the craft was sinking with a stern-down angle of 85 degrees. Within a few moments the motor and the battery were both flooded, the latter giving off thick chlorine fumes which soon filled the whole boat.

Inside four minutes the craft was on the bottom in over a hundred feet of water. *Present Help* had seen signs of the disaster and had passed the emergency signal "Tripper," this being the local equivalent of the now so unfortunately well-known "Subsmash." Hydrophones were quickly rigged over the side of the drifter, but no signals could be heard.

It did not take Lorimer more than a few seconds to realize that they would need to bail out. At 110 feet they would have to wait a while before the craft could flood completely and the pressure equalize to allow the hatch to be opened. In this difficult situation, one without precedent in the short annals of the flotilla, Lorimer handled himself and his two trainees calmly. For some reason Laites had trouble with both of the D.S.E.A. sets he tried, and when, after an unpleasant forty minutes, Gay managed to produce the effort needed to open the hatch, escaping himself as he did so, Laites was in process of changing from one set to another. He might never have survived had not Lorimer literally thrown him out of the hatch by the seat of his trousers, sending him up to the surface with no set at all. Then Lorimer let his own shoulders slide through the narrow circle of the hatchway.

By this time the emergency signal had been taking effect. With the news of the escape of *X.3*'s crew things slowed down a little, but it was still not long before the deep-diving and salvage vessel H.M.S. *Tedworth*, arrived on the scene with a team of the Navy's most experienced helmet-divers. By 11 P.M. on the day of the incident *X.3* was raised.

As the salvaged craft was sent by rail to Portsmouth to be repaired, her crew went to Barrow to take over *X.6*, the second of the operational boats. Meanwhile, another training craft, *X.4*, had arrived at Loch Striven under the command of Lieutenant Godfrey Place, D.S.C., R.N.,[1] and was shortly conducting an endurance trial in Inchmarnock Water, to the north of the Isle of Arran. During the first evening of the exercise a Clyde 'stinker' blew up, and *X.4*'s First Lieutenant, Sub-Lieutenant Morgan Thomas, R.N.V.R., was washed off the casing and drowned. The same wave that caused this tragedy also flooded the escape compartment, leaving the craft suspended in a more or less perpendicular position on the surface, with Place for'ard, E. R. A. Whitley aft, and the flooded "W and D" between them. Neither could speak to the other, and so Whitley had no inkling of what was happening when Place managed to send out distress signals to *Present Help*, in near-by Loch Ranza.

Over two hours later the craft had been found and towed to a

[1] Now Commander B. C. G. Place, V.C., D.S.C., R.N.

position of shelter and a hawser had been secured to her submerged stern. Slowly the drifter's capstan took the strain and the craft was able to resume a more normal angle. As the open hatchway broke surface the compartment was bailed out and Place and Whitley were released. They had been imprisoned, with only scanty information as to what was happening to them, for several hours. Whitley, in particular, had not even had the means of knowing the craft's depth. During the early part of the proceedings she might have been on the bottom for all he knew.

Two technical modifications were made to all the craft as a result of this tragedy: a horizontal bar and a buckled strap were fitted to the induction trunk for securing the watch-keeper on the casing in rough weather, and a device was incorporated for closing the hatch from the control-room. The bar and strap were known semi-officially as the "Hezlet rail," taking their name from the flotilla's Training Officer, Lieutenant A. R. ("Baldy") Hezlet, D.S.C., R.N.[1] This officer had already made a name for himself as a submarine commander, and played a large part in the development of the flotilla in its early stages, both in the training of officers and men and in the design of various items of equipment.

But the whole of the flotilla's existence was by no means a succession of unhappy floodings and sinkings. For the most part life went its normal busy way. The acquisition of technical efficiency came first, second, and third. The accustoming of oneself to discomfort and, to a lesser extent, to an element of risk, were only poor 'also-rans.' The aspects of the technical knowledge required were manifold. Some of them could be taught on the blackboard, but it was the practical training that mattered. The officer-trainee had to learn to manipulate hydroplanes, wheel, pumps, and the main air-line all at one and the same time; to con and navigate by periscope (which above water was literally of no greater diameter than an ordinary fountain-pen); to charge batteries; to start both motor and engine; to test electrical circuits; to repair faults; to scrub and clean. It was a full life.

A feature of the complicated equipment with which the craft were fitted was the induction trunking. This item was used for more than merely 'snorting' on the engine at periscope-depth. With the main hatch only a foot or so above water, even when the craft was at full buoyancy, the trunking was needed to ensure a supply of fresh air while the craft was on the surface, when, as usually seemed to happen, the sea was too rough to allow the hatch's remaining open.

[1] Now Captain A. R. Hezlet, D.S.O., D.S.C., R.N.

If encouragement were needed to sustain the early training-classes in their work, it came with the turn of the year. On December 31, 1942, *X.5* was launched at Faslane. *X.6* arrived on January 11, and the remaining four craft were not long in following. Preliminary plans had already been put in hand at Submarine Headquarters, and advanced training was immediately commenced with a view to attacking main units of the German fleet in the spring of the year, before the hours of darkness should become too short.

The "5–10" class were very different from *X.3* and *X.4*. Although of the same dimensions, they had a completely changed interior lay-out. The battery compartment was for'ard. Then came the "W and D", the control-room, and the engine-room. With the control-room amidships instead of for'ard this was more the orthodox submarine design, even though conceived on a very, very small scale.

There was much less room, for instance, than in the smallest types of domestic air-raid shelters. In a way, living in an *X*-craft was rather like being cooped up beneath the stairs. Under the periscope-dome a small man could stand upright, but elsewhere in the craft there was scarcely head-clearance from a sitting position. Progress from one part to another was made bent double, and nowhere could one stretch one's arms apart without encountering either external pressure-hull or internal equipment. The small hatchways were roughly two feet in diameter and presented quite a problem for anyone wearing lots of woollens and oilskins. When the three—and later, four—members of the crew were at action stations the skipper, in the centre of the control-room, could touch each of the others without moving his feet and without undue stretching. Aft, in the engine-room, conditions were even worse. To work on the engine or motor one had to lie flat on a foot-wide fuel-tank, with the pressure-hull rising only two or three inches clear of one's head and shoulders. And to operate the air-compressor it was necessary to pass one's arm through a six-inch gap between a red-hot exhaust trunking and a fly-wheel turning at anything up to two thousand revolutions a minute.

And yet life was not really uncomfortable. More correctly, one found a new type of domesticity and homeliness in basically uncomfortable circumstances. And from the three cooking appliances of hot-plate, double boiler, and electric kettle many an attractive meal was prepared. Even after a five-day endurance trial in foul weather one could feel surprisingly fit, and on one occasion the crew of *X.6* actually went to the length of having a last-minute shave lying on their tummies in the battery compartment.

H

But on that particular occasion they did not receive the admiration and wonderment that were really their due. During their absence a rival had come to steal their thunder, in the shape of a converted Clan Line merchantman which, as H.M.S. *Bonaventure,* was to become the *X*-craft depot-ship. She was under the command of Captain W. E. Banks, D.S.C., R.N.[1]

[1] Now Captain W. E. Banks, C.B.E., D.S.C., R.N. (retired).

CHAPTER FIFTEEN

Depot-ship Number Two

His Majesty's Ship *Bonaventure* was no beauty. Her single black-topped, upright merchantman's funnel was set exactly midway between stem and stern. For'ard of this her thick, wide bridge-unit rose four decks high from the depths of the for'ard well. Abaft the funnel and the boat-deck lay another well, from which—as from the one for'ard—ascended a huge derrick. A raised cable-deck and poop completed the up-and-down outline of her upper deck.

Her captain, "Willie".Banks, was, like Sladen, Fell, Ingram, and Hezlet, a former submarine commander. Charming to talk to and possessed of a good sense of humour, he was made up of a mixture of Sladen's aptitude for getting things done, Fell's understanding of people, and Ingram's industry. He shared their love of, interest in, and capability with things underwater too. But he had something else as well: a creative imagination large enough to countenance, plan, and administer the development of the flotilla that was to take place. Under Willie Banks midget submarines surprised the Navy by growing into a major force in the conduct of the War.

"B.V.," as the new depot-ship soon became known, made little immediate difference to the flotilla. Admittedly *X*-craft were berthing alongside her, and were, on occasions, being lifted inboard by "Jumbo," the large 50-ton derrick for'ard; but no new elements were being introduced into the training programme. The reason for this was the reluctant realization by those in command that the time in hand before the advent of the lighter nights was insufficient for crews and craft to be fully worked up. Nor had the vital problem been solved of how to transport the craft to within striking distance of a target. Various towing methods were still being tried, and it had not been concluded that the only satisfactory 'tug' was a big submarine. Accordingly Flag Officer Submarines was compelled to inform Vice-Chief of Naval Staff that the operation would have to be postponed until the autumn.

In March *Bonaventure* proceeded to Loch Cairnbawn. With her went the first division of operational craft: *X.5*, *X.6*, and *X.7*. For the ensuing month they were hard at it. The working-up programme included exercises for the recently formed passage-crews. The theory about the latter was that the operational crew should travel in the towing submarine while on passage to the target-area, exchanging places with the officer and two ratings of the passage-crew by means of a rubber dinghy.

During the month of April *X*-craft and chariots changed their name from the Experimental to the Twelfth Submarine Flotilla, and Captain Banks was appointed to command the new organization from Port Bannatyne. He relinquished *Bonaventure* to Captain P. Q. Roberts, D.S.O., R.N.,[1] yet another ex-submarine commander. At about this time *X.5*, *X.6*, and *X.7* returned to *Varbel*, their places in Cairnbawn being taken by *X.8*, *X.9*, and *X.10*. Most of the activity in Loch Striven still consisted in the training of new classes, although the operational crews were also extending their own range of experience by doing some practice net-cutting. This involved a member of the crew getting out through the escape-compartment, suitably clad in a self-contained diving-suit, cutting the craft through the net and then returning inboard. Everything went quite peacefully until, late in May 1943, Sub-Lieutenant David Locke, R.N.V.R., was lost after having cut *X.7* through an A/S net.

Locke's place as First Lieutenant was taken by Sub-Lieutenant Bill Whittam, R.N.V.R., and a major change in *X*-craft policy was resolved. It was decided to incorporate some charioteers under training into the *X*-craft side of the flotilla. Operational crews were to be increased to four persons, one of the ex-charioteers being carried as a specially trained diver.

An average few minutes in a craft's control-room during any of the more interesting exercises from Striven or Cairnbawn might have sounded somewhat as follows. The C.O. is looking through the periscope and standing, bent at the waist, in the middle of the small space between bunk and pumps and helmsman's seat and chart-table. The First Lieutenant is seated aft, facing to starboard and operating the motor- and engine-controls, the hydroplanes, the pumping systems, and the auxiliary machinery board. For'ard the E.R.A. is on the starboard side of the control-room, just for'ard of the periscope-well, and is concentrating on the wheel and on the gyro-compass repeater. The diver is plotting courses and bearings on the chart. Everything is silent, except for the quiet purr of the main motor.

[1] Now Captain P. Q. Roberts, D.S.O., R.N. (retired).

Although the hatches are battened down the craft is still on the surface, the C.O. just having come below preparatory to diving.

A click is heard, then a highly pitched buzz. The periscope slides down into the well and the C.O. is able partly to straighten his bent back. "Dive, dive, dive. 30 feet. 850 revolutions. Course 350 degrees. Let me know when you're happy about the trim, Number One."

As the E.R.A. opens the main-vent valves the air is heard rushing out of the ballast-tanks. In a matter of a few seconds they are full of water and the craft is moving unhurriedly down. The First-Lieutenant is juggling with pump-controls and the hydroplane wheel. It takes him two or three minutes of pumping in from sea to compensating tank and backward and forward between fore and after trim-tanks before he is able to feel the craft's bows respond gently and obediently to the slightest movement of hydroplanes and before the little tell-tale bubble in the inclinometer—which, with the depth-gauge, must receive his constant attention—is resting motionless and showing that the craft is lying perfectly horizontal in the water.

"Craft trimmed for diving, sir," he is then able to report.

"Very good. 250 revolutions. Periscope-depth."

As soon as the depth-gauge needle steadies at nine feet the C.O. presses the button of the periscope hoist-switch, and the narrow tube runs slowly up. It is stopped when it is barely a foot or eighteen inches above the Corticene of the control-room deck-boards, and the C.O. has to crouch on his knees in order to get to the eyepiece. The submarine's speed through the water is no more than one knot.

"Take down a fix. . . . Now! Strone Point bears Green 124, Bracken Point bears Green 9."

"Ship's head, 351," calls the E.R.A.

"Give me a course to reach position AA, George. We'll alter at exactly 1407, that's in five minutes from the time of the fix."

A brief pause while the diver-cum-navigator works out speed, course, and tidal corrections, then: "New course will be 315, sir."

In a few minutes' time the periscope is up again. "There's a launch dead ahead, distance about one and a half cables. She's coming straight towards us. Flood 'Q.' 30 feet."

No sooner is the launch heard to go over than more propellor effect is picked up.

"Periscope-depth, please," calls the C.O.

"Blast. Two more launches. They'll force us to go deep just as we're entering the narrows. And there's not much water there. What's the depth of water just this side of position AA?"

"Three-and-a-half fathoms, sir."

"Twenty-one feet. It will be a tight squeeze. Take her down to 18, Number One."

Within a very few minutes the two launches are heard to draw closer until they are almost right above the submarine. Just as the reverberations of their diesel engines are at their loudest the craft jolts. This is followed by a fair-sized bump, and then another. Altogether this bumping, jolting, banging, and scraping lasts for more than two minutes, before the C.O. is able to give the order for a return to the more comfortable depth of nine feet.

"You had better enter that in the log as 'Bouncing along the bottom,' George. And now stand by for another fix. . . . Now! Colintraive Pier, Green 165; a church, or possibly it's an isolated house, Green 90."

"Ship's head, 315."

"Good. Let me have a new course and a convenient time of alteration within the next few minutes to reach the north-west corner of Area F. Twenty feet."

And so it would continue. The target-area would be reached without any too serious mishap. A mock attack would be made on the battleship, aircraft-carrier, or depot-ship lying there. A listening-watch would almost certainly be waiting for them, but as often as not they would manage both the inward and outward journeys without being detected. And on the return trip various experiments would probably be arranged.

"We'll imagine that revs are restricted to 400, Number One. I won't use the periscope more than once every half-hour. Disconnect the for'ard gyro-repeater, Jones, and we'll run on the emergency direction-indicator. Then, if all that is a success, we'll run on the engine at eight feet and hope too much water doesn't come down the induction. All right?"

Two minor tragedies that belonged to this period were the departures of George Washington and Willy Meeke. Right from the start the former had intended to renew his First War acquaintance with submarines by serving in *X*-craft instead of merely serving with them. His age had made this a virtual impossibility, and he had not improved his chances by making himself so invaluable. In the end, however, he came to realize that the authorities did indeed mean "No," and he left for a more active appointment. Meeke had taken the opportunity of transferring back to 'big' submarines, feeling that he could not stay away from offensive action any longer.

As the time passed and September approached, Cairnbawn became crowded. *Bonaventure* and the six craft were joined, late in

August, by *Titania* and the six towing submarines. Teams were immediately paired off for last-minute operational exercises. In command of *Thrasher* was Baldy Hezlet, who had left Loch Striven some time previously and was now renewing his association with the flotilla in a second capacity.

Shortly before September 11, the day fixed for the departure for Norwegian waters, the craft were hoisted inboard to have the live side-cargoes fitted. While this was going on a slight fire was caused by sparks from a welding apparatus. As there were six pairs of charges lying close to one another on the deck, this was the signal for a large-scale 'panic.' Two officers who were passing immediately coupled a hose and got to work. In a short time there was no fire to be seen—only a lot of water. All concerned felt more than somewhat crestfallen when it was explained to them that there had been absolutely no danger. The amatol in the charges, it transpired, would only melt with the heat, requiring detonation to make it explode.

During the last few days the commanding officers of all vessels concerned received a briefing from Commander G.P.S. Davies, R.N.,[1] on the staff of Flag Officer Submarines. The excellence of this must have been the result of an enormous amount of work behind the scenes.

Three days before the 'off' Sir Claud Barry arrived. The inspections that he carried out were undoubtedly exacting, but they were in no way irksome to the crews.

Of his impressions of this visit one cannot do better than quote his own account. He described the crews as being

> like boys on the last day of term, their spirits ran so high. Their confidence was not in any way the outcome of youthful dare-devilry, but was based on the firm conviction, formed during many months of arduous training, that their submarines were capable of doing all that their crews demanded of them, and the crews were quite capable of surmounting any difficulties or hazards which it was possible for human beings to conquer. It was in this spirit that they went out into the night in their tiny craft to face a thousand miles of rough seas before they reached their objective, which itself, to their knowledge, was protected by every conceivable device which could ensure their destruction before they could complete the attacks. And the *Tirpitz* herself was tucked away close under the cliffs at the head of a narrow fjord sixty miles from the sea.[2]

[1] Now Commander G. P. S. Davies, O.B.E., R.N.
[2] From *His Majesty's Submarines* (H.M.S.O., 1945), p. 61.

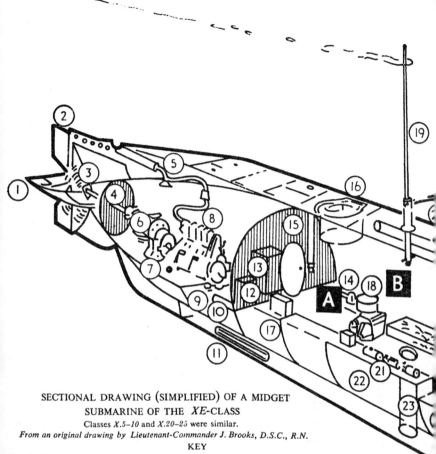

SECTIONAL DRAWING (SIMPLIFIED) OF A MIDGET SUBMARINE OF THE *XE*-CLASS

Classes *X.5–10* and *X.20–25* were similar.

From an original drawing by Lieutenant-Commander J. Brooks, D.S.C., R.N.

KEY

A, Position of First Lieutenant at hydroplane, pump and main-motor controls.
B, Position of Captain at periscope.
C, Position of E.R.A. at steering controls.
D, Position of Diver in "W and D."

1, hydroplanes
2, rudder
3, propeller
4, after trim-tank
5, exhaust muffler
6, main motor
7, air-compressor
8, diesel engine
9, fuel-tank
10, oxygen-cylinders
11, compressed-air cylinders in keel
12, tool-locker
13, fresh-water tank
14, miscellaneous machinery: air purifier and cooling plant, compensating pump, etc.
15, magnetic compass
16, after-hatch
17, No. 3 main ballast-tank
18, gyro-compass
19, attack periscope
20, search periscope under periscope-guard
21, periscope hioisting-motor
22, compensating tank
23, periscope-well
24, bunk and chart-table
25, induction trunk
26, fore-hatch
27, control-room door
28, "Q" tank (for quick diving)
29, battery-compartment door
30, No. 2 main ballast-tank
31, stores
32, battery boards (for'ard sleeping position)
33, main battery (fuel-tank under)
34, fore trim-tank
35, No. 1 main ballast-tank
36, vent-valve
37, free flooding space

CHAPTER SIXTEEN

Success in the North

F IRST away was *X.6*, towed by the submarine *Truculent*.[1] When the tow was secured and final orders received the operational and passage-crews were seen off by Admiral Barry. It was a tense moment. The testing time was beginning. Eighteen months' training of men and working-up of craft—some men lost—weeks of planning and preliminary reconnaissance—years of research. All these were being invested in the shape of six small steel cylinders, which were now setting out to brave the unfriendly North Sea and the wrath of a strong and watchful enemy. Would the investment bring its dividend? Would any of the 40,000-ton *Tirpitz*, the 26,000-ton *Scharnhorst*, and the 12,000-ton *Lützow* be sunk or disabled? The chances might well have seemed slight.

So began eight days and nights of towing. For the passage-crews this meant eight days and nights of unrelenting hard work and constant vigilance. Two people out of three had to be on watch for most of the twenty-four hours. Some one had to have an eye glued to the depth-gauge and inclinometer bubble all the time the craft was submerged. There had to be unceasing preparedness for emergency signals from the parent submarine. Hour in and hour out there was maintenance and still more maintenance to be done. Air-bottles and batteries needed recharging. There were battery-readings to be taken every few hours, insulation readings on all electrical circuits every day, and a thousand and one odd jobs to be attended to, plus the cooking and cleaning. There was never any doubt that the hardest-working people in the whole of the Twelfth Submarine Flotilla were the *X*-craft passage-crews.

On the first night out one of our own trawlers just missed running down *X.6*, but apart from this incident the first four days' passage was uneventful for all concerned. The weather was amenable and the six teams made good speed. Three or four times every twenty-four hours the craft surfaced to ventilate for about fifteen minutes, remaining

[1] Lieutenant R. L. Alexander, D.S.O., R.N., in command.

approximately forty feet deeper than the parent for the other twenty-three hours of the day. The operational crews were enjoying a much more generous allowance of fresh air, for the big submarines stayed 'up top' for the whole of each night.

During this comparative inaction the R.A.F. had been busy. Spitfires based in Russia had undertaken photographic surveys of the Altenfjord area, and the results had been flown to England by Catalina, arriving in time for final instructions to be sent to the six submarines by radio on the fifth day of the passage. These instructions listed *X.5*, *X.6*, and *X.7* to attack *Tirpitz*, *X.8* to attack *Lützow*, and *X.9* and *X.10* to attack *Scharnhorst*. There were some exciting hours spent poring over charts and harbour-plans when these signals were deciphered.

The tempo of the whole proceedings was increased on this Tuesday. Not only did the final operational instructions come through, but the first obstacles presented themselves and had to be overcome.

About 0400 the bows of the submerged *X.8* gave a sharp tilt downward, indicating that the tow had almost certainly parted. Within seconds main ballast-tanks were blowing. As the air rushed in with its comforting "whoosh" the depth-gauge needle slowed, quivered, and then returned hesitatingly towards the lower numbers. When the craft surfaced, and Lieutenant Jack Smart[1] clambered out on the casing, some five minutes must have elapsed in all since that first plunge. And yet there was no sign of the submarine *Seanymph*. This was a complete mystery, for the visibility must have been a good five miles and the two vessels could scarcely have been a mile apart. Smart philosophically decided to plough along on his own at a steady three knots in the hope of being picked up. If necessary he would try to reach Altenfjord and carry out an attack with his passage-crew.

Aboard *Seanymph* the fact of the tow's having parted was not noticed until some two hours later, when the craft was due to surface to ventilate, and as the previous surfacing had been six hours earlier the distance between "parent" and "offspring" could have been anything up to thirty-five long, lonely, grey sea-miles. Faces were long as *Seanymph*'s captain, Lieutenant J. P. H. Oakley, D.S.C., R.N., swung the submarine through 180 degrees and increased speed to retrace the previous hours' track. Extra look-outs were posted, every man was keyed up, but at noon they had still failed to sight the midget, and the log-entry read ominously "sea rough to very rough."

[1] Now Lieutenant-Commander J. E. Smart, D.S.O., M.B.E., R.N.V.R.

At about this time *Stubborn*'s[1] log-entries read as follows:

1213.   Submarine sighted, believed to be *U*-boat. *Stubborn* dived.
1323.   Surfaced.
1550.   Tow parted. *X.7* surfaced and auxiliary tow passed.
1700.   Proceeded.
1718.   Closed and joined by midget submarine *X.8*. Proceeded in company to look for *Seanymph*.
1900.   Dusk. Resumed course for Altenfjord.
1954.   Signal made to Admiral Submarines, to be passed to *Seanymph*.
2359.   Contact lost with *X.8*.

So once again Jack Smart was on his own. This time, as it later transpired, amid the noise of sea and wind an ordered course had been misheard and *X.8* was steering 146 instead of 046. Consequently when dawn broke there was no sign of *Stubborn* from *X.8*'s casing, and there was no sign of *X.8* from *Stubborn*. But, if *Stubborn* failed to sight *X.8* again on the morning of the 16th, she did the next best thing when at 3.15 A.M. she sighted and identified *Seanymph*, giving her the latest information about the errant midget's likely position. But it took almost another fourteen hours' searching before *Seanymph* and *X.8* made contact again at five o'clock that evening. Jack Smart had been on his own for thirty-seven weary hours, during which time he had scarcely been off his feet. By eight o'clock the craft was in tow once more, and, as the weather was favourable and to relieve Smart and his crew after their last exhausting day and a half, the operational crew transferred to the craft and took over the tow.

At nine o'clock on the morning of the 16th the submarine *Syrtis* (Lieutenant M. H. Jupp, D.S.C., R.N.) fired the customary three hand-grenade-type S.U.E.'s (signals-underwater exploding) to surface her charge, *X.9*. But there was no response. At 0920 the tow was hauled in and was found to have parted. *Syrtis* followed the same pattern that *Seanymph* had observed the day before, turning to a reciprocal course and searching diligently. But neither she nor any other submarine ever sighted *X.9* again. Craft and passage-crew had to be considered missing. Until the end of the War there was always hope. Flag Officer Submarines wrote in his dispatch: "It can only be hoped that the Passage Commanding Officer (Sub-Lieutenant E. Kearon, R.N.V.R.) made the Norwegian coast, scuttled his craft, and made his way ashore with his crew." But this was not to be. To the training casualties among *X*-craft personnel had been added the first three men to be lost on an *X*-craft operation. Undoubtedly the small

[1] Lieutenant A. A. Duff, R.N., in command.

submarine—trimmed bow-heavy to counteract the normal upward pull from the parent vessel and then suddenly burdened with the extra weight of the heavy tow-rope—had been carried below the danger limit before any corrective action could succeed. Her plates would have buckled in and the crushing inrush of the water would have done the rest.

The next day Lieutenant Jack Marsden, R.A.N.V.R. (the First Lieutenant of *X.8*) reported that the trim seemed all to blazes and that the craft was being confoundedly difficult. Throughout the day whoever was on the main controls had to be constantly pumping and continually using very large hydroplane angles to keep depth, and, as things gradually got worse and the main ballast-tanks had to be used for trimming, the source of the trouble was eventually traced to an air-leak from the buoyancy chambers of the starboard-side charge. The craft was developing a list to starboard, and at 4.30 P.M., with the compensating tank dry, No. 2 main ballast fully blown, and the trim still difficult to hold, her C.O., Lieutenant B. M. McFarlane, R.A.N., decided to jettison the starboard charge, which was set to 'safe' and released in approximately 180 fathoms. In spite of the 'safe' setting, however, the charge exploded fifteen minutes later, about a thousand yards astern of the craft. The explosion was loud, but caused no damage either to *X.8* or to *Seanymph*, both of whom were dived at the time.

Trim was still difficult to maintain, and the craft—to the accompaniment of various witticisms from her crew—slowly took on a list to port, indicating that the port charge also had flooded buoyancy chambers. This obviously had to go too, and although the witticisms continued they were only the outward signs of a very brave attempt to cover up an intense disappointment. But once McFarlane had made and announced his decision there was still plenty to think about, apart from 'what might have been.' Both vessels surfaced and, distrusting the efficiency of the 'safe' setting, both C.O.'s agreed that the charge should be set to fire at two hours. For some reason *Seanymph* succeeded in towing *X.8* only three and a half miles from the position of release by this time. The force of the detonation felt inside the midget was tremendous. Serious damage was caused. The "W and D" compartment was flooded, doors were distorted, pipes were fractured, and in general such damage was caused as to render the craft no longer capable of diving.

It is not so clear why the second explosion should have caused so much damage at an apparent range of three and a half miles, but whatever the reason the efficiency of the charges would appear to have been convincingly illustrated. The results of the explosion, emanating in water of over 500-pounds-per-square-inch pressure, were indeed remarkable.

At first light on the 18th McFarlane informed *Seanymph* of the extent of the damage aboard the craft; and, as *X.8* could no longer serve any useful purpose in the operation, and if sighted on the surface might indeed compromise the success of the others taking part, it was decided to embark her operational crew in the submarine and scuttle her. Accordingly she dived for the last time. *Seanymph* did not return to home waters directly her charge had disappeared beneath the waves. Instead, she was instructed by Flag Officer Submarines to patrol the area outside Altenfjord in case the *X*-craft attack should 'flush' any of the enemy forces known to be located there. *Seanymph* was also directed to be prepared to pick up any of the returning *X*-craft that she might encounter after the operation. It was also decided at Northways not to alter the operational attack plan for fear that the news of the *X.8*'s scuttling might have a dampening effect on the other crews taking part. This meant that the pocket-battleship *Lützow* would not be attacked.

The weather during the 17th and 18th had not been good, and the sea conditions had still been "rough to very rough." But by dusk on the 18th the weather had at last begun to go down a little, and Godfrey Place had taken Bill Whittam and the operational crew aboard *X.7*, "Uncle Peter" Philip (the South African) and his henchmen having joined *Stubborn*. Commenting on the whole operation some years later, "Uncle Peter" wrote: "When we changed over outside Altenfjord Godfrey borrowed my boots—enormous, fleece-lined, leather jobs—five guineas at Gieves and the apple of my eye."

The remaining submarines—*Thrasher* with *X.5*, *Truculent* with *X.6*, and *Sceptre*[1] with *X.10*—waited until the following day before deciding that the sea had sufficiently moderated for crews to be transferred. Of *X.6* at this juncture John Lorimer wrote subsequently: "We transferred at about 6 P.M. and found Willie Wilson[2] and his crew had left the craft in A 1 condition. How they stood eight days being towed in that confined space I have no idea. It must have been very grim."

The position at midnight on Saturday was that the operational crews of all the four *X*-craft still remaining had been transferred successfully, a night ahead of schedule. *Truculent*, *Thrasher*, *Sceptre*, and *Syrtis*—the latter with no *X*-craft—had all made successful land-

---

[1] Lieutenant I. S. McIntosh, M.B.E., D.S.C., R.N., in command.
[2] Now Lieutenant A. Wilson, M.B.E., R.N.V.R.

falls and were in their patrol sectors. *Stubborn*, who had been delayed by the incident of the tow parting and by locating and nursing *X.8*, was closing to make her landfall with *X.7* still in tow. *Seanymph*, having scuttled *X.8*, was on patrol some sixty miles to the westward of Altenfjord.

The first excitement occurred at 3 A.M., when *Syrtis* sighted a submarine on the surface. Five minutes later this was identified as a *U*-boat. In order not to compromise the operation in any way submarines had been forbidden to attack anything below a capital ship while on passage out to or in their patrol-areas. So poor Martin Jupp had no option but to let this tempting target pass by, at 1500 yards' range and a sitting shot. It reflects credit on the look-out kept by our submarines that, with six of them in the vicinity, of whom four had *X*-craft in tow, none was sighted. A single sighting might well have prejudiced the whole operation, and would have at least led to anti-submarine activity in the area.

Later in the day *Stubborn* sighted a floating mine. The mine itself passed clear of the submarine, but the mooring wire caught in the tow and slid down along the hawser until it became impaled on the bows of *X.7*. This brought Godfrey Place up on the midget's casing, where, by deft footwork, he was able forcibly to persuade the mine to become disentangled and proceed on its unhealthy way, remarking as he did so, "You know, this is the first time I've ever kicked a mine away by its horns."

This was the last of the several introductory incidents that were to precede the big adventure, and during the early evening of the 20th the four remaining *X*-craft were slipped from their parent submarines and started to make their way independently into the Soroy Sound, the submarines withdrawing to seaward. That four out of the six *X*-craft which had set out from Port HHZ should have made these passages of anything up to 1500 miles, in tow of submarines, without major incident, to be slipped from their exact positions at the time ordered after nine gruelling days, was more than could reasonably have ever been expected. In the words of the late Admiral Barry:

> The passage-crews of the *X*-craft deserve great credit for the way they stuck the long and weary passage and for the efficient state of the craft when they were turned over to the operational crews. The passage-crews played a big part in the subsequent success of the operation. I consider this passage a fine example of seamanship and determination by all concerned.[1]

[1] Cmd. 38204/993, p. 998, paragraphs 68 and 69.

The crews of all four *X*-craft were in great spirits and full of confidence when they parted company from their towing submarines. The craft were in an efficient state. Indeed, two of them were in completely faultless condition, and *X.10*'s only defects were in her periscope hoisting-motor, in the motor of her "W and D" pump, and in a slightly leaking gland. These were new occurrences, which had cropped up in the hours immediately preceding the change-over, and were ones that the operational crew were positive they could easily repair. Finally, the starboard charge of *X.6* had been flooded since the first day of the tow, but experiments with the stowage of stores and spare gear had put the boat into a working trim, provided that the inland waters of the fjords should prove sufficiently saline.

From this point onward *X.6* and *X.7* kept extraordinarily well together, although at no time did they encounter each other. "We had an uneventful passage across the minefield off Soroy during the night of the 20th–21st," wrote John Lorimer, "and successfully made our way up Altenfjord during the daylight hours."

Both the craft had been finding trimming rather difficult, presumably because of the presence of freshwater layers. *X.6* developed a defect on her periscope, and *X.7* encountered several enemy vessels during the day, all of which were easily avoided. Perhaps the biggest thrill was when Place sighted a large vessel in the lee of Aaroy Island at about 4.30 P.M. He was almost sure that this was the battleship *Scharnhorst*, but beyond noting the sighting in his log he could pay the battleship little regard. His target was very definitely the *Tirpitz*.

Everything was going according to plan, and *X.6* and *X.7* both spent the night among the Brattholm group of islands in waiting billets. They had no firm contact with each other, nor with *X.10*, who must have arrived there before they left. "We had to dive several times that night," wrote Lorimer, "as we were very close to the main shipping route to Hammerfest. At one point we were almost rammed when I was on watch, as the steering jammed." The crew of *X.7* enjoyed similar experiences, trying to charge batteries amid the constant interruptions of unwitting small boats and minor vessels. During the waiting hours they fitted the spare exhaust pipe— no easy job at the best of times—only to find that it did not fit properly. However, the difficulty was soon remedied by 'make do and mend' and the employment of judicious amounts of sticky tape, canvas, and chewing-gum. For this effort E. R. A. Whitley was heartily congratulated.

Next morning the entrance of Kaafjord began. *X.7* left the lee of the Brattholm islands shortly after midnight, and *X.6* followed an

The Illustrations

KING GEORGE VI EXAMINING A CHARIOTEER'S KNIFE ABOARD
H.M.S. "BONAVENTURE" IN 1944

Peering over His Majesty's shoulder, Admiral Sir Bruce Fraser, C.-in-C. Home Fleet:
on the left, Captain W. R. Fell.

[See p. 167]

FIRST CHARIOT TRAINING-CLASS AT LOCH ERISORT

Back row, left to right: Stoker Petty Officer C. E. T. Warren, Lieutenant
D. C. Evans, Lieutenant C. E. Bonnell, Lieutenant A. Moreton. *Front row:*
Corporal J. Allandar, Sergeant D. Craig, Able Seaman J. Brown.

MEMBERS OF THE FIRST
SUCCESSFUL CHARIOT
OPERATION AT
BUCKINGHAM PALACE
AFTER INVESTITURE

Left to right: Lieutenant R.
T. G. Greenland, Leading
Signalman A. Ferrier, Lieu-
tenant R. G. Dove.

[*See pp.* 77–93]

Photo "Universal Pictorial"

TIRED MEN
A chariot team is helped aboard after a training run.
Photo "Illustrated"

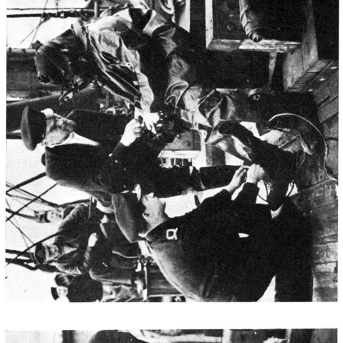

Two Stages of Charioteer Dressing

The charioteer waits for the headpiece and apron to be passed over his head before his boots are secured and his belly-clamps tightened.

Photos "Illustrated"

MARK I HUMAN TORPEDO BEING HOISTED OUTBOARD
In this photograph no warhead is fitted. The controls are as shown
in the diagram at p. 29.

Photo Associated Press

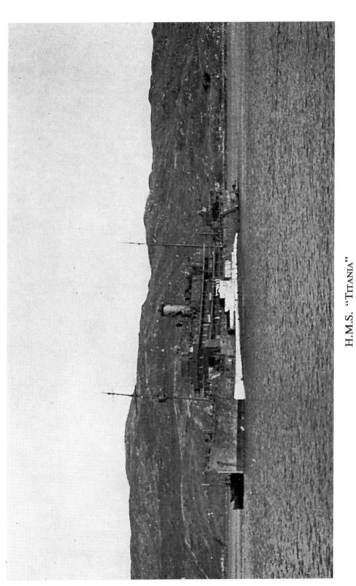

H.M.S. "Titania"

A submarine with chariot container fitted for'ard lies alongside.

chariot comes to
surface to find position

HUMAN TORPEDO SURFACING
Photo "Illustrated"

LEIF LARSEN (*left*) AND CAPTAIN W. R. FELL AT THE FIRST
REUNION DINNER OF THE TWELFTH SUBMARINE FLOTILLA
ASSOCIATION, LONDON, 1951

Photo Key Hollan

T-class Submarine with Mark I Chariots and Containers Mounted Aft

X-CRAFT ON THE SURFACE
This shows X.21 and her commanding officer, Lieutenant J. V. Terry-Lloyd.
Photo "Illustrated"

X-CRAFT DIVING
The periscope has just been raised.
Photo Associated Press

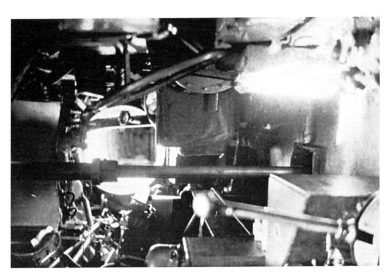

(*Left*) Interior of *X*-craft
Control-room, Looking Aft
from Sill of "W and D."
The Attack Periscope is
raised

The equipment is as shown in the
diagram at pages 120 and 121.

(*Right*) Interior of *X*-craft
Control-room, Looking
For'ard from First
Lieutenant's Diving
Controls

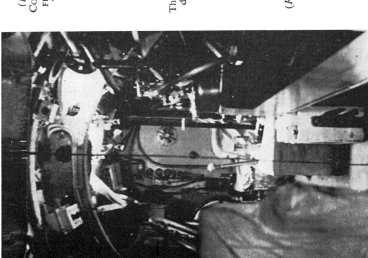

Four Operational *X*-craft of "5-10" Class in Dry Dock

X-craft on Chocks on After Well-deck of "Bonaventure"

LOCH CAIRNBAWN (PORT HHZ)

Bonaventure (foreground) is shown with *X*-craft on well-decks, *Titania* (middle distance) with towing submarines alongside, prior to departure on the *Tirpitz* operation.

SEPTEMBER 11, 1943

X.5 prior to hoisting out for the *Tirpitz* operation. Her port side-cargo
can be clearly seen.

[*See p.* 119 *et seq.*]

C.O.I. Crown copyright reserved

H.M.S/M. "THRASHER" AND *X.5* LEAVING LOCH CAIRNBAWN

The tow-rope can just be seen.

C.O.I. Crown copyright reserved

X.10 LEAVES LOCH CAIRNBAWN UNDER TOW

The passage commanding officer, Sub-Lieutenant E. V. Page, is on the casing.

"TIRPITZ"

Drawing by Adolf Bock from *Voelkischer Beobachter* (1939), showing Tirpitz-class battleship at speed.

THE OPERATIONAL AND PASSAGE CREWS OF *X.5* AND *X.6*

Back row, left to right: Lieutenant J. V. Terry-Lloyd, Sub-Lieutenant A. D. Malcolm, Lieutenant H. Henty-Creer, and Sub-Lieutenant T. J. Nelson. *Seated, right:* E.R.A. R. Mortiboys.

Back row, left to right: Lieutenant A. Wilson, Lieutenant D. Cameron, Sub-Lieutenant J. T. Lorimer. *Front row, left and left centre:* Sub-Lieutenant R. H. Kendall and E.R.A. E. Goddard.

THE OPERATIONAL AND PASSAGE CREWS OF X.7 AND X.8

Back row, left to right: Sub-Lieutenant R. Aitken. Lieutenant B. C. G. Place, Lieutenant L. B. Whittam, Lieutenant P. H. Philip. *Seated, left and right:* Leading Seaman J. J. Magennis, and E.R.A. W. M. Whitley.

Back row, left centre to right: Lieutenant B. M. McFarlane, Lieutenant J. E. Smart, Lieutenant W. J. Marsden. *Front row, left and right:* E.R.A. J. Murray and Leading Seaman H. A. Pomeroy.

Back row, left to right: Lieutenant T. L. Martin, Lieutenant M. H. Shean, Sub-Lieutenant J. Brooks, Sub-Lieutenant E. Kearon. *Seated centre:* E.R.A. V. Coles.

THE OPERATIONAL AND PASSAGE CREWS OF *X*.9 (*above*) AND *X*.10

Back row, left to right: Sub-Lieutenant G. Harding, Lieutenant K. R. Hudspeth, Sub-Lieutenant B. Enzer, Sub-Lieutenant E. V. Page. *Seated, left:* E.R.A. Tilley.

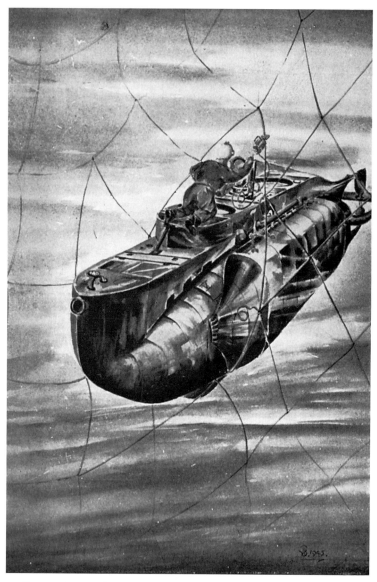

X-CRAFT DIVER CUTTING A CRAFT THROUGH AN ANTI-SUBMARINE NET
From a painting by Lieutenant-Commander J. Brooks.
Imperial War Museum. Crown copyright reserved

THE OPERATIONAL CREW OF *X*.24 ON THE BRIDGE OF H.M.S/M. "SCEPTRE"
RETURNING FROM THE SUCCESSFUL ATTACK ON "BARENFELS" IN BERGEN
HARBOUR

Left to right: Sub-Lieutenant J. Brooks, Lieutenant M. H. Shean,
E.R.A. V. Coles, and Sub-Lieutenant F. Ogden.

X.24 AND THE JOLLY ROGER
Sub-Lieutenant J. Britnell and craft in Loch Cairnbawn.

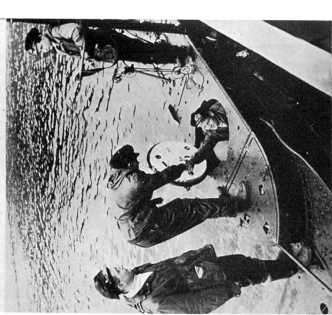

THE OPERATIONAL CREW OF X.21 (AUTUMN 1944)

Centre left: Lieutenant J. V. Terry-Lloyd. *Centre right:* Sub-Lieutenant A. J. Renouf. The picture shows the size of the "W" and "D" hatch.

THE CREW OF XE.12, LOCH STRIVEN (SPRING 1945)

Standing, left to right: Stoker Warner, Sub-Lieutenant J. Benson, Petty Officer G. Ives. *Seated:* Lieutenant W. D. C. Simonds.

ADMIRAL JAMES FIFE (U.S. NAVY) AND CAPTAIN W. R. FELL

The photograph was taken on the bridge of *Bonaventure* prior to *X*-craft operations against Singapore and Saigon, July 1945.

[See p. 220]

XE-CRAFT IN SYDNEY HARBOUR

XE-CRAFT IN SYDNEY HARBOUR, PASSING "BONAVENTURE"

hour later. Within three hours Place had taken his craft successfully through the first obstacle, the anti-submarine net at the entrance to the fjord. With Cameron, however, things were a little more difficult. The periscope flooded soon after they left the billet and continued to flood and reflood time and time again. It was a mystery how he conned them throughout the rest of the attack, for he could hardly see anything. But luck was with them. They surfaced in the wake of a small coaster and followed her through the nets in broad daylight. Cameron had acted in the coolest manner. They must have been invisible.

Meanwhile life in Kaafjord in general and in *Tirpitz* in particular pursued its normal course, as the following extract from the battleship's deck-log shows:

0500–22. Called the hands.
          Set normal anti-aircraft and anti-sabotage watch ashore and afloat.
          Boat-gate in anti-torpedo nets opened for boat and tug traffic.
          Hydrophone listening office closed down.

Once his craft had entered Kaafjord Cameron went to sixty feet and proceeded by dead reckoning, taking the opportunity to strip the periscope, but without managing to effect a permanent repair. To add to the difficulties the periscope hoisting-motor brake burnt out, resulting in manual control of the brake being necessary when raising or lowering the very dimly lensed 'stick.' It is no wonder that twice they only just avoided collisions by a coat of paint. "Once," wrote Lorimer, "we passed under the bows of a destroyer, between her stem and her mooring buoy." A few minutes later they were so close to the tanker *Nordmark*, lying half a mile from *Tirpitz*, that a periscope sight came just in time for another mooring buoy to be avoided by a very sharp alteration of course. E.R.A. Goddard was kept busy on the wheel.

By 0705 *X.6* had closed the anti-torpedo shore-net defence of *Tirpitz* and was through the boat-entrance and within striking distance of her target.

After entering the fjord at four o'clock *X.7* had her first piece of bad luck when she was forced deep by a patrolling motor-launch. While she was thus temporarily 'blind' she got caught in the unoccupied square of A/T nets, once used to house the *Lützow*, but by then empty. They spent a busy, if cautious, hour or more in getting free. Place had no wish to put a diver out unless it was really necessary, especially as this was a case of getting free from a net as

I

opposed to getting through one. After much pumping and blowing the craft shook herself free and shot up to the surface. Luckily she was not spotted during the brief moments before she dived again. All this violent action seemed to have put the gyro-compass "off the board," as Place wrote, and the trim-pump was also out of action. Then the craft was 'hooked' again, this time by a lone wire across the periscope standard. But by six o'clock she was free once more, and although, without a trim-pump, her trim at periscope-depth was somewhat precarious, she was soon headed down the fjord for her target.

At 0710 Place having decided in favour of passing under *Tirpitz*'s A/T-net defences, *X.7* endeavoured to do this at seventy-five feet (which should have been well below the maximum depth of such nets) and was surprisingly caught. Up to this point no suspicions had been aroused in *Tirpitz*, and normal harbour routine was in progress. That the two craft should have reached the innermost defences of the battleship after so long a journey and through so many hazards to arrive within five minutes of each other, was a supreme credit to careful and intelligent planning and to able and determined execution.

X.6 made her way through the boat-gate, following close behind a picket-boat. Once the latter was through, the gate was closed, which fact Cameron was able to discern on his periscope and report to his crew.

"So we've had it now as far as changing our mind," joked Goddard.

The water was very calm, and it was unfortunate that the craft should run aground on the north shore of the netted enclosure. As she was at remarkably shallow depth when this occurred it was impossible for her to be freed without just breaking surface for a few moments. This surfacing was observed in *Tirpitz*, but, although reported as a "long black submarine-like object," there was a five-minute delay in passing the information on to higher authority as it was thought that the object sighted might be a porpoise. So *X.6* was enabled, by some German's fear of ridicule, to close inside the range of *Tirpitz*'s main and subsidiary armament. Five minutes later their luck, hitherto so good, deserted them again. They hit a submerged rock and were pushed to the surface.

Lorimer took her down immediately, and from her position some eighty yards abeam of the battleship her head was again turned to close. But this time she had been clearly sighted and correctly identified. The gyro had been put out of action by the grounding and by

the subsequent acute angles that the craft had taken, and the periscope was almost completely flooded, with the result that progress in
the target's direction was blind. Indeed, Cameron was hoping to fix
their position by the shadow of the battleship.

After another five minutes *X.6* got caught in an obstruction which
she took to be the A/T net on the far (starboard) side of *Tirpitz*, but
which was probably something hanging down either from the battleship or from one of the small vessels alongside. She surfaced where
she was, close on *Tirpitz*'s port bow, to be greeted with a brisk fire
from small arms and hand-grenades from the deck that loomed above
her. Don Cameron realized that escape was hopeless, so, directing
the crew to destroy the most secret equipment, he had the craft go
astern until the hydroplane guard was scraping *Tirpitz*'s hull abreast
'B' turret. There he released the charges, both of which had been
set earlier to detonate one hour after release, and scuttled the craft.
It was 7.15 A.M.

"Bail out!" came the order.

"This we did," wrote Lorimer subsequently, "and we were very
sad to see *X.6* go. She went down on top of the charges, under 'B'
turret. It was the end of an old friend."

They were picked out of the water by *Tirpitz*'s picket-boat, which
also made unsuccessful attempts to secure a tow to the *X*-craft before
it sank.

On board *Tirpitz* and in Kaafjord the alarm had now been properly
raised, and it is clear from entries in the battleship's log-book that
complete surprise had been achieved. "Action stations" was
sounded in the battleship, steam was ordered, and the ship prepared
for sea, in order to get her outside the nets. This order was apparently
not given until all the watertight doors were closed, twenty minutes
after the crew of *X.6* had been embarked. It is not clear why there
was this delay, nor why the Germans initially took the four of them
for Russians, unless because of their unshavenness or because of their
presence in such northerly waters, or both. The four of them—
Cameron, Lorimer, Goddard, and Sub-Lieutenant "Dick" Kendall—
were huddled together in a group while orders were shouted and
divers put down over the side. Their interrogation was being left
until later, but an attempt was made to warm them up after their
'dip' with generous amounts of hot coffee and Schnapps. They all
recall that as the time neared 8.15 there was a certain amount of
anxious and surreptitious looking at watches, mingled with specula-
tion as to what effect the charges would have, and connected, in
Lorimer's mind at least, with the knowledge that the divers were still

under the ship. These unfortunate men had been given the unpleasant task of examining the hull for limpet mines, although it appears that some form of charge dropped under the ship was also expected, as the extract from the log recording the preparation for sea reads: "in order to leave the net enclosure if possible before the time-fused mines detonate."

The interrogation was just starting when the charges went off—at 0812.

"I was thrown off my feet with the force of the explosion," Lorimer recalls,

> and we all ended up on the deck. I could not help thinking that the two divers must have come up much more quickly than they went down—with the aid of what I knew would be at least four tons of amatol and which I now know to have been eight.

"There was panic on board the *Tirpitz* as our charges went off," wrote Kendall after his return from Germany.

> The German gun-crew shot up a number of their own tankers and small boats and also wiped out a gun position inboard with uncontrolled firing. Everybody seemed to be waving pistols and threatening us to find out the number of midgets on the job. The Germans lost about a hundred men all told, mostly due to their own lack of discipline.

While *Tirpitz* was first catching sight of *X.6*, and making up her mind how to deal with the situation, *X.7*, so far unseen but stuck in the nets ahead of the battleship, was trying to extricate herself. In his report Godfrey Place wrote:

> 0710. Seventy-five feet and stuck in the net. Although we had still heard nothing, it was thought essential to get out as soon as possible, and blowing to full buoyancy and going full astern were immediately tried. *X.7* came out, but turned beam on to the r 't and broke surface close to the buoys.
> We went down again immediately . . . and the boa. stuck again by the bow at 95 feet. Here more difficulty in getting out was experienced, but after five minutes of wriggling and blowing she started to rise. The compass had gone wild and I was uncertain how close to the shore we were; so we stopped the motor, and *X.7* was allowed to come right up to the surface with very little way on. By some extraordinarily lucky chance we must have either passed under the nets or worked our way through the boat-passage for, on breaking surface, I could see the *Tirpitz* right ahead, with no intervening nets, and not more than 30 yards away. . . . "40 feet." . . . "Full speed ahead." . . . We struck the *Tirpitz* on her port side approximately below 'B' turret and slid gently under the keel. There the starboard charge was released in the full shadow of the ship. . . . "60

feet." . . . "Slow astern." . . . Then the port charge was released about 150 to 200 feet farther aft—as I estimated, about under 'X' turret.

After releasing the port charge (about 0730) 100 feet was ordered and an alteration of course guessed to try and make the position where we had come in. At 60 feet we were in the net again. . . . Of the three air-bottles two had been used and only 1200 pounds (less than half) was left in the third. X.7's charges were due to explode in an hour—not to mention others which might go up any time after 0800.

A new technique in getting out of nets had by this time been developed. The procedure was to go full ahead blowing economically and then to go full astern, the idea being to get as much way on the boat as the slack of the nets would allow and thus to have a certain impetus as well as the thrust of the screw when actually disengaged from the net. In the next three-quarters of an hour X.7 was in and out of several nets, the air in the last bottle was soon exhausted and the compressor had to be run.

At 0740 we came out while still going ahead and slid over the top of the net between the buoys on the surface. I did not look at the *Tirpitz* at this time as this method of overcoming net-defences was new and absorbing. . . . We were too close, of course, for heavy fire, but a large number of machine-gun bullets were heard hitting the casing. Immediately after passing over the nets all main ballast-tanks were vented and we went to the bottom in 120 feet. The compressor was run again, and we tried to come to the surface or to periscope-depth for a look so that the direction-indicator could be started and as much distance as possible put between ourselves and the coming explosion. It was extremely annoying, therefore, to run into another net at 60 feet. Shortly after this (at 0812) there was a tremendous explosion. This evidently shook us out of the net, and when we surfaced it was tiresome to see the *Tirpitz* still afloat. . . . So X.7 was taken to the bottom.[1]

Place and his crew surveyed the damage to the craft. Compasses and depth-gauges were out of action, but there appeared to be little structural damage. Whittam found the boat impossible to control, however, and on subsequent handling she broke surface on several occasions. On each of these fire was opened by *Tirpitz* causing further damage to the hull, and it was finally decided to abandon ship. Place brought the craft to the surface for the last time, rather than use D.S.E.A., owing to the depth-charging that was being experienced. The boat surfaced close to a gunnery target, but before the three members of the crew could escape from the control-room she sank again, due to the persisting gunfire all round her. Before she went down, however, Place was able to step from the casing on to the gunnery target, from where he was rescued by a German picket-boat and taken aboard *Tirpitz*.

[1] From Cmd. 38204/993, p. 1007.

"Godfrey was wearing an enormous pair of boots," wrote Lorimer, not knowing of Uncle Peter's great loss, "a submarine sweater, and long submarine-issue pants, with no trousers. He was a cheering sight, standing shivering underneath the guns of 'Y' turret."

Two and a half hours later, at 1115, Sub-Lieutenant Bob Aitken broke surface, having escaped from the sunken craft using D.S.E.A. He was given a very warm welcome by his five companions, and the Germans even managed to provide some more coffee and Schnapps.

He had spent a very gruelling two hours and forty minutes. Just as the craft took its last dive he had heard his skipper's voice proclaiming, "Here goes the last of the Places." Within a few moments they were on the bottom. Fortunately the hatch had been shut in time, the boat was more or less dry, and there was no panic. Bill Whittam took charge, had the D.S.E.A. sets cut down from their stowage positions, and started to flood the craft. As the diver, Aitken took the other two through the correct escape-drill. He remembers feeling absolutely confident himself. "I gave Chadwick and his training full marks," he said afterwards. "He had made us realize that the pressure at 120 feet was a mere nothing."

It was decided to use both hatches for getting out. Whitley and Whittam would have one apiece and Aitken would use whichever one was clear first. However, when they tried to assume the appropriate positions for this manœuvre, they found it impossible to pass each other with D.S.E.A. sets on. Aitken was thus left for'ard by the "W and D" hatch. Flooding was proving a very slow process, too slow for their general peace of mind, and they discussed how to speed it up. The water was extremely cold, and the icy depression that was engendered as it reached calves, knees, thighs, and waist can perhaps be imagined. Unfortunately the remaining inboard vents all seemed to have stuck, and it was impossible to let the water in faster. They just had to stand and wait. In time, as was bound to happen, the water reached an electric circuit. Something fused, the boat filled with fumes and the three men were forced to start breathing their escape-oxygen.

When the boat appeared to be about fully flooded Aitken tried the for'ard hatch, but with no luck. On climbing back into the control-room he found that Whitley, whom he had left propped up against the periscope and not looking too happy after the fumes, had slipped. Guessing that he had perhaps demanded too much of his oxygen, Aitken groped under the water to find that the breathing-bag was flat and that the two emergency cylinders had each been consumed. Whitley could not therefore be living.

The next job was to feel about in the darkness to find if Bill Whittam was still all right. But as he straightened up from Whitley's body, Aitken found himself drawing breath in vain. His oxygen-bottle had given out too. Hurriedly he broke open the two emergency-oxylets, but at that depth they seemed to give him no more than a breath apiece. Whether or not he realized it, he was very near to death. His last oxygen-reserves had gone, he was in a flooded sub-marine at 120 feet with two men, both presumably dead, and the hatch was still shut.

His only remaining asset was the breath he was still holding in his lungs, plus, of course, his guts.

He remembers scrambling back into the escape-compartment for one more go at the hatch. Then things went black, until his eyes opened to see a stream of oxygen bubbles all round him as he sped up to the surface. His black-out had been only momentary, but during it he managed to open the hatch and had also remembered to carry out the correct D.S.E.A. drill, for he was very pleased to find that he had unrolled the apron of the escape-apparatus and was holding it out in front of him to check his ascent.

Then he broke surface. He was alive, thank God!

As soon as he was deposited aboard *Tirpitz* a surly officer in-structed him to strip naked. The upper deck was both public and cold, and he was glad to go below to a warm reception and a hot drink. After a brief questioning he was given a blanket and told he could sleep on a hammock-rack. On the principle of first come, first served, the whole of the cell accommodation had been taken up by Place and by Cameron and his crew.

So there were six newcomers asleep in *Tirpitz* that day. They sadly regretted that they could not number eight.

At 0843 a third *X*-craft had been sighted some five hundred yards outside the nets. *Tirpitz* opened fire and claims to have hit and sunk this craft. Depth-charges were also dropped in the position in which the craft disappeared. This was obviously *X.5*, Henty-Creer's[1] command, which had last been seen off Soroy on the previous day by *X.7*. Nothing is known of her movements nor was any of her crew saved.

Place had been disappointed to see *Tirpitz* still on the surface following the explosion. The fact that she survived at all was largely due to the limited evasive action she was able to take after the sinking of *X.6*. This was achieved by heaving in on the starboard cable and veering port to take the ship as far away as possible from the position

[1] Lieutenant H. Henty-Creer, R.N.V.R.

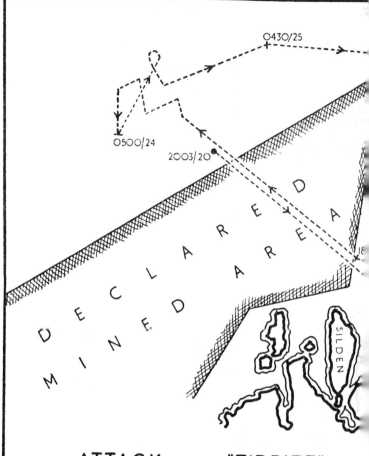

0430/25

0500/24

2003/20

D E C L A R E D A

DECLARED

MINED

AREA

SILDEN

ATTACK ON "TIRPITZ"
OPERATION "SOURCE"
Showing movements of X.10
September 20th - 28th 1943

ALL TIMES ARE G.M.T.

Scale in Nautical Miles

0   5   10   15

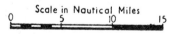

Based on map in Cmd. 38204/993 (H.M.S.O.).

22° E.

1525/25

150/28
X.10
recovered

Ofjord

Ytre Reppafjord

SOROY

SOROY SOUND

SEILAND

0205/21

2350/22

STJERNOY

2135/21

STJERNSUND

2320/21

Storelokkerfjord

ALTENFJORD

2100/22

0110/22

0215/22 - 1800/22

Brattholm

70° N.

"TIRPITZ"

Kaafjord

in which the craft had gone down. The battleship's log records at 0812 "two heavy consecutive detonations to port at one-tenth of a second interval." The first explosion was abreast 'X' turret about six to eight yards from the ship, the other fifty to sixty yards off the bow in *X.6*'s last position. The latter explosion was almost certainly composed of three charges going up together, for a subsequent examination of the sea-bed failed to discover any of the charges, or even fragments.

With the explosions the giant ship was heaved five or six feet upward, and a large column of water was flung into the air on the port side. Members of the ship's company on deck were hurled off their feet and several casualties resulted. The ship took on an immediate list to port of about five degrees. All the lights failed. Oil-fuel started to leak out from amidships. From the damage reports compiled in *Tirpitz* during the morning after the attack the following items of the battleship's structure and equipment were put out of action: all three main engines; one generator room; all lighting equipment; all electrical equipment; wireless telegraphy rooms; hydrophone station; 'A' and 'C' turrets; anti-aircraft control positions; range-finding gear; port rudder.

One person was killed and about forty wounded by the explosion, in addition to those killed and injured by the German's own gunfire, and five hundred tons of water were taken aboard. In all, the final effect of the attack was completely satisfactory. Even though the *Tirpitz* was still afloat, and even though many of the minor disablements she suffered were only temporary, she was certainly immobilized as far as undertaking any sea-action was concerned. On November 22, two months after the attack, the German Marine-gruppenkommando Nord reported to the German Naval War Staff that "as a result of the successful midget-submarine attack the battle-cruiser *Tirpitz* had been put out of action for months." It was, indeed, considered by the War Staff that the 40,000-ton ship might never regain complete operational efficiency. The truth of the estimates was borne out by the fact that it was not until April of the following year that *Tirpitz* was able to limp from her anchorage, only to be further damaged and finally destroyed by air-attack.

The six survivors of the *X*-craft crews—who were well treated aboard their victim, where their bravery was greatly admired—made their way slowly through Norway to Dulag Nord in Germany for a dose of solitary confinement and interrogation, and then to Marlag-Milag Nord on November 28. There Kendall and Aitken, two of the charioteers who had been talked into *X*-craft by Captain Banks, were by chance quartered in the same hut as Greenland and Dove, two of the charioteers who had been so successful in Palermo. When the two former members of the quartet were also awarded the D.S.O., the hut contained four holders of the highest award to be won by an R.N.V.R. officer in the 1939–45 War. Other awards, including the V.C. for Cameron and Place, were made to all the surviving members of the operational crews of *X.6* and *X.7* and to officers and men from the other craft.

Not long afterwards the operation was the subject of a signal from Sir Max Horton, by this time in command of the Western Approaches. Remarkable for its length from a man whose congratulations normally amounted to a curt "Well done," it read:

> Will you please convey to the Twelfth Submarine Flotilla my warmest congratulations and profound admiration for their unique and successful attack on the *Tirpitz*.
>
> Having been closely associated with the inception and early trials of the *X*-craft I fully realize the immense difficulties which have had to be surmounted, and I know also what devoted service has been given by those who designed the craft and its special equipment, by the original trial crews, and by those responsible for training the operational crews and for planning the operation itself.
>
> The long approach voyage in unparalleled conditions, culminating in the successful attack on the target, called for and produced the highest degree of endurance and seamanlike skill.
>
> While deploring with you the loss of officers and men whose gallantry is unsurpassed in the history of the Submarine Service, I rejoice at the success which crowned this magnificent feat of arms.

Meanwhile, the six submarines had been waiting off the entrance to Altenfjord. They started their return journey on September 29, after having remained for seven days after the attack. *X.10* was in tow of *Stubborn.*

CHAPTER SEVENTEEN

Tail-clutch

W<small>HEN</small> *X.10* slipped from *Sceptre* at 8 P.M. on September 20 she
was dived to adjust her trim, and when this proved satisfactory she
was set on a south-easterly course and proceeded to close the land at
maximum surface speed. Her crew consisted of Lieutenant Ken
Hudspeth, R.A.N.V.R., Sub-Lieutenant Bruce Enzer, R.N.V.R.
(First Lieutenant), Sub-Lieutenant Geoff Harding, R.N.V.R. (diver),
and E.R.A. Tilley, a regular from big submarines. The short hours
of darkness were uneventful, and when the craft dived she was in a
position five miles west-north-west of the island of Stjernoy.

Geoff Harding was the youngest person taking part in the whole
operation, being just a couple of months over nineteen. Just before
the craft had left HHZ he was still a midshipman and had been
wearing an Army battledress dyed navy blue, with his maroon
midshipman's patches on the lapels. The general effect of this had
been very odd, so much so that Tiny Fell had said that the Germans
would probably take him for a railway porter or something similar.
To be on the safe side he was instructed to put up a Sub-Lieutenant's
single ring, even though he had officially another four months to
wait. So his first acquaintance with operational business was a very
happy one.

He had served with *X*-craft for a bare two or three months prior
to the operation, having joined a chariot training-class at Blockhouse
with the express purpose of being trained as an *X*-craft diver right
from the start. By the time the operation came off he felt he knew a
fair amount about diving for and from *X*-craft, but little enough
about the craft themselves. He had no watch-keeping certificate and
supposed himself to be very much of a passenger. In actual fact he
was able to undertake a large amount of the relief depth-keeping and
navigation.

The trip in *Sceptre* had been free from incident, but, especially for
him, far from uninteresting. He was having to cipher and decipher
for the first time in his naval career, and although he was rarely

getting any sense out of his deciphering he found it more fascinating than any crossword. Then, of course, this was his first trip in a big submarine, and his own feelings and other people's attitude towards him were just as though he were a small boy being given a ride on the footplate of a train. It was grand.

He had enjoyed the changeover in the rubber dinghy too; not least because it meant seeing big, tall, red-bearded, Irish "Ernie" Page,[1] the passage C.O. And then there was all the excitement of the night's surface run across a minefield. They were still in the field when they dived.

"I was sleeping in the battery compartment," Harding related afterwards,

> and awoke to hear a wire scraping the hull. I looked aft and saw three white faces in the control-room looking just as worried as I felt. We all held our breath. The noise stopped and we all breathed again—for a few minutes. Then it all happened again. This performance was repeated several times in the next hour, until we all felt that this was the thickest minefield ever. It was not until we were on the surface some time later that we discovered that our auxiliary towing pendant had come adrift. It had been this which had been swept backwards and forwards along the side of the craft every now and again.

Difficulty had been experienced in trimming ever since the craft had dived, and the earlier defect in the periscope-motor had become worse. Further electrical defects also developed, and the gyro-compass failed. Bruce Enzer had so much to do that he didn't know where to start.

"Bruce," called Hudspeth, "come and look at the chart. I think we'll make for Smalfjord, here, on the north coast of Stjernoy. We can have a go at getting things right there. There'll probably be less chance of our being disturbed than in one of the small fjords off Stjernsund."

This was agreed as being the best plan, in spite of its being a change from their original intention. Accordingly *X.10* altered course.

It was 0700 when the craft arrived and bottomed in her new hiding-place. All hands immediately turned to the making good of defects. During part of the day the craft was kept on the surface, there being little apparent risk of being discovered.

Harding was the only one not busy the whole time.

"I spent part of the day sitting on deck, looking at giant jelly-fish and fishing," he remembers. "Tilley was playing about with bits of metal beside me and seemed to be very intent."

[1] Now Sub-Lieutenant E. V. Page, M.B.E., R.N.V.R.

Within a few minutes Harding's curiosity got the better of him.

"What are those bits of metal, Tilley?"

"Only the tail-clutch."

"Oh," replied Harding, resuming fishing.

Then, a short time later; "What does a tail-clutch do?"

Tilley smiled. "It connects the engine and/or the motor to the propeller and makes the boat go." Then he went on working on the slippery, narrow casing.

"His reply sank in after a suitable interval," Harding reported,

and I continued my fishing wondering what would happen if he dropped those pieces of metal into the hundred and fifty feet of water that lay beneath us. Tilley seemed too absorbed to worry. . . . I believe there was a Jerry camp of some sort just over the hills from where we were, and I remember it seemed very odd to be sitting so comparatively close to them spending a quiet hour or so fishing, eating, and every so often putting on an extra sweater to keep warm. Smalfjord sticks in my mind as being a beautiful place in the bright clear sunshine we had that day. In a way I was sorry to leave.

It was 6 P.M. when they left. Although everything was by no means cured, Hudspeth judged that sufficient progress had been made for the approach to be continued. The log read:

2035/21. Entered and proceeded up Stjernsund, keeping to the north shore.

2135. Sighted a small ship of fishing-craft type, burning navigation lights. Ship appears to turn into Storelokkerfjord.

2320. Reach Altenfjord. Course shaped to the southward.

"On our way in up Altenfjord one of the side-cargoes flooded," ran Harding's story.

We had great fun impersonating a mad porpoise. On one occasion we had to blow main ballast to avoid going down too far, and a few seconds later we were on the surface doing everything possible to get down again. We were close to the shore and near a guard-post at the time. It was still more or less daylight, and my recollections of that moment are of combined anger and fear—mostly the latter, I think!

The boat was leaking above the main switchboard, and very shortly after the worst of the porpoising episodes, when we were getting fairly near to the target, all the fuses blew. I spent a while putting in new ones by the handful as they continued to blow. There was a real firework display of sparks shooting all over the boat. We had to use a fire extinguisher at one point, and it wasn't until then that somebody noticed the label on it that read: "Not to be used in confined spaces." This struck us all as being highly amusing.

At this stage of the proceedings there was so much 'loose' electricity about that we could probably have boiled the kettle by touching the plug against any piece of metal in the craft. Bruce would probably have tried it if he hadn't been so busy.

At two o'clock the following morning periscope-depth was ordered, only for the periscope hoisting-motor to burn out immediately the switch was pressed. The craft filled with smoke and had to be surfaced for ventilation. Luckily there was no sign of life either seaward or landward, and in a few minutes they were able to dive and remain undetected.

In this early class of X-craft there was no periscope hand-winding apparatus, so the best that could be done was for the hoisting wires to be cut, the periscope manhandled up to a suitable height, and then lashed in a fixed position with codline. Near to it was hung a sharp knife. The whole arrangement was known as the Enzer Periscope Motor: "To lower, cut the cord and stand clear."

The damping bottles of the gyro-compass were not working, with the result that the card was wandering. The magnetic-compass light refused to function, and they suspected it of being flooded. They were in no state to carry out an attack and could really not go much farther as they were. So, at 2.15 A.M. the craft was bottomed in 195 feet of water, four and a half miles from the entrance of Kaafjord, where her target lay.

"Ken Hudspeth asked each of us whether we wanted to go in and do the attack," stated Harding,

and we all said, "Yes." But after consideration he said that we would be bound to be seen and that this would not only do us little good but might also spoil the chances of the others, which was more important. We would stay on the bottom to hear if any of the bangs occurred at the appointed times. If they didn't we would go in to 'have a bash' ourselves. It was reassuring to know that while we were near enough to the *Tirpitz* and *Scharnhorst* to hear the bangs, we were far enough away to be out of the range of the big blast that we hoped the morning would bring.

They continued their hard but almost fruitless toiling at the long list of repairs that were necessary. As they worked they could not rid themselves of the feeling of waiting, waiting, waiting. Nor was this helped by the occasional slight sounds they could hear, but had not the means to identify.

We felt like kids at a Punch and Judy Show, knowing that Punch was about to hit Judy and enjoying the fact that Judy didn't know. The bangs came (at approximately 0815—the exact time for exploding charges as laid down in the operational instructions) and were a lovely sound. Soon after and on and off for a longish period lots and lots of other bangs banged, and we had to consider which were other side-charges, if any, and which were depth-charges.

We stayed on the bottom all that day, and I think we were all feeling very mixed inside. We were glad about the bangs, but sad that they weren't ours. We were glad that we didn't *have* to take our wreck of a boat in to attack, but sad because it was a wreck of a boat by this time and could not really make an attack.

By 1800 we had been on the bottom nearly sixteen hours. Early on we had worked on some of the defects, but for the last few hours we had just been lying still and waiting for a good time to get away. The air we were breathing was getting worse every hour. It was not a happy party there, for we were desperately disappointed at having had so much bad luck. Nobody said much, but I think each of us knew what the others were thinking. I looked at Ken and Bruce and Tilley on different occasions. Conversation was obviously pointless.

At 1800 Hudspeth finally decided that it was off. Without a periscope in full working order and with no compass at all any attempt to attack the *Scharnhorst* would have been doomed to failure from the outset and would merely have been an unnecessary waste of valuable lives. And they had the heartening conviction that some of the craft had almost certainly been able to press home an attack. But, all the same, Ken Hudspeth's was undoubtedly the greatest disappointment in the whole of the operation. It is now known from German naval records that *Scharnhorst* had not been in or near her anchorage during the whole period in question, so that in any case *X.10* would not have found her quarry. Perhaps it would have been an even greater disappointment to have struggled into a makeshift attack and found the anchorage empty.

In the relevant section of his report to the Lords Commissioners of the Admiralty, Admiral Barry wrote:

The Commanding Officer [of *X.10*] expresses the highest opinion of all his crew throughout the whole of the time they were on board. They worked long and arduously in the face of ever-growing disappointment and at no time did their zeal or enthusiasm fail. I consider that the Commanding Officer himself showed determination and high qualities of leadership in a gallant attempt to reach his objective. He was frustrated by defects for which he was in no way responsible and which he made every endeavour to overcome. He showed good judgment in coming to his decision to abandon the attack, thereby bringing back valuable information.[1]

[1] From Cmd. 38204/993, p. 1000, paragraph 92.

Harding's story continued:

Eventually we surfaced and went flat out down the fjord with the skipper on deck. We dived once or twice under patrol-boats, and at these times Ken would come below caked solid with ice and refusing all offers to take over from him on top when we surfaced again.

He had to 'con' us all the way out as we had no compass. Once we tried running on the D.I. [an aircraft-compass type of direction indicator, which, although it had no power to seek north, was supposed to seek and maintain a set direction for periods of up to twenty minutes]. This was when Ken was down for a spell. When he got back up on top he found we had turned 180 degrees and were running up the fjord again. Down below we all got cross with the D.I. and, being somewhat flimsy, it didn't work again after that.

By this time we had ditched the side-cargoes as both of them were flooded and our speed was being considerably reduced. The charges had, in the past, made an unhappy habit of exploding even when set to safe, particularly when dropped in deep water, and we had a worrying few minutes after letting them go. But the terrific bang we were waiting for never came. We were, of course, going hell for leather away from the dropping-zone at the time—but hell for leather was only a matter of six knots, so we wouldn't have got very far clear.

Smalfjord was reached just before dawn. It was completely deserted and with the frequent snowfalls that were prevailing it was considered safe to leave the craft on the surface, securing her to the shore with the grapnel. The risk of detection was negligible with shore and craft covered in snow. The opportunity was then taken to get some rest and to try and make good some of the defects.

Later that day they set out and recrossed the declared mined area that they had traversed on the way in. They waited in what Ken Hudspeth could best judge to be the planned recovery positions for five whole nights.

Harding found it a dreary business. "The days were the longest I have ever known. None of us seemed a bit worried, however, and we talked mostly about where we should go if no submarine turned up at all and about what had probably happened up in Kaafjord."

It was at 4.30 A.M. on the third day 'in waiting' that Ken Hudspeth decided to leave the first planned recovery position and try elsewhere. He set course for Sandoyfjord on the northern coast of Soroy Island, some miles to the north of the entrance to the main Altenfjord. At 10 A.M. he dived—just to be on the safe side—and two hours later he was entering Sandoy. Off to starboard he saw a narrow inlet which looked promising. He followed it and, after a time,

K

was able to surface and secure the craft to the beach. The time was then 1525.

The place bore the peculiar name of Ytre Reppafjord. "It was crescent-shaped," the young diver recalled,

with very high cliffs all around and a good depth of water. A waterfall emptied into it on one side, and we had great plans to swim ashore to get some fresh water. The sea was practically ice and it would have been a cold swim. As we considered this possibility—we were all on deck— we suddenly heard an aircraft. The last man was down and the plugs were pulled out in about five seconds.

Our periscope was still showing above the surface when we hit the bottom at about nine feet! The chart had showed a lot of water there too. It was a very funny feeling doing a crash-dive from the surface and ending up nine feet lower.

Soon we surfaced and were all up top again. We all felt very cold, but thought we had better wash over the side to brighten ourselves up a bit. It took us about half an hour to undress and I started making a list of what I took off. After getting as far as one pair of padded buoyant trousers, four pairs of ordinary trousers, and one pair of pyjama trousers I gave up. We discovered that since we had got really cold the many layers of clothes we were wearing were just keeping us that way, and we were all very much warmer with much less on. We tried the specially issued salt-water soap and found it about as much use as a piece of coal would have been, so we used Chemico instead.

We followed the wash with a wonderful meal. Tinned tomato soup; tinned chicken, tinned peas, tinned spuds; tinned fruit; and a Bruce Enzer cocktail. The latter was malted milk made as thick as porridge. Excellent!

None of us took the benzedrine tablets that we carried on board, though this was not because we got plenty of sleep to keep us going. On the contrary, all the blankets were so sodden with condensation that they did nothing but make us feel colder.

On the morning of the 27th they set course a little way down the coast to the southward to investigate the planned position in Ofjord, where it was expected a submarine would close that night.

During the trip down the coast the diver did some watch-keeping on the hydroplanes. But the needle of the after depth-gauge was not registering, and by the time some one for'ard realized it I was at a periscope-depth of 180 feet.

We planned to make for Iceland or Russia if we made no contact with a submarine that night. We patrolled close inshore [in Ofjord] all during that evening and into the night. Just after midnight Ken announced that we would give up waiting in another hour's time exactly. There was a large amount of quietness aboard.

As the minutes ticked on towards one o'clock *X.10* was lying motionless on the surface. Hudspeth and Enzer were on the casing and Harding and Tilley were maintaining a thoughtful silence below. Russia or Iceland—either would mean a dickens of a long and difficult journey. The clock showed exactly 1 A.M., some six or seven minutes to go before the time-limit expired.

"Bruce, there she is!"

Hudspeth's voice resounded from the casing above. Harding and Tilley leapt into each other's arms in the middle of the restricted control-room and hugged each other vigorously—"just like a couple of schoolgirls," they both admitted afterwards.

A few minutes later there was the mother and father of all crashes as the boat was lifted up by a wave and dropped back on the saddle-tank of what turned out to be H.M.S/M. *Stubborn*.

This procedure was repeated twice more, until diver and E.R.A. felt they could happily wish themselves many miles away, back off the entrance to Kaafjord, with all that would mean. They were both made miserably sick by the violent movement.

"Geoff on the casing!" called Hudspeth at this point, so up Harding went, dressed rather unprotectedly in battledress and gym-shoes.

> I saw that we were *very* close to the rocks inshore. Bruce tied a line around my waist and threw the other end to the submarine. Having come up out of the light into the dark of the night I could see practically nothing, so that when some one shouted, "Jump," I had to jump almost blind. As I jumped a horrible thought flashed through my mind—I hope they meant me—I must still have been a bit dazed. Anyway I landed safely on the side of the conning-tower and had kept my feet dry.
>
> "Down below," a voice instructed me. I had no idea that I had landed on *Stubborn*, so I jumped down the hatch expecting to find the ladder on the for'ard side, as it was in *Sceptre*. But *Stubborn*'s ladder was secured on the port side of the hatch, so I dropped straight down to the hatch below, where I landed very surprised and bruised.

He was greeted by Peter Philip, who was ready to take over the craft for the tow home. But no more changes could be made at that moment as it was all that could be done to get the tow rigged before both vessels went on the rocks. Indeed, weather soon became so bad that it was not until 10 P.M. the following day—that is, some forty-four hours later—that the transfer could be completed.

Harding slept uninterruptedly for a full twenty-four hours, and for a long while after that he had a feeling of floating along, not being really connected with all that was going on round him. He was, indeed, too tired to undertake any conscious action, except that of eating at regular intervals.

The tow home towards Lerwick was very slow indeed, due largely to the makeshift towing equipment that had to be used. In the end the craft was on the end of a spare periscope hoist-wire, which did not encourage any great speed being attempted. With the worsening of the weather and the rapidly deteriorating conditions in the craft, Peter Philip and his crew were having an uncomfortable time.

By the 3rd October, having had three days in which to recover some of their depleted energy, Hudspeth and Enzer decided to rejoin their craft, relieving Philip's seamen and stoker in so doing. This manœuvre was achieved, and the three-officer passage-crew had been in possession for a mere hour or so when a signal was received in *Stubborn* from Flag Officer Submarines. All *X*-craft personnel were to be embarked in *Stubborn*, and *X.10* was to be scuttled. A gale was due to reach the area to the north of the Shetlands in the immediate future and could be expected to reach Force 8. The risk of losing three gallant men if the makeshift tow should part was too great to be justified.

By 8.30 P.M. the three officers had been re-embarked and the craft had been scuttled. They had another four hundred miles to go.

"I had to go over to the craft in the rubber dinghy," Harding described.

> The sea was pretty bad. I got aboard the craft and collected a pair of shoes I wanted, but, of course, I had to leave all the other odds and ends that one collects aboard. Just before we abandoned ship some one threw me up the ship's crest. This was a heavy, solid-bronze effort, and I remember a few laughs about weighting me with the crest and sending me down with the craft. This very nearly happened for, as I jumped for the dinghy, I slipped and landed half on the rubber rim and half in the water. With the weight of the crest inside my battledress I would certainly have 'dived' if I had missed the dinghy altogether.
>
> It was a sad business sinking the boat, and we all felt it pretty badly. Nevertheless we sang very lustily—"Three Men in a Boat"—until we reached *Stubborn*. We all went in the drink getting aboard the big boat, and that was about the end of the operation.

At Lerwick they changed submarines and embarked in *Truculent*. The trip down from the Shetlands to Rothesay was quiet and uneventful. They ate well, *Truculent* seeming to have an inexhaustible supply of eggs and bacon. And they talked. The need for reticence seemed to have gone, and once tongues were loosed there was much that wanted to be said.

As *Truculent* came past Rothesay to Port Bannatyne they were all on the bridge. They were put aboard *Bonaventure*, where their reception was terrific. However, their immediate descent into the wardroom for dinner—unwashed, unshaven, and in battledress, as they were—evoked a complaint from one of the ship's officers. This they thought strange. But in all fairness it must be stated that this was one of the rare occasions when lack of understanding between age and youth, between R.N. and R.N.V.R., was the cause of any friction.

Soon afterwards they went ashore—to *Varbel*. Here the reception was even more enthusiastic. Modestly they deplored all the fuss—after all, they had achieved nothing, they said.

CHAPTER EIGHTEEN

Practice and Theory

W ITH the return of the parent submarines from the attack on *Tirpitz* the atmosphere at *Varbel* was very definitely one of anti-climax. Not merely was this because the nervous tension of eighteen months had been finally relieved, nor because no further operational plans were yet forthcoming. The real reason was the sending back of a large number of trained *X*-craft personnel to General Service.

By the end of September 1943 there was a considerable number of people at Loch Striven and at the Hydro who had completed every phase of their training, at least as far as the now limited capabilities of *X.3* and *X.4* would allow. The new deliveries of craft were not due to arrive for a few months. So part of the winter had to be spent in a cruiser, destroyer, frigate, or corvette.

Concurrent with the *Tirpitz* attack and the subsequent enforced idleness of *X*-craft the chariot-crews remaining in Home Waters were finding much to occupy their time. Trials were carried out with a view to carrying two chariots under the fuselage of a Sunderland flying-boat. This means of delivering machines and crews to an operational area would have obvious tactical advantages, it was thought. The trials were completed in every stage and seemed fairly satisfactory. However, no further move was made to employ this new technique operationally.

On September 24, thirteen days after the departure of the six *X*-craft for Altenfjord, four chariots and twelve charioteers left HHZ in *Alecto*. At Lunna Voe, in the Shetlands, they met with M.T.B. 675, who was fitted with davits to carry two chariots, one on either quarter. There followed several days' intensive training in the new 'M.T.B.' technique.

The operational plan called for a British agent to be landed in a Norwegian-type rowing-boat, with concentrated rations, a short-range wireless-set, and other equipment, on a small island overlooking the harbour of Askvoll, some seventy-five miles north of Bergen. M.T.B. 675 would then withdraw to a near-by inlet and camouflage herself with nets and other impedimenta. A listening watch would be continuously maintained on the agent's wave-length. Should suitable targets materialize the chariots would then be able to be dropped in the most advantageous position and proceed as instructed by the agent.

In actual fact the operation was only partly successful, and then not in the way that had been planned. The M.T.B. found the weather difficult on account of her greatly increased load, but decided to struggle on. The agent was landed and the agreed hiding-place was reached. But it was not long before the suspicious attentions of a dubious-looking fishing-vessel made a move out to sea desirable. Then the situation deteriorated rapidly with three separate and fierce attacks from enemy aircraft. In the course of these actions one Focke-Wulf was shot down into the sea and one Messerschmitt was badly damaged. The casualties aboard the M.T.B. were severe, numbering thirteen out of a total complement of forty-four. With the wounded in poor condition, two of the four engines out of action, and the compass destroyed, it was necessary to abandon the agent and limp home. The return trip took eight precarious and worrying hours.

Five days later another M.T.B. returned to pick up the agent. On its way back to the Shetlands this craft torpedoed and sank a large merchant-ship. So, with planes being shot down and a ship torpedoed, there was some good coming out of the operation, even if Fate had not allowed the charioteers to engage the enemy. Further similar operations were attempted during the month of November, but still there was no luck. Heavy snowstorms and incessant rough weather intervened on two occasions; wireless contact broke down on another; and more often than not there were no targets to be had. Conditions ashore had reduced escape-chances to nil, and it was finally decided to cease all further chariot operations in Norwegian waters for the remainder of the winter.

Some of the charioteers transferred to other branches of the Service, but many others continued training and working-up. During the spring and early summer of 1944 they shared *Bonaventure* and HHZ with the *X*-craft crews. It was thus that a Sub-Lieutenant Jim Warren and a Midshipman Jimmy Benson[1] travelled north together on the same train. The former was a charioteer and had recently been commissioned after having started his chariot career as a Stoker Petty Officer. The latter was reporting for spare-crew *X*-craft duties.

Now Sub-Lieutenant J. Benson, R.N.V.R.

The chariots housed in *Bonaventure* were mainly the new Mark II's, in which Numbers One and Two sat back to back and with legs inside the structure of the machine. During the summer there were two chariot accidents, both within shouting distance of *Bonaventure*'s quarter-deck. The second of these was fatal, the casualty being Sub-Lieutenant K. V. F. Harris, R.N.V.R. He was the Number One of a machine attacking *Bonaventure*. His Number Two reported that the disaster seemed to be caused by speed being suddenly increased instead of decreased as the heavy bilge-keel was approached. The unfortunate Number One took the full weight of the collision, with the fast-revving motor forcing him hard against the unyielding metal. With great skill Able Seaman Hutton, the Number Two, brought the chariot under control and to the surface. But Harris was already dead.

Two days before this had come the first accident. Warren was taking down one of the few Mark I machines for a trial dive. Everything seemed in order, but no sooner had they left the surface than the hydroplane controls stuck at 'hard to dive.' At sixty feet Warren gave up wrestling with the joystick and turned to see whether his Number Two, Leading Stoker Jack Harman, wanted to bail out. As he did so his elbow knocked the by-pass valve full open, at 2200 pounds per square inch. Instinctively he spat out his mouthpiece to save his lungs, but in so doing he let the pressure flood into his suit. He immediately became the perfect imitation of the Michelin man, with his arms forced straight apart.

In the brief second while all this was happening Harman acted. In a flash he had cut open one of Warren's cuffs to allow the pressure to escape, and then he made his way up—from what must have been ninety to a hundred feet—with Warren and the chariot. After several weeks in hospital nursing a distended lung, Warren was pronounced fit for diving, but not for charioteering, and so left the Flotilla.

These two accidents brought home to the charioteers in "B.V." how much they feared the only accident that mattered—the one that was fatal. It was a frightening thought that death could be so close even in the most domestic of exercises. The fact that sanity was preserved could only have been on account of the strength of the universal conviction: "It can't happen to me."

If the chariot activity from *Bonaventure* was the more unfortunately sensational during this period, the *X*-craft programme was certainly the busier. There were towing exercises, navigational exercises, practice-attack exercises, and escape exercises. The last two of these always brought the spare-crew personnel most into the picture. In the mock attacks several observation posts had to be set up for thirty-six hours or so, each being under the command of a spare-crew officer with two or three spare-crew ratings as look-outs. On very few occasions were the craft ever spotted, which made for great confidence when the same spare-crew personnel eventually joined operational boats.

One other form of spare-crew activity was to serve aboard M.L. 235 (Lieutenant Peter Kern, R.N.V.R.), which was attached to *Bonaventure* as a permanent tender. It was her job to take part in depth-charge trials with various *X*-craft, steaming on a parallel course to the submarine, dropping a single charge, waiting for the craft to surface and compare notes, and then resuming the operation at closer distance. When the odd light-bulb began to go in the craft it was considered time to bring the exercise to an end. All this provided valuable information about the depth-charge danger-radius for the craft, as well as giving the crews experience in recognizing which bangs were big enough to worry about.

There had been twelve new craft delivered early in 1944: *X.20* to *X.25* and *XT.1* to *XT.6*, the 'T' in the latter indicating that they were built for training purposes only, at less expense and with fewer fittings. The "20-class" craft were thus left free for operational working-up and for actual operations.

Two passage-crews were later appointed to each operational craft. This was symptomatic of the general state of the War. Official eyes were resting to a much greater extent on the Far East, and operations in that part of the world would probably call for longer tows than could reasonably be attempted by the same three or four men.

The larger numbers in the new total complements made an *X*-craft C.O.'s job more responsible. In addition to this, it was still by far the most interesting. In any submarine the knowledge that one is the only person who can see what is happening makes the whole business of captaincy ten times more entrancing.

Most *X*-craft were happy ships. This was partly due to the fact that the crews were not assembled by the normal arbitrary methods, but were 'hand-mixed' in the Staff Office at *Varbel*. Thus, any obvious anomalies, such as the choice of a very Bohemian R.N.V.R. First Lieutenant for a very strait-laced R.N. Commanding Officer could be avoided.

The good *X*-craft C.O. had to be blessed with a large amount of initiative. He had always to be prepared to try new ideas, even if some of these should seem somewhat risky. Occasionally, a brainchild would run astray and a craft would lose some paintwork or sustain a minor dent, but the keynote of 'nothing venture, nothing gain' still seemed an admirable one for conducting the working of an X-craft at sea. Furthermore, the good C.O. had to know how to take command. The problem of what degree of familiaiity between officers and men should be allowed was potentially great. Conditions at sea meant that the four members of the crew must get to know one another very well indeed. But the routine of shore-base and depot-ship would not, and could not, permit the same degree of equality being continued. In most craft the problem seemed to solve itself satisfactorily. It was common for the captain to be "Derek" or "Nobby" to his fellow-officers whenever and wherever non-duty matters were being discussed, but he was "Captain, sir" on all other occasions. He had probably never given any instructions to this effect. It just happened naturally, and the two forms of address would fit in side by side in the same conversation.

Possibly the side of the working-up programme that had developed the most since the days of X.5 and her contemporaries was the business of net-cutting. No longer were X-craft divers converted charioteers. They were people who joined specially for the job, and were almost entirely young R.N.V.R. officers or senior regular ratings. Most of these men, as well as being expert in their own particular department, developed into capable navigators, and could have doubled jobs with their First Lieutenants if such had ever been necessary.

In addition to the diver proper, either the First Lieutenant or the E.R.A. of each operational crew had to qualify fully as a diver. So, throughout the working-up period, two divers from each craft were undertaking net-cuts of different types and under different conditions, until each of the two had more than completed the required numbers of successful penetrations. For those poor unfortunates who had to do their net-cutting during the winter months conditions could be very cold and unpleasant.

For a normal 'cut,' the craft would leave one of the two piers at Loch Striven Head, manned by the operational crew. The diver would usually have dressed ashore, as dressing inside the craft had only a nuisance value that, once experienced, could satisfactorily be dispensed with. The diving-tender, with Warrant Officer Jack Passey in charge, would be already in position at the net, and the craft would dive to close directly under her at periscope-depth. A few hundred yards away a final course would be set, and then she would be taken deeper, usually to about thirty feet.

The first contact with the net always came as a sudden jerk, and speed would immediately be reduced to dead slow ahead. Inside the "W and D" the diver would have his oxygen-supply connected, his nose-clip would be fixed, and the circular window would be fitted into the face-piece of his new-style, streamlined suit. Then the door connecting the compartment with the control-room would be shut, and he would be alone.

He was cramped for space. The only possible posture was for him to sit on the 'heads,' when he could enjoy just a little freedom of movement in the box-shaped space that was scarcely wider than his shoulders and less capacious than the normal cabin-trunk.

Flooding- and pumping-controls for the compartment were duplicated on either side of the control-room door. To conserve his strength the prudent diver would give a valve one turn, and then it would be opened for him from inside. Then, with the pump started, the water would be forced in from No. 2 main ballast-tank. The first sensation for the diver was always that of the rubber suit being pressed tight against his legs. As soon as it was practicable he plunged his hands into the dark and—probably—icy liquid, to accustom them to the temperature of the loch in which they would have to work. Hands were the only part of the body left unprotected from the cold, although string-mesh gloves were sometimes worn to guard against the worst effects of the rough wires of the net.

Up and up would come the water, over chest, mouth, eyes, and head complete. In another few seconds the compartment would be full and the pump turned off. One arm would float up and release the hatch-clip. Then would come the whole body, pushing upon the hatch. Pausing as he cleared the rim and facing aft to the night-periscope, where he knew the skipper to be looking, the diver would give the appropriate signal, float clear, and shut the hatch.

There would be the net—a series of wire rectangles, each three feet by eighteen inches. With luck the craft might have remained at right angles to the line of the net, for which purpose the motor had been kept running ahead. Taking the cutter out of the for'ard casing, the diver would crawl up to the bows and climb through the most amenable-looking rectangle. Then he would go down, counting.

It was usual to make the cuts in the shape of an inverted letter 'V.' There would be nine cuts in all for a straightforward penetration, four in each leg and the final one at the apex, where the craft's bull-ring was resting. The cutter was easy to use, but somewhat heavy. Often two hands were needed to operate it, and if the diver

had forgotten to have one arm locked round a firm strand of the net
he risked plunging downward when the knife-edge bit through the
section of wire on which the cutter—and he himself—was suspended.

With the ninth cut the whole V-shaped piece of net would drop
forward, and the craft come slowly through. Thankfully keeping a
firm grip on the casing, while remaining near the net to clear any of
the aftermost parts of the superstructure, the diver would see the
craft through and then re-stow the cutter and climb back into the
"W and D."

In a way, the worst was still to come. The hatch would have to be
shut before the compartment could be drained, and this could prove
to be the very dickens of a job. It was surprising how difficult it was,
especially with a well-fitting hatch, to overcome the slightly greater
resistance afforded by the water in the compartment. Added to this
there was the lack of room for manœuvring to get a good pull, and
then the net-cut itself might have been quite tiring. But the hatch had
to be shut or the whole exercise was pointless. The average diver
wedged his shoulder, cracked his by-pass valve, and strained his
biceps and stomach muscles perhaps a dozen times before success
was achieved. Then he relapsed to the comfort of the seat on the
'heads.'

With the hatch shut he was almost 'home.' As soon as he had
regained his breath he had to turn a valve-handle, and then wait until
the water came down and down and down, until the control-room
door could be opened and his face-piece removed. The air inevitably
tasted good.

Of course, things did not always go smoothly. Divers would
occasionally 'pass out' and have to be carried up to the surface by
attendants operating from the diving-tender in Sladen suits. Jack
Passey would treat it all very much as a matter of course.

"Relief-valve stuck?" he would say. "Try this set, then, it's all
right. Down you go."

He was right, of course, but it would have been pleasant to disobey
him.

Then there was the bugbear of broadside cuts. Occasionally
a strong current would take charge and force the craft almost broadside on to the net. Even several increases in speed would not enable
the rudder to straighten her up. And so the diver would have to
make a matter of twenty cuts. To balance this there were the very
infrequent occasions when one was lucky enough to hit the net
immediately alongside a previous penetration. A couple of cuts
would see the craft through and clear. But the careful attention of

the boom-defence people made sure that this did not happen too often.

And so the days and weeks would pass. Working-up was completed for one set of crews, and the craft had then to be handed over for further exercising. The scarcity of operations during 1944 made life rather disappointing. It couldn't be helped, one supposed, but Jerry might have been sporting and provided a few more targets, and Admiralty might have made more use of the craft.

In the end there was the usual bromide of leave. London saw a succession of parties, and then one went home. Sports jackets and flannels seemed quite pleasant for a while, but the bombs and doodle-bugs brought the War rather frighteningly near.

CHAPTER NINETEEN

Bergen

T HE X-craft attack on the *Tirpitz* had been highly successful, thanks to the perseverance of Place and Cameron and their crews. Many lessons were learnt in respect of design and equipment for new classes of craft, and at least one tactical lesson was learnt too— namely, that except in very special circumstances future operations should be planned on the basis of one craft, one target.

This was the motto adopted in the scheming of Operation "Guidance," to be carried out by *X.24* (Lieutenant Max Shean, R.A.N.V.R.).

Working-up had been started in January 1944, and was continued right up to April. During the best part of four months, therefore, the craft was able, by carrying out endurance trials and making countless attacks on *Bonaventure*, to acquire a high standard of efficiency.

Previous to the operation, and towards the end of the period of working-up, *X.24* paid a visit to Scapa Flow, for the purposes of testing the anchorage's boom-defences. Originally this should have been undertaken by "Digger" McFarlane in *X.22*. But in the course of a towing exercise that continued through the height of a gale *X.22*'s parent submarine, *Syrtis*, turning suddenly to rescue her Officer-of-the-Watch, who had been washed out of the conning-tower platform by heavy seas, rammed her small charge. "22" sank immediately, with the loss of the four members of her operational crew.

A short time later therefore "24" started the series of test-runs on the Scapa defences. These exercises had been planned because it was thought—happily, in error—that the Germans had captured complete one of the craft from the *Tirpitz* raid, and would possibly be returning the compliment with a midget-submarine attack of their own on the Home Fleet. If this should have happened it would have been of value for the boom-defence people to have heard the noises made by an *X*-craft, or appreciated the lack of them. The success achieved by *X.24* must have caused a few sore heads at Admiralty among those responsible for the safety of the fleet anchorage.

The craft's presence was kept fairly secret, and after each day's exercise she had to return to *Bonaventure* by the longest possible route, always avoiding the main body of the Fleet. However, the senior officer in charge of the trials was eventually prevailed upon to take the craft back through the Fleet on the last day, "provided you keep good station on my M.T.B.," as he put it.

The 'buzz' must have gone round in a very few minutes, for there were large numbers of interested spectators lining the various guard-rails. It was only when passing *Duke of York* (battleship and flag-ship of the Commander-in-Chief Home Fleet, Admiral Sir Bruce Fraser, later Admiral of the Fleet Lord Fraser of North Cape) that one of the officers hit upon the idea of coming to the salute. There were two solitary bodies on the casing of the tiny *X*-craft, and they were soon splitting their sides with laughter as they saw the best part of 1000 officers and men aboard the "Duke" spring smartly to attention.

Not content with this, as he stood peering up at the huge edifice towering above him, the same officer picked up his Aldis signalling lamp and flashed across: "What a big bastard you are!" Back from the flagship came a formal receipt-of-signal code group—and nothing more.

The next morning's panic can be imagined when a signal was received from the C.-in-C., reading: "R.P.C. [request pleasure of company] dinner to-night."

This was followed shortly afterwards by a visit from Admiral Fraser himself, who remarked that it must have been very wet for whoever had been on the casing the previous afternoon. Still no one knew whether the great man had seen the signal.

That evening, when the officers of *X.24* went to dinner aboard the flagship, they were entertained to a more than first-rate party. Not until very shortly before the festivities closed did they learn through the Flag Lieutenant that the Admiral had not in fact received the signal. They were very relieved.

Soon they were back in HHZ, and with the beginning of April all leave had been completed and they were ready to start. They had been told that they were to enter the Norwegian harbour of Bergen—one of the most heavily defended ports under German control—and attack the Laksevaag floating dock. Briefing was very thorough indeed. In addition to information from underground sources, first-hand details about the dock, the harbour, and the approaches were provided by three Norwegians, one of whom had worked for the floating-dock company prior to the German occupation. The target, one of the largest floating docks available to the Germans, was being used by *U*-boats and was also supplying power to two other docks in the harbour. If it should be sunk the other two docks would thus, temporarily at least, be rendered inactive as well.

X.24 sailed from HHZ at 10 A.M. on the 9th of April 1944, in tow of the submarine *Sceptre* (Lieutenant Ian McIntosh, D.S.O., M.B.E., D.S.C., R.N.[1]). Also present on the first stage of the journey were the depot-ship *Alecto* and His Norwegian Majesty's Ship *Narvik*.

The *X*-craft passage-crew, under Sub-Lieutenant John Britnell, R.N.V.R., had a quiet trip to the Shetlands, where the operational crew took over after a brief rest in the Burra Forth, leaving there, still in tow of *Sceptre*, at noon on the 11th. *Alecto* and *Narvik* were to wait at Burra for the return of the two submarines.

Two and a half days later they slipped the tow at a point some thirty-five miles from the target. The time was ten minutes to eleven o'clock. It was a calm, dark night, and for several hours the craft was able to proceed at full speed on the surface, sometimes reducing from six and a half to four and a half knots to charge her batteries. They travelled along a wide fjord and then across a minefield, clearing the latter by about midnight. By 1.15 A.M. their course was 140 degrees, and they were faced with the problem of passing between two small islands about half a mile apart, across which gap no fewer than five searchlights were playing. It would have been inconvenient to dive, as there was a battery charge 'on,' so Max Shean contented himself with lying flat on the casing and lowering the induction trunk to its housed position. By this means they were able to pass through unobserved.

At half-past two they dived. Sub-Lieutenant Joe Brooks[2] (the First Lieutenant) found depth-keeping difficult owing to freshwater pockets, which state of affairs continued throughout the attack. Apart from this, which was unavoidable, there was no single technical difficulty experienced. All the equipment worked perfectly, and paid a handsome dividend for the hours of preparation.

Max felt quite satisfied with their progress. They had travelled twenty-five miles up the fjord before diving and had successfully negotiated the outer of the two minefields guarding the harbour, as well as the searchlight trap. On diving, speed was reduced to two

[1] Now Commander McIntosh.
[2] Now Lieutenant-Commander J. Brooks, D.S.C., R.N.

knots, and the craft was kept at periscope-depth so that Max could investigate a little opening that was marked on the chart as Langholm. He intended to enter this little bay and bottom for a few hours in order to make the next part of the passage in the full light of morning. However, Langholm was by no means as deserted as he had hoped, so there was no option but to continue.

'Normal attack stations' were being maintained for the whole of this stage of the penetration. This meant Shean at the periscope, Brooks at the controls, E.R.A. Coles at the steering position, and Sub-Lieutenant Frank Ogden helping Shean with the navigation. Periscope-depth was maintained almost continuously for the next three hours, a tribute to Brooks's skill and concentration. And so when Max sighted their first enemy ship at 5.30 A.M. they were some six miles nearer the target. The contact was a medium-sized fishing-vessel coming out of the entrance to the West Byfjord swept channel, where *X.24*'s course lay. They passed well clear of her, and then, twenty minutes later, themselves started to cross the inner minefield, the last lap of the passage into Bergen harbour.

The craft was taken to twenty-five feet and brought back up to periscope-depth approximately once every five minutes. Life soon began to be hectic and exceedingly difficult. The channel through the minefield was simply alive with traffic. Shean counted forty ships that passed near to them and there were always many more in the middle distance. The fairway was so crowded that collision often seemed imminent, but was always avoided at the last moment. The traffic consisted in the main of small coastal craft, though there was a sprinkling of fishing-vessels, landing-craft, ferries, flak-ships, and—to Max's dismay—anti-submarine patrol vessels.

One of these was transmitting Asdic from its patrol course in the middle of the channel and in due course established contact with *X.24*. The four men could hear the 'ping' striking the stern of the craft at horribly regular intervals. "It was just like water dripping into an enamel bowl," one of them wrote subsequently.

Immediately a twenty-degree zigzag was ordered, and the craft was crossing and recrossing from side to side of the channel for fully fifteen to twenty minutes before the 'pings' became irregular and eventually ceased. Presumably the patrol vessel's Asdic operator had regarded the smallness of the echoes he was receiving as indicating that he was on to a shoal of fish or something similar, and certainly not a submarine. It was a relief to be able to resume a normal course. The zigzag had greatly increased the danger from the over-head traffic. Indeed, on one occasion when the periscope was raised

L

X.24 was so near to the stern of an assault-craft that Max got a 'periscope full' of the coxswain's sea-boots.

By 0745 they were right into the harbour, and a quarter of an hour later Max sighted the floating dock. It was flooded down and apparently empty, which was disappointing. Max didn't like to be too dogmatic about things, because from where he was situated the dock was partly obscured by the stern of a large merchant-ship. As far as he could see there were no net-defences round the dock, which was surprising. Again he couldn't be absolutely certain, because parts of the harbour were covered with a light haze.

They approached the target on a steady course. A small harbour-defence trawler gained Asdic contact with them on the way in, but her attentions were soon evaded by the orthodox expedient of turning 'end on' and going deep. Harbour traffic was probably busier than anything the craft had encountered during its working-up programme. Small boats, tugs, and fishing-vessels were continually passing overhead. This caused considerable worry among the crew lest one of these many vessels would spot the pencil-slim periscope and ram or otherwise sink the craft before the attack could be carried out. Each time Max ordered the craft to come to periscope-depth four breaths were held. The nearest they actually came to being undone in this respect was when a minesweeper came so close that all Max could see through the periscope was the number painted on her side. Then she passed clean alongside with a loud rushing noise.

"Sixty feet. Revolutions for one knot. Course 166 degrees to close the dock." Max was making a practice run-in before he embarked on the attack proper.

After the right number of minutes had ticked away on the control-room clock they passed under one dark object and then under another. The second they judged to be the dock, and they were still making their reckonings when the craft grounded at sixty feet. Stop. . . . Astern. . . . Out again to the middle of the harbour.

They tried the run-in again, both for practice and to make completely sure that course, speed, and depth were correct. A stopped trim was obtained to get the attack bearing—then ahead—then the darkness of the target overhead again. A second time "24" buried her nose in something at 60 feet. Through the scuttle in the periscope dome Max could distinguish what looked like sloping, loose-stone foundations. That would be the pier connecting the dock with the shore, they agreed. Disengaging the craft's bows from the stonework, Max slowly ran along the full length of the object above him, checking its length by a stop-watch calculation from the craft's

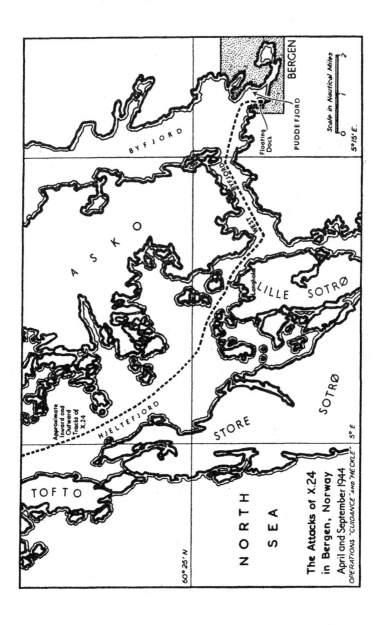

BYFJORD

BERGEN

Floating
Dock

PUDDEFJORD

Scale in Nautical Miles

0   1   2

5° 15′ E.

A S K O

WEST DROFAL...

Langholm

LILLE   SOTRØ

SOTRØ

Approximate
Inward and
Outward
Tracks of
X.24

HJELTEFJORD

STORE

TOFTO

N O R T H

S E A

60° 25′ N

5° E

The Attacks of X.24
in Bergen, Norway
April and September 1944
OPERATIONS "GUIDANCE" AND "HECKLE"

known speed through the water. Sure enough, this gave an estimated length for the object of 500 feet overall—the exact length of the dock. The general shape was straight-edged and rectangular, so Max withdrew the craft once again into the centre of the harbour, feeling very satisfied.

A likely-looking billet was found in Puddefjord, an opening off the main harbour from which the dock could be observed. Max took occasional peeps through the periscope, but was prevented from getting one good long look by the amount of traffic. As he edged the craft out again into the main fairway the traffic was so congested that it was scarcely possible to raise the 'stick' at all. Indeed, his last periscope observation before diving to seventy feet to attack was made from fully 250 yards away from the target, a greater distance than would have been really desirable in the circumstances and with the strong currents that were known to exist.

They were eight minutes at this new depth before Max sighted an object above them through the thick glass scuttle in the dome. The time was 0856, less than an hour after the first sighting. Everything was in order.

The dock was lying due north and south. From its extreme northern end Max took *X.24* along for a distance of a hundred feet and then stopped. The starboard side-cargo was released with a four-hour setting. They had attacked. A perceptible thrill ran round the four occupants of the control-room as the final turn on the huge basket-wheel allowed the charge to slide away from the hull and descend, falling leaf fashion, to the bottom.

"Bring her up to forty feet." This was speedily done, and the tense quartet in the *X*-craft's control-room were distinctly able to hear the sound of one or more reciprocating pumps functioning above them. Dock machinery, without doubt. At dead slow ahead the *X*-craft continued until she was within a hundred feet of the southern extremity of the dock. There she was brought up short by the loose-stone pier that she had encountered earlier.

This was just ideal. A slight positive buoyancy was induced and the craft slowly rose until she squeezed herself in and was wedged between the pier foundations and the target.

"Let go the port cargo."

Through the scuttle the cargo could be seen partially to disengage from the craft's pressure-hull and then rest against the rocks. The space was so congested that it was not until *X.24* withdrew astern that the charge lay completely clear.

The time was 0911. The attack had been completed. Two two-ton side cargoes, each with a four-hour setting, had been released and would be going up soon after 1 P.M. It was time to turn tail and run, and speed was accordingly increased to two and a half knots. There was a feeling of complete relief from all care, and they cruised blithely out, ignoring every danger. Nothing seemed to matter now that they had achieved their goal. The traffic, anyway, was not so thick on the outward journey, and on no occasion did anything out of the way occur until well into the evening, by which time *X.24* had almost reached the open sea.

By 6 P.M. the air inside the tiny submarine was becoming noticeably foul and breathing was difficult. But it was still not possible to surface with safety. Three hours later Max was on the point of bringing the craft from periscope-depth to the surface when a largish vessel coming towards them appeared seemingly out of nowhere. 'Q,' the emergency quick-diving tank, was immediately flooded, and they stayed deep, out of harm's way. Half an hour after this slight escapade, at half-past nine, they were finally able to surface.

All four members of the crew were in very bad shape by this time, the craft having been submerged for nineteen hours without a single 'guff' of fresh air. The symptoms of what they knew to be a combination of lack of oxygen and carbon dioxide poisoning were violent headaches and acute burning pains in the stomach. Nor did the inrush of good, clean air, which flooded the boat as soon as the captain opened the hatch, bring their troubles to an immediate end. On the contrary, and as is always the case when a submarine surfaces with badly deteriorated interior air-conditions, they all felt very sick. Shean and Coles were subjected to spasms of vomiting. But it was still good to be on the surface. They felt they were as good as home.

Sceptre was soon sighted, and the two submarines proceeded in company for an hour and a half before passing the tow and changing crews in the early minutes of April 15. There was a very large meal waiting in *Sceptre* for "24's" operational crew, which, in spite of their earlier stomach-upsets, they were all able to tackle with gusto. In celebration of the occasion an unwritten law was broken and the submarine's wardroom bar was opened on patrol. Its contents had never tasted better.

In a little over three days they were back in HHZ. Britnell and his crew had brought the craft to tiptop condition, the only defect being the parted telephone cable, which they obviously could not rectify. Arriving a few minutes after 0630, they found their base looking more like Hampstead Heath on Bank Holiday Monday than the desolate

Scottish loch that it really was. Ships were beflagged, sirens were being continuously hooted, a veritable fleet of small boats had come out to greet the returning heroes, and *Sceptre* and *X.24* were welcomed home to the strains of Harry Roy playing *American Patrol* and *In the Mood* through some one's loud-hailer.

"Nelson no doubt turned in his grave," was the comment of one member of the operational crew. But the ensuing, and very alcoholic, celebration was in the best tradition of the Service. None of the participants remember any part of it.

It was most unfortunate, however, that this day of rejoicing should be marred by the news that "24" had not sunk the floating dock. Instead, she had laid both her charges under the 7500-ton merchantman *Barenfels*, now a complete loss, which had been lying almost next to the dock and obscuring it from view during much of the attack.

This was a grave disappointment. It was typical of Willie Banks that he should assume the whole responsibility for this having happened, instead of just ascribing the misplaced charges to "force of circumstances" or "bad luck." He was adamant that his insistence on extreme caution in the use of the periscope was to blame for the mistake having occurred, saying that in point of fact there had been so much shipping about that the risk of detection was considerably lessened and the risk of being rammed correspondingly increased. Had Lieutenant Shean felt freer to use the periscope more often he might have achieved complete success in his attack. This opinion Captain Banks made very firmly in his report to Flag Officer Submarines.

It had been of the greatest coincidence that the 7500-ton motor vessel should have been of the same overall length as the floating dock (490 feet as against 500); that her draught of twenty-eight feet should have been exactly that of the dock when flooded down; that both ship and dock should have been lying precisely on the same north-south line; and that the shadows cast by the ship into the water should have shown a square-ended silhouette, presumably due to their combining with the shadows of neighbouring ships or of the jetty-wall.

Nevertheless, the attack had been a success. A powerful unit of the German-held merchant fleet had been destroyed and considerable damage had been inflicted on the jetty and harbour installations. Another of the objects of the operation had been achieved in that, at a critical stage of their career, it had been proved that *X*-craft could successfully enter and return from a harbour in which the defences were as strong as, if not stronger than, those at Altenfjord. Moreover, the Germans did not know what had hit them. Later in the year the Commander-in-Chief, Home Fleet, described the operation as a "magnificent achievement, ably planned and most daringly carried out."

Among the flotilla there were a number of persistent rumours concerning the outcome of this attack. The principal content of these was that the *Barenfels* had been carrying a cargo of high explosive and had consequently taken half the waterfront of Bergen up with her, after which occurrence the Germans had taken fifty Norwegian hostages and shot them in reprisal for an "act of sabotage." The resultant discussion on this subject always revolved round whether the British Government, to save the fifty lives, should have published the cause of the sinking. Whatever was the truth of this matter, there was no doubt that the Norwegian Embassy officials felt some grievance in respect of Operation "Guidance."

During the summer King George VI carried out an inspection at Scapa Flow at which *Bonaventure*, with chariots, and *X.24* were ordered to be present. Max Shean was recalled from leave to have the honour of showing His Majesty over the small submarine. The King was most impressed and remarked particularly upon the lack of comfort in the ordinary matter of living that must have been occasioned. Max was completely charmed by the interest and wit which the King displayed concerning what was, after all, only a very small unit of his naval forces.

When Max had brought *X.24* back from Bergen he was succeeded in command by Lieutenant H. P. Westmacott, D.S.C., R.N.[1] With the latter's considerable knowledge of big-submarine theory and his equally wide experience of big-submarine practice, he was an obvious candidate to be groomed for early stardom. Soon it was decided that "24" should return to Bergen, still with the intention of sinking the floating dock.

It might well have been that this rapid promotion for a comparative newcomer would have been unpopular with the flotilla at large, for Westmacott had only transferred from 'big boats' some two months previously. But this was not the case. It was very soon apparent to all concerned that Westmacott was a first-rate submarine officer. He was, admittedly, soon dubbed with the nickname of "Pusser Perce"; but this was only a gentle leg-pull on his somewhat formal ideas about the administration of a craft at sea, and there was implicit no more than an admiring, and perhaps smilingly, grudging recognition that

[1] Now Commander H. P. Westmacott, D.S.O., D.S.C., R.N.

an R.N.-trained submarine officer had no equal in any underwater field.

Operation "Heckle" took place in September 1944. Its terms of reference were exactly the same as Max Shean had received for the previous visit to Bergen. The initial briefing was also much the same except for the addition of a wealth of information from the previous crew.

Lieutenant Ian McIntosh and *Sceptre*—"Bring-'em-back-alive *Sceptre*," as she was called in an official report to Flag Officer Submarines—again performed the towing honours, and in company with *Alecto* the two submarines left Rothesay at 1615 on the afternoon of September 3. For seventy-four hours the passage-crew battled against bad weather, which became extremely severe round Cape Wrath, until they berthed in Balta Sound, among the Shetland Isles.

The operational crew left again at noon on September 7. With Westmacott were Sub-Lieutenant Beadon Dening, R.N.V.R., Sub-Lieutenant D. N. Purdy, R.N.Z.N.V.R. (diver), and E. R. A. Davison. The weather was far from good, and by the night of the 8th a full gale was blowing. Conditions 'up top' and 'down below' were both absolutely intolerable. For several hours the tow was maintained with both submarines at 120 feet—and "24" still rolled.

It was on surfacing during this atrocious weather that the induction trunking was seriously damaged by the force of the water. Not long afterwards there came tragedy. Purdy was washed off the casing and lost.

Nothing could be done but continue, and it was not until the weather moderated slightly, more than twenty-four hours later, that Sub-Lieutenant K. St. J. V. Robinson, R.N.V.R., of the passage-crew, was transferred from *Sceptre* to fill the vacancy.

When the tow was slipped at 8 P.M. on September 10 the operational crew had completed a passage of eighty hours across open sea in the foulest possible conditions. Strange to relate, the telephones had performed absolutely perfectly, although the air-compressor was completely out of action.

The approach story was much the same as Max Shean's. Conditions inside the fjords were better than out in the open sea, but they still left a lot to be desired. During the middle watch visibility was considerably restricted, often to about half a mile, owing to fierce rain-squalls. There was a long, low swell in the more seaward of the fjords, and the surface seemed uncommonly prone to phosphorescence. Westmacott had to consider the desirability of slowing and/or possibly of trimming down in the very bright moonlight, and he had to weigh this against the advantages of an early arrival in the West Byfjord. The latter won.

The craft was manœuvred down the final swept channel at periscope-depth, Westmacott making frequent observations to avoid all the traffic. On one occasion "24" was forced to go deep and was actually at thirty-five feet when a ship went immediately over the top of her. It was educative to ponder how small had been the gap between keel and casing. Fortunately, there was no sign at all of any anti-submarine patrol, so in this respect life was somewhat easier.

Puddefjord was entered at 0705. Westmacott was still taking frequent looks through the periscope, as the following reconstruction of the log shows:

0712. In the entrance to Puddefjord. Identify the observatory, the cathedral, and various harbour installations. Sea surface like a mirror. The town looks delightful, wreathed in an attractive mixture of light haze and blue sky.

0730. Observed *U*-boat pens.

0739. Dock observed. At full buoyancy. Unfortunately empty. No nets to the north, some nets to the east.

0748. Passing the coal wharf, course 140.

0754. Passing a mast sticking out of the water. The *Barenfels*. Notice reads "Langsam Fahren," or "Go Slow." Excellent—our speed only 2½ knots.
        Periscope jams and starts to smoke. Fixed with a screwdriver.

0810. Run in to attack.

0815. Periscope constantly up—down—up—down.

0820. Under dock at 25 feet, 'Q' tank having been flooded.

0840. On the bottom 60 feet below the north end of the dock. Let go port charge.

0850. Southern end. 50 feet below. Let go starboard. Set course for West Byfjord.

At 8.30 P.M. Westmacott was able to allow the craft to surface, and within half an hour they were in contact with *Sceptre*. The small craft followed the big submarine out to sea for a while before the tow was passed and the crews changed. The return-trip was uneventful except for the 'phones ceasing to function after the first eight hours. Balta Sound was entered at 9 A.M. on September 13, almost six days having elapsed since the two vessels' departure.

In his report on the operation Westmacott claimed damage to the ship or ships secured to the west side of the floating dock as well as the probable sinking of the dock itself. Subsequent observations confirmed that the floating dock and one smallish merchant vessel had both been sunk.

An interesting item in the final report was a domestic one. Meals at sea had been restricted to two a day. With the advent of bad weather the various items on the menu that were deleted fell off in the following order: soup, spam, eggs, fruit, tea, and orange juice.

X.24 had been magnificent. Hers were the only offensive actions undertaken by "20-class" craft, in spite of a persistent rumour that some one would have the task of cutting out a German capital ship from her anchorage in Trondhjem, and in spite of a suggestion from one of the crews that they should be allowed to attempt a mining expedition to the Kiel Canal.

PART IV: THE COAST OF EUROPE

CHAPTER TWENTY

No Better Charioteers

THE little Italian lieutenant looked at his watch. It was half-past seven; half-past seven on the 21st of June 1944. Almost an hour had elapsed, he thought, since the *Grecale*—a sleek, streamlined race-horse of a destroyer to which he had been newly appointed as junior watch-keeping officer—had steamed out of the little Corsican harbour of Bastia.

He had enjoyed the few days they had spent on the island. The French, he believed, called it the "scented isle," but its appeal was surely as much to the eye as to any of the other senses. The sharp-pointed mountains seemed to rise up right out of the sea. Indeed, one could take in a view of blue sea, golden sand, and grey-white peak without even turning the head. Yes, he had really enjoyed himself, in spite of the uncomfortable journey he had been obliged to make on the stupid narrow-gauge railway between Bastia and Ajaccio; in spite of the bustling, business-like atmosphere in Bastia itself, with its trading traditions struggling to survive among a welter of semi-derelict tourist shops that reflected a far-off past; in spite of the *vin rosé* in the wine parlours—good though it may have been, he would have preferred an indifferent Chianti; and in spite of the way their 'passengers' had spoiled his afternoon on the tiny bathing beach to the north of the harbour. Perhaps horseplay was part of their make-up. He didn't know.

Of course, they should have sailed at 1730. The fact that they did not proceed until an hour and ten minutes after that had not pleased the 'passengers.' Nor had it pleased his Comandante, who had had something pointed to say about engineer officers, who allowed boiler-trouble to develop at times like this. Needless to say, the M.T.B. that was to accompany them had been ready to leave right on the dot, which hadn't improved matters.

Ship's head was a few degrees north of east, and they were speeding along in perfect conditions—calm sea, bright sun, good visibility. The 'passengers' seemed a bit worried about the visibility being so

good, and he could well understand. He looked up at the group of
them on the bridge, and thought how strange it all was. It didn't
seem long since Italy had been resounding with glorious news of the
doings of the gallant men of the Decima Flottiglia Mas (the Tenth
Submarine Flotilla). They had attacked the British fleet in Alexandria and Gibraltar, they had been the spearhead of Italian naval
offensive action. And now, what was happening? The Italian Navy
was transporting British human-torpedo people to attack two
Italian cruisers—admittedly now in German hands—and the famous
De la Penne was even now in the *Grecale*, organizing a subsidiary
attack by the "Gamma" boys, the Italian Navy's frogmen. It all
seemed so strange. He had still not accustomed himself to being on
the 'other side' in this peculiar war.

"Lorenzo."

He turned at the sound of his Christian name, and found that his
cabin-mate was calling him over to meet the British charioteers, as
they named themselves. After a brief introduction he found himself
talking a little, in his hesitant English, listening a little to a mixture of
English and Italian, but mainly looking and observing.

There were two crews—four men. The first team were a Sub-
Lieutenant, Malcolm Causer, and an Able Seaman, Harry Smith.
Causer was on the short side of medium height, about five feet,
eight inches. The first things one noticed about him were his
extraordinarily broad chest and the apparent strength of his hands.
In spite of being rigged in khaki battledress, he looked every inch a
seaman, exuding that indescribable quality of 'fitting in' among
things nautical. He was always cheerful, but never appeared silly or
childish. And yet he was quite young, twenty-two or twenty-three.
The little Italian officer found him a likable personality, and thus
agreed with the universal verdict. It was in his favour, of course, that
in some lights he looked a Latin. If his dark hair had been straight
instead of crinkly, and if the accent that his Brazil-learnt English bore
had only been a little more pronounced, he could well have passed
unnoticed in an Italian community. Not so the Able Seaman, however. His pink young face would give him away as an Englishman in
any surroundings. But for all his youth he looked a formidable
character, this Smith. His build was every bit as strong as that of his
Number One, and if, guessed Lorenzo, he lacked imagination, then
he certainly made up for it with staunchness. He seemed to personify
the phrase he was so often using, "What the hell?"

The Number One of the second team was called Conrad Berey. He
was a Petty Officer Cook. What sort of a Navy was this? thought

Lorenzo. How could a cook, even a Petty Officer Cook, get the job of piloting a human torpedo? How could a cook even be that type of person? It was all very unusual, but he had to admit to himself that Berey looked very much the part. In many ways he was a more commanding personality than Causer, slightly taller, though not so broad. His dark, smooth hair framed a face that looked tough in the extreme. Mentally and physically hard, he allowed nothing to distract him from his job. He had no time for idle conversation, spoke little in compliment, and when he did speak in criticism he was ruthless and spared no one. The oldest of the four, he was in his late twenties. His life was the sea and the Navy—his own Navy. And for foreign navies or foreign anything—especially, it seemed to Lorenzo, for things and people Italian—he had nothing but scathing disrespect. "Me, in an Eyetie ship; downright disgusting!"

Berey's Number Two was Ken Lawrence, a Stoker. He was tall and thin—by far the tallest of the four. His outstanding characteristic was his blind faith in his Number One, and the fact that Berey would never have changed his Number Two showed that the young stoker was a first-rate diver.

This much Lorenzo either knew or saw or guessed. He also knew that the rest of the party included the Gamma crews and two special motor-boats, as well as British Staff Officers and dressers for the divers.

The mountains round La Spezia were easily visible, and in a short time they could see a column of smoke, seemingly of considerable size, rising near the Italian coast a little to the south-east of the naval base. This was soon distinguished as a small coaster on fire, presumably through the action of the R.A.F. The two ships decreased speed, as, owing to the exceptionally good visibility, the coast seemed uncomfortably near, and, although it would probably be difficult to spot a destroyer and an M.T.B. from such a distance, a certain amount of concern was being felt on board.

At 8.30 P.M. the order was given to stop engines. The two M.T.S.M.'s (the frogmen's special motor-boats) were lowered, on board one of which went the three Gamma men. The other was being used merely as a spare. Once they were clear the M.T.B. came alongside and embarked the chariot party.

Lorenzo watched them go, waving and shouting his good wishes, just as several of his shipmates were doing. There they go, he thought, off to attack the *Bolzano* and *Gorizia* in our own Italian human-torpedo base of La Spezia. One wishes them well, of course, but it does seem a topsy-turvy world.

Under the direction of the Senior British Naval Officer, Commander P. E. H. Heathfield, R.N., the M.T.B. shot off at twenty-three knots. She was heading due north, direct for La Spezia. Heathfield found the evening dragged terribly. He thought dusk would never come, and he could detect signs of impatience among the four charioteers. The light was certainly lasting longer than they had expected, and before ten o'clock speed had to be reduced to thirteen knots, which seemed a virtual snail's pace in a craft of that type.

They were able to discern details of the smoke that was coming from Leghorn. As Heathfield suspected, the R.A.F. had given that town especial attention. And there was still that burning coaster. It was good to see the enemy being chivvied at every turn, even though a spell of quietude might have made them less watchful and less likely to intercept the attack that was soon to commence.

Closer in, speed was reduced still further to six knots. The two M.T.S.M.'s were waved off, and they quickly sped away in the direction of the breakwater. The M.T.B. was not far off the chariot-dropping position, and Heathfield went over for a few words with her commanding officer.

"Lieutenant Carminati. May I have a chat with you?"

Heathfield knew that the M.T.B. was very noisy when starting its engines or when idling, so he made it clear that he wanted the engines stopped, as soon as the dropping position was reached, and not left running in neutral.

"The shore seems only just off the starboard bow, and I can't risk our being heard. There's a shore battery and a searchlight abeam of the position, which doesn't ease my mind at all. We'll wait for a quarter of an hour after the chariots leave before we start the engines again. Let them get well away before the searchlight picks us up, as I'm sure it will as soon as the throttles are opened. All right? Thanks."

Position was reached at twenty minutes to midnight. The crews were dressed and ready to enter the water the moment the propellers had stopped turning, and within a few minutes they would be away. As the au-revoirs were being said and the good wishes exchanged, Heathfield stood apart for a few moments. The visibility, damn it, was still excellent. Couldn't be better from the Jerries' point of view. And it was just then that a tubby Italian seaman caught his eye, indicated the sky and the shore with an expressive, almost grand-opera, gesture, and remarked, "A pain in ze neck, eh, Comandante?"

It was a pity that no one could know what was going on in Berey's mind at that moment. It would have been especially heartening to the Italians, after his scarce-suppressed lack of respect for their methods, could they have heard him thinking. The two machines were lowered from the specially cut-away stern of the M.T.B. with very little noise. Entry into the water from the low freeboard was easy for the divers, too. In fact, thought Berey, the whole thing is perfect, and certainly the best means of transportation I have had anything to do with.

The divers were in the water; the machines had been slipped from their cradles. The four men mounted and checked the trim, putting the motors to slow ahead. In a moment or two they passed the port bow of the M.T.B. and headed into the darkness. There was a wave from Causer, and then they were gone—Causer to find and sink the *Bolzano*, Berey the *Gorizia*. Everything was black and quiet. Even aboard M.T.B. 74 all voices seemed to have died.

It is relevant here to record a difference of opinion. The captain of the M.T.B. and Commander Heathfield both stated after the operation that the chariots had been launched from the agreed dropping position, approximately three miles from the breakwater. The Number Ones of both chariots, however, were then convinced that the run-in distance was considerably greater than three miles. Causer reckoned the position was eight miles out, Berey that it was six at the very least. It subsequently appears that the charioteers were wrong and that their misapprehension was due to the machines' batteries producing considerably less than the usual maximum speed.

The fortunes of the two teams differed widely right from the start. Causer and Smith enjoyed a straightforward run-in, apart from the unpleasantly long time it took them to reach the breakwater of the harbour. Within a few minutes of waving good-bye to the M.T.B. Causer turned his head for another glimpse, but could see nothing but blackness, not even the suspicion of a silhouette. It was only at this time that he actually realized that Smith and he were now entirely on their own, making towards a heavily defended enemy harbour. This caused an odd feeling in his stomach—the sort of tension or excitement he had occasionally experienced before an important game or examination.

For the first hour they ran in on the surface without seeing any signs of the enemy, but shortly after the hour had elapsed they heard the *put-put* of a diesel engine approaching, so they dived immediately to about twenty-five feet and reduced speed. The noise appeared to be coming in their direction, became louder, and eventually passed right over them to die away in the distance. As soon as Causer thought it reasonably safe they surfaced again and stopped the motor, while with signs and much pushing and pulling Smith was instructed to sit facing aft—a most unusual manœuvre on this type of chariot—to keep a watch against things happening astern. They then continued on the surface, and Causer was much intrigued by the considerable activity in the direction of the harbour. There were tracer patterns shooting off all over the place, searchlights and various assortments of flares.

Soon he could pick out a black shape in the middle distance. This turned out to be the boom-defence vessel that he had been given to expect. She was supposed to carry a listening-post, and he accordingly varied his speed at intervals and exercised even greater caution in all his manœuvring. Altering course to starboard, he found the marker-buoy that lay midway along the breakwater. No snags so far. Half a minute later he turned the machine's head still farther to starboard and commenced running parallel to the breakwater and about fifteen yards away from it. There ought to be no trouble about finding the east entrance, he thought.

Meanwhile Berey and Lawrence were also approaching the breakwater. Everything was going smoothly until Berey decided to trim the machine down, when she suddenly became possessed of a queer assortment of tricks and antics. When he pushed the stick forward the screw came out of the water with a shattering amount of noise. When he corrected this by pumping aft she stood on her tail with a foot of warhead above the surface and Berey's visor still under the water. A stealthy approach was out of the question if it should be needed later on. Also, it was impossible to surface her gently. She insisted on breaking out of the water with a rush.

Berey's brain became ice-cold. Coolly he investigated the trimming difficulties as the machine was kept headed in towards the harbour. There was an air-leak into the ballast-tank, so that couldn't be used for trimming. Of the nature of the remaining fault, his own conclusion at the time was that something had broken inside and was accentuating any angle put on the machine by the hydroplanes.

His operational narrative continues the story:

I now proceeded towards the breakwater. On the way in I noticed a light flashing at presumably either the main or the western entrance to the harbour. Also heard a motor-engine, very subdued. Concluded this was one of the M.T.S.M.'s. Eventually sighted the two masts which we had been told at briefing were in the middle of the breakwater and which should have given us a bearing on the gaps. Time 0230. On getting closer I found the 'masts' to be two factory chimneys on a hill. Could still not see anything else, Spezia being surrounded by hills, which made silhouettes out of the question. Saw two small islands next, which fixed my position at the eastern end of the breakwater. My visor had been misting up and soon became hopeless. From the time of sighting the islands I had to keep it open. I had decided to make my entrance into the harbour on the surface, anyway, both because I could not see the instruments when dived and also because of the machine's impossible antics. This was my second operation, the first having been a failure. I was determined to carry things through, somehow.

We now proceeded along the breakwater in a westerly direction, investigating what I thought to be gaps, but only succeeding in badly denting the head on submerged rocks. After about an hour we came to four wireless masts which, owing to their number and description, I thought could not be 'our' masts. My next plan was to go in at the main entrance, and we reached there, only to find plenty of lights in the form of Aldis-type signalling lamps and heavy torches, and, of course, plenty of voices. It was quite apparent that they were looking for something in the water. I realized now that if I was detected, which was almost bound to happen with the machine permanently on the surface, they would know what they were looking for, and the whole operation would be ruined. To go back to the other entrance was not possible, as dawn was breaking and the battery was showing signs of being weak. Due to lack of facilities for charging during transport they had been standing about for nearly a week. I now decided, although it was an awful thing to do, that we had to give up, as nothing more could be done. It only remained to find a quiet place to land quickly, so we proceeded farther along the breakwater until we ran into a current and could make no headway. Turning inshore, we found a little bay and set the clock on the warhead for 0800, sending the machine seaward with the pumps flooding and the motor running full speed ahead. Time 0430 on the 22nd.

Meanwhile, Causer's body was feeling a bit stiff as he guided his machine along the line of the breakwater. He would be glad, really, to be inside the harbour and beneath the surface. Even in good weather the slight slap-slap of the wavelets on the top of the guard just in front of his eyes, together with the crouching forward position that every Number One assumed on the surface, could be a little tiring; whereas below the surface everything was relaxed, natural, and free from worry.

All along the breakwater he kept a close watch for any gap that might let them through, and once they actually attempted such an entry, but found there was not enough water for the chariot's draught. By this time they were a good three hours behind schedule and every minute was precious, so Causer decided not to waste any more time and made straight for the old entrance at full speed.

M

As they neared the end of the breakwater speed was reduced to the minimum, and the machine was headed round to port to close and pass through the entrance. They had a perfect diving-trim and all that was above the surface was just enough of Causer's head, for him to see where they were going. Then, suddenly, from the end of the breakwater came the sound of heavy boots taking a few steps and the distant click of a gun being cocked.

"We were so close that I hardly dared breathe," recalls Causer, "and did not even dive for fear that the movement would attract the attention of the guard. Instead, we just carried on straight ahead, and soon I felt we were reasonably safe again."

By this time they were right in the middle of the disused entrance and could make out the shape of a half-sunken ship. Negotiating their way round this vessel, they found, to their dismay, three rows of anti-torpedo nets. This was not funny! They let the machine come right alongside the first net, and then the two of them began pulling themselves and the machine down in the hope of passing under the net at about forty-five feet. But they reached bottom at thirty-five and the amount of surplus net lying on the harbour-bed was too much for them to lift up and pass under. So they surfaced again. Admittedly they had net-cutters with them, but time was short and net-cutting always was a slow business. And there were three rows of nets. Some other way in had to be found.

In the blackness that surrounded them they groped their way about. Sladen suits were not designed for playing a glorified hunt-the-thimble. The creases of surplus suit at one's elbow-joints didn't encourage rapid movement. Leaning across one's breathing-bag at an acute angle could tend to deprive one of vital oxygen. And the machine would begin to float away if one's leg slid off the saddle. The water, of course, was just a confounded nuisance. Why did it always have to push against you? To blazes with everything! But, at least, it wasn't freezing cold, thought Causer, with memories of Trondhjemsfjord flooding back into his mind.

And then they found it, a gap big enough for them to get the chariot through. Rejoicing, they eased the machine between the strands and ran on at slow speed. Would their luck hold with the other two nets? They had little time to wonder for soon they were up to the second line of buoys. Their luck had held. Indeed, it had improved, for they found gaps in both the remaining nets with no difficulty at all. They were so badly damaged that a submarine could have been taken through. There must have been some 'softening-up' going on.

Still keeping the machine on the surface, Causer set course for where recent reports and the latest aerial photographs had indicated the *Bolzano* to be lying. Unfortunately, as they left the last of the nets they ran into a patch of oil, which obscured their visors. Smith fished out the little cotton waste which he had stowed away aft against just such a mishap and with the aid of this they were both able to clear their glasses of most of the film. They soon sighted the *Gorizia*, like their own target, the *Bolzano*, a 10,000-ton and 8-inch-gun heavy cruiser and sharing the same streamlined appearance that seemed to typify Italian warship design. The chariots had been expected to have completed their attacks by 0130, and all attackers, including the Gamma men, had been instructed to set their charges to go off as near as possible at 0630. But the planned times were now hopelessly irrelevant, and as he passed the *Gorizia* Causer wondered whether the other chariot had been successful or whether it was at that moment under the cruiser.

From Berey's target Causer was able to alter course for where he knew his own target lay.

We were still on the surface when we sighted her dark outline. I reduced to slow speed and continued until we were within about 200 yards' range. Then a last look and a good compass-bearing to make for just aft of her bridge structure before pushing the stick forward and diving to about twenty-five feet.

Shortly afterwards we could distinguish clearly, by looking up, the shape of the *Bolzano*. I continued until I judged the intervening horizontal distance to be approximately fifteen yards, when I turned to starboard and reduced depth by about five feet. In a few moments we came scraping along the underside of the huge hull. We switched off the motor, clamped on with the magnets, and immediately began to pull ourselves and the chariot along the ship's hull, moving one magnet at a time. We continued this progress underneath the ship until I reckoned we were half-way along, and, as far as I could assess, under the boiler-rooms.

Once settled on this position I proceeded to stick magnets on the ship's bottom without myself getting off the chariot. The loose ends of the lanyards hanging from the magnets I secured to the torpedo warhead. As soon as several of these were safely made fast I got off my saddle. That was a mistake in the circumstances, in that I was holding one heavy magnet in my hand. The weight of this was such that I immediately started on my way to the bottom, so I quickly let the offending item slip out of my fingers and rose up again on my slightly positive buoyancy. Smith by this time was also off his seat and was up alongside the warhead making sure it was properly secured. These things could not be too well checked. As it was almost exactly 4.30 A.M. when we decided the charge was well and truly fast, having exchanged the 'thumbs up' with a fair degree of swagger about the gesture, I turned the handle of the time-fuse setting until I felt two distinct clicks. Two clicks, two hours—so the balloon should go up as near as damn it at 0630. Back to our seats therefore, a final check of everything, and then I pulled the release-gear that freed the warhead from the chariot.

It had been arranged that the charioteers should land on a little beach inside the harbour and then cross over a range of hills to reach the open sea to the west of La Spezia. This landing-place, of course, had been schemed against the background of an operation that was to finish well before daybreak. In the present circumstances it seemed to have little to recommend it. Causer had no liking for the idea of suddenly popping up on a chariot, dressed in diving-gear, in broad daylight on a populated beach. The rest of the original plan had been that they should wait at a prearranged rendezvous on a cliff-edge throughout the whole of the day and at 2230 an attempt would be made to pick them up.

But with the time fast approaching 5 a.m. the first part of this plan was not to be thought of. A quick decision was called for, and the only temporary way out that Causer could see was to make for the familiar breakwater, which he knew lay in a southerly direction. Dive to thirty feet, therefore, course due south, full speed ahead. Course and depth were immediately achieved, but the speed was a mere mockery. The battery was getting very low and haste was impossible.

Exactly at 5.45 a.m., however, the breakwater was reached, the machine slowly burying its nose against the jagged rocks at the base of the structure. Causer stopped the motor and flooded the chariot completely. He turned to Smith and made signs that he was dismounting and that he wanted Smith to follow suit. This information was not received with any enthusiasm by the Number Two, who, indeed, was so reluctant to move that he just stayed seated where he was. Eventually Causer managed to persuade him, and he let himself float clear. No sooner was he dismounted than, to his further surprise, he saw his Number One climbing up the rocks and beckoning him to do the same. This was getting past a joke, he thought, as he saw Causer disappear above him. Then, within a few moments, the ripples over his head betokened the surface.

But that wasn't all. There was Causer partly out of the water and already cutting away his suit with his greasy diver's knife. By the time Smith was completely surfaced and on a firm footing his companion was stripped of all his gear—suit, breathing-set, boots, everything. Before Smith could get his visor open he saw the other bundle all his equipment together and send it down to join the chariot.

Smith shook his head, gave up trying to undo his visor's wing-nuts, ripped his headpiece off with his knife, and said, "Well—what the hell are we doing here?"

CHAPTER TWENTY-ONE

Sailors Ashore

BLAST!" said Berey.

He and Lawrence had just scuttled their chariot and were making their way inshore when he stumbled. Righting himself, he stepped forward again, only to fall.

"Blast!" heard Lawrence again, and as this expletive was followed by the unpleasantly familiar gurgling sound of water rushing into something, he turned—to see Berey's head disappearing beneath the surface. A couple of paces, a long reach with a long arm, and Berey was grabbed by the shoulder harness of his breathing-set and hauled above the surface. There was much spluttering, a little coughing, and a look of thanks.

"Blast!" he repeated.

He had fallen down a hole, and, with his visor still open, his suit had started filling up, from which uncomfortable set of circumstances he could almost certainly not have extricated himself had not his Number Two come to his aid. With Berey now feeling a trifle too wet and heavy for congenial walking the two of them continued the last few yards ashore. It would indeed have been ignominious to have been drowned within the proverbial stone's throw of the beach.

Once out of the water they undressed as quickly as possible under an arch of the small pier which stood, spindly and deserted, over-looking the scene of what might so easily have been a disaster. On further inspection the hole into which Berey had fallen turned out to be a place that had seemingly been specially dredged to allow a ferry steamer or the like to come alongside the pier. The hole seemed to have taken a liking to diving-suits, so they gratified its desires, and two lots of everything went tumbling, splashing down.

Having no plans ready-made for a landing in this position, they walked along the beach, looking for a means of getting inland through the rolls of barbed wire.

"I think we'll have to give it up," said Berey. "There doesn't seem to be a gap in this part of the world. We'll climb over."

And so they did. It was obviously a good day for climbing, because they followed the rather prickly negotiation of the first fence of the course with a hand-and-foot scramble up a fifty-foot bank.

"There'll be a road at the top," whispered Berey during a pause half-way up. "Remember the torch we saw being carried along from down on the beach?"

Sure enough the road was there. They turned left along it, and had a quick look where they were. To their right there rose a steepish cliff-face some twenty feet or more in height. From the base of this wall were sticking out, horizontally, some more rolls of barbed wire. Above cliff, road, bank, and beach there was the mountain. They both knew from the briefing that La Spezia was surrounded with hills, but this, briefing or no briefing, was "the mountain."

They needed to get away from civilization and from risk of being discovered. The mountain would be ideal. Once established at or near its top they would be able to check their bearings and plan the best way to reach the rendezvous.

But there still remained the business of getting up the mountain. The wire and the cliff were not very encouraging, so they walked on a little way, passing a small pillbox which either was unoccupied or else all its inhabitants were asleep. Farther down the road they came to a house. A car drove out from its gateway while they were still ten or twenty yards away.

"Better go easy," Berey warned Lawrence. "That place must be occupied by Germans or by Fascists. No one else would have a car or use it at this time of the night."

It soon became clear that the wire barricade, like its predecessor on the beach, was not going to provide a gap. It had to be tackled by the same straightforward method and to the same accompaniment of muttered curses. The wire surmounted, the cliff had to be scaled. This did not prove as difficult as they had feared, and in no time they were on the slopes of the mountain proper. Daylight was already beginning to break, but there was fortunately still not very much activity. This would give them a chance to get well clear before the working-day really commenced.

By the time they were far enough up the mountain to feel reasonably safe from casual discovery their bodies were bathed in perspiration. In the scramble away from the beach they had not removed their diving undergarments. It had seemed a wee bit chilly then, but now the sun was well and truly up, and its rays carried appreciable heat even at the early hour of six o'clock in the morning. They looked

about until they found a suitable bush to hide under, stripped off all
their clothing, which in Berey's case was still wet from his ducking,
laid it out to dry, and then curled up close to each other and fell
straight asleep.

They were awakened by a terrific explosion at exactly 0800. This,
they concluded, was their own charge going off. They experienced a
certain satisfaction, but within a few minutes of the echoes dying
they were back underneath the bush, unconscious.

It was about midday when they woke again. Their clothes felt
well aired and crisp, so they dressed in battledress blouse, shirt, and
trousers, leaving the diving-woollens rolled up in their sleeping-
place. Feeling refreshed, although by this time devilish hungry, they
made their way to a higher vantage-point, from where they reckoned
the harbour would be visible. It was: and their first glance revealed
what was left of the *Bolzano*. She was heeled over on her side,
resting on the harbour-bottom, a complete loss. They realized then
that it had presumably been Causer's charge that they had heard
explode, unless his had gone up earlier and they had both been too
sound asleep to respond.

They stayed where they were for the rest of the afternoon, moving
across the side of the mountain in the early evening to get a better
idea of the whereabouts of the night's rendezvous with the M.T.S.M.
As they had thought—and feared—it soon became apparent that
they would have to cross a small valley and cover a great deal of
ground along the perimeter of the mountain. There would be no
hope of doing this between nightfall and the arranged time of 2230.
The only way the rendezvous could possibly be made in time from
where they were was for them to keep walking through the remaining
hours of daylight, as well as after dark, and risk meeting anybody
who might be looking for them.

They started off straight away, and in an hour or so they were down
into the valley, along part of its length, and were beginning to climb
the farther slope. From this they gained access to the mountain
again, only to find that if they were to continue at all it had to be
along a sheer cliff-face. The only alternative was to turn back. Tired
and hungry, they searched the rock-slab with weary eyes. They were
rewarded—encouraged, at least—by the sight of a narrow, crumbling
goat-track which they eventually managed to reach after a repetition
of the morning's tooth-and-nail manœuvres. Along this track lay
their way to freedom.

"Last lap," said Berey.

"I flicking hope so," said Lawrence.

And so, with noses to the ground, they began scrambling along the eighteen-inch-wide ribbon. It was some while before they sighted, several hundred feet below them, the rock which was to be their rendezvous with the M.T.S.M. They just had enough time to cover the remaining distance, bearing in mind that darkness was already beginning to close in, and they were both inwardly rejoicing. It was just at this point that they negotiated a sharp bend to find that the track disappeared. There was no mystery about it. The track just stopped. And there was nothing but steep rock-face. Further horizontal progress was impossible.

"Trust these foreigners not to mark a blooming cul-de-sac," chirped Lawrence.

"H'm," vouchsafed Berey. "We'll have to go downward, that's all."

When Lawrence recovered from his surprise at hearing this, and at realizing that it was a serious statement, he was able to follow his Number One in a very hazardous undertaking. They launched themselves off the edge of the track and just slid, trying to make a little horizontal progress on their way down.

"We descended almost entirely on our bottoms," recalled Berey, "putting the brakes on by grabbing at trees and bushes that flashed past us."

Darkness was coming down fast, but the descent was prevented from becoming completely suicidal by the narrow ledges that appeared in the cliff at more or less regular intervals. As long as Berey could see the next ledge he felt they could justifiably continue. By 10 P.M. it was completely dark and they were both resting on a ledge that was narrower even than usual. Nor could they see the next step in the descent. Indeed, it looked as though the cliff probably continued unbroken for the remainder of what they judged to be two hundred feet separating them from the beach-level. Furthermore, as Berey unwillingly had to admit to himself, their descent to their present resting-place had demanded an all-out effort, which their vitality had not been in a state to withstand. They were done in. The beach was totally inaccessible to them, at least until the morning—even then they might find themselves in a position from which they could move neither upward nor downward. If and when the boat came they could do nothing about it.

They sat and watched the darkness that they knew to be the sea. At about half-past ten, the time planned for the rendezvous, a convoy of small boats or landing-craft, escorted by E-boats, passed their position, going north. Still no sign of the M.T.S.M., and as they half lay, half sat on the narrow ledge they both wound their legs round the trunk of a stunted tree to save themselves from falling out of bed and into eternity. Soon they were asleep. Their eyelids had been threatening to close for some time, and once it became clear that they could do nothing until the morning there was no point in resisting.

They dozed until 4.30 A.M. Berey vaguely remembers hearing an engine that might well have been the M.T.S.M.'s, but he didn't really awaken. In fact, for part of the night they probably did more than doze, incredible though the thought of sleep may have been in such circumstances. With the dawn they realized that further downward progress was absolutely impossible, but that it would be a practical proposition to retrace their way up the cliff-face. This they found easier than it looked, and soon they had reached their goat-track, traversed the valley, and were reclining in their first hide-out. All this they achieved by seven, which was remarkably good going, even though this time they had the advantages of knowing which way they wanted to go and also where the major snags lay.

Just as they arrived at their patch of bushes they saw and were seen by an old Italian woman. She immediately turned in her tracks and made off with agitated step. They could not be bothered to do more than hope that she would say nothing to anyone. Perhaps she would be too scared, for they were aware that they looked a pretty sight. Their hair was all over the place, they were unshaven, faces and hands had been badly lacerated by brambles, clothes had been torn and worn by their descent of the cliff. But their appearance was not their first concern. Nor even was the risk of being caught. First and foremost they wanted water. They had come across none so far in their morning's travels, and there didn't seem to be any in the vicinity of the hide-out. They had to have some. Their last drink had been on the previous day, and they had perspired plentifully since then.

In the distance they could see an isolated cottage. Should they try there? Perhaps it wasn't wise—but nothing could be wise in the circumstances. They didn't care.

In front of the doorway stood an old Italian. By repeating the one word *acqua*, and by making a cup of his hands and repeatedly bringing it to his lips, Berey was able to convey their need. The old man shouted a few words into the main room of the dilapidated little whitewashed hut, and out hobbled a bent old woman with an earthenware jug. The water was far from cool and tasted of something neither of the charioteers could afterwards define, but it was a godsend nevertheless.

As they walked away from the cottage, back towards the hide-out, it began to rain. Soon they were soaked to the skin, and the clouds showed no sign of a break in the downpour. The bushes under which they were lying were providing little protection, so in the early afternoon they decided to move on. Not far away they had noticed a shed overlooking one corner of the harbour. This they tried, and their luck was in, for it was both unoccupied and rainproof.

"Look, Chef!" called out Lawrence excitedly later on in the afternoon. He was standing in the doorway of the empty shed, looking out over the fishing-boat quay. "There's a fisherman just coming ashore—there, down at the end of the quay. He's left his boat with everything rigged and she's the only one there. Wonder if he'll leave her rigged all night."

Berey smiled. "By God, it would be fun. Imagine sailing out of the harbour in a Wop fishing-boat. Getting out might be a bit difficult, but once we were out it wouldn't be any trouble to take her to Corsica. That would give old Heathfield a shock. But we mustn't build up our hopes. He'll probably unrig her before dusk."

Sure enough, just after six, back came the fisherman. Little knowing that he was working to the accompaniment of some very round British curses, he stripped the little craft of her sails, bundled them up, and walked cheerily away. It was another exit closed.

At dusk they started off again. This time Berey knew what he would do. He knew the broad outline, at least. The detail would have to be worked out as they went along. It would be good to be completely on their own, and not to have to attempt to fit in with other people's arrangements. And so they began making their way round the outskirts of Spezia. From the trough of the valley they had crossed the previous evening they followed a footpath which eventually joined a road. Traffic on the road made them jump down into the ditch on occasions, and once they found themselves in the garden of an isolated house. They weren't worried about that until they discovered that the lawn was sprinkled with machine-gun nests, whereupon they exercised the utmost stealth and were glad to get back to the road unseen and unheard. A little farther on they were aware of a crowd of people approaching. Again they went down into the ditch, and watched several German soldiers pass within arm's length. Things were getting exciting.

They soon realized that they were coming to the dockyard. This would be well guarded, and had it not been for the thickish hedge that flanked the opposite side of the road they would probably have turned back right at the start. As it was, the hedge gave them the

chance to concoct, in whispered tones, the simplest possible plan for
getting past the guards.

Berey and Lawrence waited until the first patrol of three soldiers
was marching away from them, when they followed. As the stamping
of feet indicated a precise German 'about turn,' they dived into the
hedge and let the patrol pass them going the other way. By repeating
the procedure a second time they managed to get clear of the beat.
They were just congratulating themselves that the beats did not
overlap when they turned a bend only to see, some ten yards farther
on, a gateway equipped with a little office, the light from which
illumined all but the far side of the road.

"Right," said Berey, "we'll cross over into the dark."

Before Lawrence could whisper a reply, and every bit as though the
darkness itself had heard Berey's instruction and had something to
say on the subject, there came an unmistakable sound. A man broke
wind. Diagnosing the source of this disturbance as a hidden sentry,
Berey decided that they had reached an impasse. It was all distinctly
infuriating, but there was nothing to do but turn back. Quietly, and
following the reverse pattern, they repassed the same patrol. Another
twenty yards or so and they had left the guards sufficiently out of
earshot and were near enough to the end of the dockyard precincts to
be able to relax.

"Halt!" came the voice. It was another hidden sentry.

"Freund," gulped a surprised rather than frightened Berey.

"Soldato?"

"Si."

"Avanti."

That was their closest shave to date. Berey didn't know whether
to be amused at his success in the little piece of bilingualism or to be
disgusted from a professional point of view at the sentry's casual
behaviour. If only he had possessed fluent Italian or German he
would have braved it out still further and given the man a first-rate
reprimand.

From this point luck favoured them for a while. Coming to a
road-junction they turned off down a lane which they hoped would
lead them round the town a safer, if longer, way. It was just 1 A.M.

By daylight they were dead beat, and had collapsed under a
dilapidated bridge to fall fast asleep. Berey woke soon after ten.
Their position was still west of north from the town, and as they
aimed to get right over to the east, inland of Spezia, they were not
doing so well. Their new route was safe enough, but it was taking
them over too much high ground. If they continued to make this wide

sweep round the town they would have to negotiate several steep hill-sides, every bit as difficult as the first night's 'mountain.' This made them feel pretty fed-up, until a brief 'confab' convinced them that their best course was to go through the town itself in the half-light of evening. This would lessen the equal and opposite risks of recogni-tion in broad daylight and suspicion in the dead of night. Once this was decided they felt happier.

They lazed about, refreshing themselves with stream-water, freshly picked fruit, and the remains of their bars of chocolate, until late in the afternoon.

"Liberty-men, fall in!" joked Lawrence, as he saw Berey get to his feet.

And so they set off down the hillside—a serious, determined Number One and a light-hearted, confident Number Two. Within an hour they were sitting in a clump of trees a few hundred yards away from the edge of the town, watching some Germans playing soccer in a field just below them. Soon after the game was over and the players gone Berey and Lawrence left the trees and sauntered down to the road. It was still early enough for there to be plenty of people about in the town, so just their presence ought not to make them conspicuous, and yet it was dark enough for the badges on the sleeves of their battledress blouses not to be readily discernible.

Partly to bolster up their own spirits, and partly to deceive the enemy, they gaily engaged each other's arm, putting on a jaunty swagger which they were far from feeling. They passed occasional German troops in ones or small groups, but were not once given a second glance. The first few streets of the town were soon left behind with no incidents. To add further to their disguise—and to their confidence—they tried to whistle *O Solo Mio*. But their lips must have been too dry, for no sound came forth. They soon gave up this attempt at bravado, considering that two unsuccessful whistlers might attract the very attention they were trying to avoid.

They cleared the town and followed a road up into the inland hills. Along the early stretches of this they passed two or three sentries, but were not challenged. Indeed, apart from their own voices in very occasional conversation they heard nothing until about three o'clock in the morning. They had been walking all night and were passing through a small village when an Italian voice called at them from out of the darkness. Berey gave a cheery "Buon' giorno" in reply, and while their interrogator was presumably thinking of what to say next they carried on walking.

This incident was repeated a little later in the main street of a larger village just at dawn. They both replied and were pleased to find this received with the same silence as before. It was just as well, for the village showed signs of being heavily occupied and fortified by the Germans.

Once clear of the houses they turned off the road on to a hillside, where they slept, sheltered by a few stunted trees, until just after ten, when they continued making their way south-east, keeping off the main roads and among the hills. The afternoon was not particularly eventful. Indeed, they saw so few people that they could spend their time admiring the scenery.

After the crowded industrialization of La Spezia the countryside in which they were walking seemed peculiarly wild and unexploited. In the hills the only routes of communication seemed to be the narrow goat-tracks that abounded everywhere. The occasional houses scattered among the bare fields seemed primitive, but were remarkably clean. The hills themselves had their bareness relieved by odd patches of thickly growing woodland, mainly on the lower slopes near the sea. And it was by the sea, too, that were situated the more picturesque villages. In a way they were reminiscent of Cornwall, with red-roofed houses clustering round steep, narrow streets, and giving on to long, sandy beaches. Indeed, the shore-side scene contrasted strongly with the dull, colourless hill-land. The blue sea was flanked by a golden beach. In the harbours lay rust-red-sailed fishing-boats. The red roofs of the houses topped walls of pink or white or saffron-yellow. To add to the feast of colour there were also the delights of the individual character of the villages. During the evening the two sailors returned to the coast-road again, and were delighted with the buildings—beautiful or quaint—which stood, silent and unquestioning, around them.

There were other things besides, some of them less pleasant. In one village there was a gang of Italian sailors, at whom the two charioteers looked as though they were so much dirt. The ruse, if such it was, seemed to succeed, for the Italians said nothing. In another village there were literally hundreds of Germans, who, it turned out, were manning a large coastal battery. This meant avoiding several sentries, which was achieved without incident by means of keeping to the narrower streets and alleys, and by retracing unwise steps.

A little way past this village they came to a river which Berey identified as the Magro. He had forgotten that they hadn't crossed this already. Not that he minded the crossing. What was so depressing was that they had only put a mere fifteen or so miles between themselves and La Spezia. It just wasn't good enough. When he told Lawrence how slow their progress had been the two men felt so disgusted with themselves and with circumstances in general that they were content to find a hollow in the river-bank, curl up in it, and go to sleep.

Lawrence woke first, to hear a church clock striking five times. It was the morning of the 26th. He roused Berey, and together they walked down to the water's edge. On the far side they could see six water-barges and an equal number of dredgers aground on the low tide, but what they were looking for needed to be somewhat smaller than these and on their side of the river. Eventually they found it: a rowing boat with oars. Setting off, they decided to row downstream, keeping to the farther bank, and to make up their minds about a plan of campaign when they could see more of what went on. They had gone a few hundred yards before they were called to by a couple of German sentries on the south bank. From gestures and shouting it was quite clear that any further progress downstream was strictly *verboten*, so they turned the boat's head upstream and pulled back over the same water. They just went far enough, however, to be out of sight of the sentries and to find a suitable place for getting ashore.

They felt they had wasted too much time already, so decided that further progress was to be strictly and entirely along the main coast-road. Security measures seemed so casual, anyway, that there was probably very little risk of apprehension. It was undoubtedly due to this change of plan that they had covered a net distance of sixteen miles by dawn on the following morning, when they arrived in the small town of Pietrasanta. They were greeted by an assortment of Italian youths, who walked briskly and boldly up to them. Berey was a little unsure what to make of this, until the leader of the group announced that they were members of a Partisan organization. As they were obviously addressing two British soldiers—or were they Americans?—they were happy to offer guidance to Partisan head-quarters. Berey and Lawrence willingly agreed, were led for a distance of some two miles north-eastward into the hills that skirted the town, and found themselves in a populous clearing amid thick woodland.

"Hello, Chef," came a voice.

"Hello, Malcolm," replied Berey, miraculously never batting an eyelid or showing the slightest surprise. "How's things?"

Sure enough, Causer—and Smith—had succeeded in reaching the same band of Partisans. They had already been there some three days, and as Berey and Lawrence sat down to a plate of steaming, succulent stew, having consumed a good flagon of Chianti apiece, Causer was prevailed upon to tell his story.

"I'll tell you all the details later, Chef," he said, "but for the moment I'll just give you a quick outline. As soon as we had got out of our diving-gear we hid as best we could among some rocks at the end of the breakwater. After a short while a fisherman passed quite near to us. I called out to him, and when he came up to us I told him we were British P.O.W.'s who wanted help. He refused to lend us his own boat—not unreasonably, when you come to think of it—but promised to go back to his own village to see whether he could get us any other means of transportation. So we just waited.

"At exactly 6.23 our charge went off. We got a hell of a kick out of watching it. First of all two great waterspouts shot up into the air, one on either side of the *Bolzano*, just aft of the bridge. Only just then did it come back to me what we had really done and what Jerry would do to us if he caught us. Within a minute or two of the explosion every small boat in the harbour seemed to be on the move. There were whole droves of them going round in circles, the smaller craft going near the *Bolzano*—but obviously taking care not to go too near. For our part we wedged ourselves farther down among the rocks. It wasn't long before she began to go down heavily by the bow. Soon her whole stern was out of the water and the screws were clearly visible. When her bow was all under she looked as though she were going to settle, and I guessed that her stem had probably touched bottom. However, she suddenly rolled over with a terrific splash and sank. We felt good. All that was left visible was part of her starboard side. By this time it was almost half-past seven. She had taken an hour and five minutes to go down.

"Soon after this our fisherman friend returned. He had left a small rowing boat, with a bottle of drinking water, a little way off down the beach. He had guessed what we had been up to, said that Jerry was kicking up a considerable commotion ashore, and steadfastly refused to take any money for the boat. All he wanted was to get away as soon as possible.

"We rowed away from the breakwater to a point about two miles to the south, where there were a lot of boats fishing. We hung round the edge of this group and—we were still wearing only our pants, having carried our battledresses to be less identifiable—pretended to fish. We found this very heavy work, as there was a little breeze, and, having no anchor, we had to keep rowing so as not to drift away. We kept this up all day and the sun was very hot. Towards dusk all the boats started making their way back to Spezia until only we were left.

It was still comparatively light when we decided to row and drift in a southerly direction during the night. We had been over thirty-six hours without sleep or rest, and were feeling it. My hope was to get well away from shore by daybreak and then, if possible, to row to Corsica, about ninety miles away.

"During the night we ran into a convoy. We had to dodge backwards and forwards not to be run down by what appeared to be landing-craft going very slowly. We were thankful when at last we got clear. Later we drank the water and finished a bar of chocolate apiece and our tin of corned beef.

"At daybreak we found the sky slightly clouded, and we could see no land. We rowed a little and drifted a lot. During the forenoon both R.A.F. and German fighters passed low over the top of us. Seemingly we were seen by neither, in spite of our frantic waving to the former. Nothing else of note happened until that evening, when there was a slight fall of rain. We succeeded in catching some of this in the silk escape-maps, but by the following morning our mouths were very dry and we could feel our tongues beginning to swell. We were by this time completely exhausted and had no idea of our whereabouts. I was reluctantly forced to decide to alter course to an easterly direction, with the result that when the clouds lifted shortly before noon we could see land—the mainland of Italy. We were convinced that we had come far enough south for this to be territory occupied by our own forces, so we rowed ashore merrily, beaching at about tea-time.

"Everything seemed deserted, and it wasn't until we had been exploring a near-by town for some ten minutes that we met a small boy. He told us we were in Forti de Marmi, which my map told me was only thirty-five miles from Spezia. We were disappointed.

"The boy took us to his home, where the women were prepared to welcome us. But the three or four men in the household were dead against it, saying that if we were discovered the whole lot of them would be shot. By this time quite a crowd of neighbours had gathered, and the head of the house must have decided that it would be less conspicuous to take us in than to argue with the womenfolk about us on the doorstep. Once we were inside some wine was produced and some bread and cheese. After the meal they gave us these old civilian clothes, into which we changed, packing our battle-dresses into an old sack. Late that night a guide led us through the quiet town and up into the hills until we reached the Partisans here."

Berey and Lawrence had finished their meal. When Causer's

N

story was ended they turned in on beds of soft turf and slept long and sound. They had some one else to do their worrying for them now.

So began for the four charioteers a period of six weeks spent with the Partisans, during which they underwent many strange experiences, ran some risks, enjoyed some laughs, took part in some exciting attacks, and met some interesting people. Among the latter were some deserters from the Italian Tenth Submarine Flotilla who told them that a machine and net-cutters (Causer's) had been recovered from alongside the breakwater, that the people who attacked the *Bolzano* had been killed, and that a permanent watch of sentries was now mounted in the superstructure of the *Gorizia*. A further contact was a Pilot Officer Rowlands, R.A.F., who gave them the information—to be passed on if and when any of them should get through the lines—that the road running northward from Lucca towards the Brenner Pass was mined on both sides and that if blown up electrically would block the entire route for some time. But all this is another story.

It is relevant to pick up the threads on the morning of the 10th of August. On that morning Conrad Leonard Berey of Bermondsey, in London, Petty Officer Cook, Royal Navy, Official Number P/MX 49845, crossed through the German lines to rejoin British forces. This was at a point on the river Arno, which he had reached after leaving Lucca. Stoker K. Lawrence, who attempted to cross with him, was wounded by a hand-grenade thrown by a German sentry, and taken prisoner. Twenty-four hours later an attempt to cross was made by Sub-Lieutenant Malcolm Causer, R.N.V.R., and Able Seaman Smith. This officer and rating also were taken prisoner.

CHAPTER TWENTY-TWO

D-Day: First Across

February and March 1944 saw the dispatch of two *X*-craft to their legitimate home—Fort Blockhouse. *X.20* and *X.23*, under Ken Hudspeth and Lieutenant George Honour, R.N.V.R., had been detailed for operational duties in the Channel. They were welcomed by Captain S/M 5 (Rear-Admiral R. B. Darke, C.B., D.S.O.). For him the arrival of these craft was a great occasion, for he had been closely associated with the early development of the idea that had grown into the Twelfth Submarine Flotilla, and it was only natural that he should be delighted at the return of the latest offspring to the parent body. He had, moreover, like Admirals Horton and Barry, served in the original Twelfth Submarine Flotilla of the First World War.

The craft were to work with the COPPs, the Combined Operations Pilotage Parties. The work to be undertaken was made up of two distinct types, for each of which either two or three COPPs were carried, never more than five persons being borne at any one time. The craft were to take the COPPs to within a short distance of the beaches that were being surveyed for the coming invasion. This was the first task. Soundings were to be taken, beach gradients studied, underwater obstacles investigated, and their presence and nature recorded. Other general pilotage observations were to be made. Secondly, the craft were to act as navigational marks for the first units of the invading armada.

X.23 arrived several weeks after her companion. The time-lag proved to be a handicap from which she never completely recovered, for Hudspeth got the pick of the jobs right up to the 'Day' itself. For George Honour and his crew, however, these were interesting weeks. There were all the small, miscellaneous exercises that everybody in *X*-craft had come to associate with the easily spoken but hard-to-live-up-to phrase, 'being on top line.' Then there were the larger operational exercises, right up to a series of full-scale programmes, including every phase of what the operation might be expected to comprise.

During the early weeks of *X.23*'s working-up the other craft had undertaken a successful 'type one' commission—"Operation Postage." The investigations had been off the Arromanches section of the Normandy beaches, and the nature and amount of the information that the several days at sea had revealed were completely satisfactory. Sufficient information had, indeed, been obtained in this one venture, and as Admiralty did not wish to risk the discovery by the Germans that midget submarines were operating in the Channel no more 'type one' operations were scheduled.

As the end of May approached, final preparations for the invasion operation were made. The COPPs' formulæ had been changed now that the job in hand had given way from military reconnaissance to beach-marking. Previously it had been necessary for three COPPs to be carried in each craft, leaving only the C.O. and First Lieutenant to accompany them and handle all the controls. For the beach-marking operation it was decided that two COPPs would be sufficient, and the craft's E.R.A. was therefore able to join the final team.

The morning and afternoon of Friday, June 2, saw much activity round the two small craft. All the gear for the operation was being stowed. This had proved a great problem in the past, but the use of specially designed canvas stowing-bags and the elimination of all unnecessary items enabled things to be sorted out. Twelve Luftwaffe bottles were struck down the main hatch. Their total capacity would guarantee an extra day's supply of oxygen, in addition to the craft's ordinary built-in cylinders. Then there was a miscellaneous assortment of three R.A.F. rubber dinghies, two small portable radar beacons, some Sten-guns, some special lightweight diving-suits, three flashing lamps with batteries and eighteen-foot telescopic masts, several taut-string reels for measuring purposes, and a few handfuls of revolvers and ammunition. All this was carried inboard.

Quite a lot of unusual items of equipment were also carried or fitted outboard. There were extra buoyancy chambers—a cross between a side-cargo and a large dan-buoy—fitted port and starboard. Two small CQR anchors were stowed in the casing for'ard, bollards were incorporated fore and aft, and an eighteen-feet-long sounding-pole had to be secured. An echo-sounder was fitted into the hull, and —still more external insulation for the First Lieutenant to worry about—an upper-deck repeater had been rigged from the master gyro-compass. They felt like a floating general store that hadn't sold a thing for years.

The COPPs' primary duties were to make certain of the craft's navigation, which in the bad weather that was expected and with the depleted *X*-craft crew that was being carried, could easily have been faulty. An accurate position was of the utmost importance; it was the crux of the whole operation, and on it depended a large part of the initial impact of the invasion itself. It had further been planned that one of the COPPs should float inshore in a dinghy on a long line from the craft in the event of their not being able to get right close in to the beach.

At half-past nine on the evening of Friday, June 2, *X.20* and *X.23* slipped from their moorings and set course to make the East Gate in the Portsmouth boom. Operation "Gambit" was on.

Three-quarters of an hour later the two tiny craft passed through the gate and met their escorts. *X.23* was astern of H.M.T. *Sapper*, and the two vessels had difficulty in joining company. The swell was as awkward as it could be, and the business of passing the tow proved so frustrating that it took another forty-five minutes before they were ready to proceed.

Communications were so bad that it was decided to keep the craft on the surface, so that all signals could be passed visually. In spite of the sea a good speed was being made, so the arrangement had everything in its favour. *X.20* was following suit, and the two teams were keeping an informal sort of company. No snags occurred until early Saturday morning, when the little fleet had to stop to allow Ken Hudspeth to clear a dan-buoy mooring-wire that had fouled *X.20*'s idle screw.

Just before dawn the two escort-trawlers began flashing to their charges with subdued lights. Final preparations were made, last-minute checks were undertaken, good-luck messages were passed. Then the two craft slipped their respective tows and proceeded independently of their companions and of each other.

Any philosophising that there might have been in *X.23* was broken by a crackling order over the phones. George Honour's voice came distorted down from the wet and cheerless casing.

"Full ahead main engine, course 172 degrees."

An hour later they dived to avoid being seen, now that the early-morning light was fast increasing. Once a trim had been caught they maintained a steady depth of thirty feet, half speed ahead on the main motor, on the same course of 172. These conditions continued for the whole day. George Honour had hopes of reaching the French coast without using any of his precious oxygen. To do this he had to be able to raise the induction once every five hours and run the engine for a few minutes to draw a fresh supply of air through the boat. This process was known as 'guffing through' and demanded a cautious inspection of the surrounding sea through the day-periscope, followed by a short spell of very careful depth-keeping while the induction was raised. The occasional wave lolloping over the mouth of the trunking would only cause a splashing in the bilges, but once the depth-gauge needle dropped below the 7–8 feet that had to be maintained the inflow of sea-water would be continuous, and in a very few moments the engine's persisting demands for air would have caused an unpleasant vacuum. Luckily both Sub-Lieutenant J. H. Hodges and E.R.A. George Vause were well used to this sort of caper.

With the later hours of evening, therefore, the boat had been ventilated, without breaking surface, on three separate occasions. Conditions inside the craft, although somewhat crowded with the extra body and the extra gear, were quite comfortable, and Vause's efforts as 'chef' had been much appreciated. The only unit to be feeling the strain was the battery, and accordingly, as soon as darkness was safely down, the craft was brought to the surface, a running charge put on, and the same course continued.

By three o'clock on Sunday morning (Day D-1, under the original invasion plan) the battery-charge had been broken and speed had been increased to full ahead. By four o'clock a 'dead reckoning' had been reached which placed the craft tolerably near its final required position. Nothing more could be done until dawn came and allowed some accurate periscope navigation, so the craft was stopped, the main ballast-tanks were slowly flooded, and she sank gracefully to settle happily on the bottom. Sleep claimed all except a single watch-keeper until about 8 A.M. Then came a quick breakfast, a few pints of water pumped out of the compensating tank, and a slow regaining of periscope-depth.

They were very definitely the right distance off shore. The coast-line was bare and flat, something like that of the East Anglian counties, except that there seemed to be few, if any, interesting creeks and inlets. It looked even less like the English Channel coast. Trees were very few and far between, and there didn't seem to be the faintest semblance of a cliff within sight. But there was, away to port, what looked like a river-mouth. And there were a couple of churches too. Perhaps they had landed dead on position, just off the estuary of the Orne. It would be almost too good to be true.

"Course due east. 650 revs. Keep her at periscope-depth."

Sure enough they were off the mouth of the Orne river, exactly as required. They were able to identify the two churches without any difficulty, and with a cross-bearing on a conspicuous eminence they fixed their position beyond doubt.

George kept the craft at or just below periscope-depth, some of the time with a stopped trim, until 11 A.M. There had been absolutely nothing to observe at all—no coastwise traffic, no signs of activity ashore. It looked as though the whole thing was going to be a complete picnic. But they still had to face the waiting.

At tea-time they came back to periscope-depth. New fixes were obtained and the position confirmed. Then they bottomed again to wait a few more hours. Supper—some sleep—a few games of liar dice—a yarn or two—and a quick check over the equipment.

Promptly on 2315 they surfaced and switched on their checked and rechecked wireless receiver. They had the right wave-length. It was the right programme. But there was no message for them. They knew that within a few minutes.

So the invasion might be on, in spite of the weather, or it might not. Within a few hours the hundreds upon hundreds of landing-craft and the thousands upon thousands of men might be approaching the French coast. And they, *X.23*, would be guiding the whole procession. Without the coded wireless message, mixed up in an innocent broadcast, there was no means of telling one way or the other. The excitement in the craft was not hard to tell, as George's quiet helm-and-speed orders conned her back to the waiting position. They could see aircraft landing not so far inshore. The field must have been dead abeam. And, of much more value, there was a fixed red light burning high above the entrance to the Orne river—a very hospitable aid to navigation, George thought.

So with their position confirmed from soundings, shore light, and previous fixes they commenced the final run-in, measuring the distance with the taut-wire gear.

They were very close in to the enemy shore when the CQR anchor was let go. It held first time, and as the cable was made fast on the for'ard bollards the time lacked a few minutes of midnight. Exactly one hour later a faint wireless message was received, to the effect that the whole operation was being postponed twenty-four hours.

"Weigh anchor—slow ahead—course 010."

Monday was much the same as Sunday. *X.23* spent over twelve hours on the bottom. They all had their fill of sleep. Perhaps there was even a little boredom. But that disappeared when one tried to imagine the immensity of the armada that the morrow would bring.

The log read:

2315. Surfaced and commenced wireless watch. Message received operation taking place, but reception was very difficult and master gyro had to be stopped during the period the message was coming in. This unsettled the compass and caused it to be unreliable. However, during the period of wireless-watch the craft had already reached and anchored in her marking position, so the compass defection did not prove as serious as it might have done.

Soon after midnight George was able to have the craft flooded down below the surface, just to remove any risk of a last-minute spotting. At a quarter to five on the morning of Tuesday, June 6, she slowly came back 'up top.' In a few minutes the telescopic mast was rigged, all connexions were made, and they were flashing merrily away. The job was 'on.'

No sound or sign disturbed the air until, from seaward, there came a throbbing. It was a dull, droning, soulless noise, with a faintly distinguishable regularity of beat. The assault forces were arriving.

They were magnificent. There were L.C.A.'s; L.C.I.'s and L.C.T.'s. There were L.C.F.'s; L.C.S.'s, and L.C.G.'s. There were landing-ships and headquarters-ships. There were 'Ducks' and 'Rhino' craft.

As they came towards him George weighed and proceeded. Steaming on a directly reciprocal course he passed between their lines. There were twenty, thirty, forty ships in a column, stretching away out of sight. There were as many columns stretching away to port and starboard. And then there were the men. Thousands and thousands were passing him, he knew. He could see a few of them. A few more could see him. Most of them probably didn't know who X.23 was or what she had been doing, but they all gave a cheery wave.

Poor devils! thought George. A brute of a crossing and then having to land and fight. Rather them than me.

And so it all came to an end. X.20's story had been much the same, and between them the two craft had made a success of Operation "Gambit," each having been dived for approximately sixty-four out of the seventy-six hours they had spent at sea. Now the infinitely larger Operation "Neptune" had developed. They could only hope that it enjoyed the same good fortune. There were less landing-craft by this time, and among the cluster of mine-sweepers, destroyers, and returning Coastal Force craft George found H.M.S. Largs and reported alongside. Soon he was being towed by another trawler, the passage crew had taken over, and all was peaceful oblivion. It was the first satisfactory sleep for five days.

This, for five people at least, had been the story of the invasion. It was not a story without sequels.

George's sleep was soon interrupted. The trawler skipper was not happy about the way the craft was bumping about on the surface. It was nothing to worry about, as it happened, but the trawler's course was—her helmsman was steering the reciprocal of what had been ordered, and they were heading back to France. George hardly dared return to his bunk.

Then there was the great reception that they were accorded by all and sundry at Blockhouse.

Finally came the surprise at hearing in the wardroom how some visiting Coastal Forces officers had been in the first naval craft off the coast of France on the morning of the invasion. Fiercely these officers disputed that any submariner could claim a right to their title.

"Where were you off the coast?" they asked indignantly.

"Off the coast!" came the reply. "We were damn near *on* it."

PART V: THE FAR EAST

CHAPTER TWENTY-THREE

Depot-ship Number Three

W ITH the virtual completion of the naval war in the Mediterranean, the majority of chariot personnel returned home to the United Kingdom. Most of them arrived at the end of 1943 or the beginning of 1944, when, after a spell of leave, they were sent to join *Bonaventure* or to do a complete submarine training-course to enable them to be generally useful when taking passage.

By this time the only theatre of war left for chariot operations was the Far East, and all training was being continued and modified with this part of the world in mind. And in between bouts of training a certain number of charioteers were temporarily drafted to different units to undertake port-clearance work and other miscellaneous diving-duties.

The complement of machines in the flotilla was almost completely composed of the new Mark II, or 'Terry,' models. These were very definitely an improved design and were much less likely to carry an unsuspecting couple of charioteers plunging to the bottom. Nor was there any doubt about the value of their greatly increased maximum speed of four and a half knots over a range of thirty miles, or about their larger and more effective warhead, with its 1100 pounds of Torpex.

Men and machines were transferred to Depot-ship Number Three in the May of 1944. H.M.S. *Wolfe* (Captain J. E. Slaughter, D.S.O., R.N.) was a new construction and seemed very different from her predecessor, the sluggish, dirty *Titania*, who had by this time joined the Third Submarine Flotilla as an auxiliary depot-ship. But, for all that, the important similarity was there—for she was a happy ship too. One month later she sailed, taking with her seven teams and the appropriate technicians, all under the command of Lieutenant-Commander John McCarter, who had so ably officiated in Malta. The trip out was pleasant in every way. Every one was in high spirits throughout, not least because of the confidence all felt both in the machines and in themselves. With the increased endurance of which they were now capable, the return journey from the scene of an attack to the parent submarine—so very necessary with the known Japanese attitude towards prisoners—could be practised time and again without its seeming a mere formality.

Soon after arriving in the fleet anchorage of Trincomalee, on the east coast of Ceylon, the seven teams started day-training. After the cold Scottish waters, from which they had come, this proved very enjoyable indeed. Every one liked getting under the water and observing the antics of the tropical fish and the beautiful colours of the sea-bed. There was white coral and red, silver sand lining the floors of underwater plateaux, sinuous valleys of jagged rock, a multitude of different underwater flowers swaying in the currents and changing colour with the varying filtration of the sunlight, and other visual attractions too numerous to mention. It almost became difficult to concentrate on the job of operating the machines.

After a few weeks' day-training night-runs were started in earnest. Soon all the teams were at the top of their form, and all that was required was an allocation of targets.

This was made at last. Six weeks' notice was given that two ships were to be attacked in Phuket Harbour, on the west coast of Malaya at the northern entrance to the Malacca Strait. When four of the six weeks had gone the final choice of teams was made: Sub-Lieutenant "Lofty" Eldridge[1] with Petty Officer Woollcott[2]; and Petty Officer W. S. Smith with Steward A. Brown. These four were sent ashore on a short jungle-training course, just in case they had to bail out and make their way into enemy-occupied territory. Escape-kits were prepared and explained, and every possible assistance was afforded. Some shark scares had also arrived. One of these was a repulsive-smelling ointment, which was supposed to be smeared over suit, headpiece, and hands. Finally, none of the scares was used at all, it being agreed that the machine itself and the grotesque figures riding it would be enough to frighten any sharks.

Back from their jungle course the two teams found that the submarine *Trenchant* was to take them on the operation. She was commanded by Baldy Hezlet—by this time a Lieutenant-Commander—so one of the last phases of Twelfth Submarine Flotilla activity was to be distinguished by the leadership of a man who had played an outstanding part in the early years of the enterprise. There remained a short period of time for training to be carried out with the parent submarine. For the final trial the two machines were taken out to

[1] Now Sub-Lieutenant A. Eldridge, D.S.C., R.N.V.R.
[2] Now ex-Petty Officer S. Woollcott, D.S.M.

sea and launched about six miles from the entrance at about eight or nine o'clock at night. Smith and Brown had an eventful run. On going under the first boom Brown felt his nose-clip come off and fall into the bottom of his face-piece. As soon as the machine came to the surface inside the net he opened the visor to fix things, hoping that Smith would not dive again in too much of a hurry. But with wet hands the replacement of a slippery nose-clip proved too difficult a manœuvre, so he decided to leave it off and shut the visor, judging the risk of carbon dioxide poisoning to be a justifiable one in 'practice battle' conditions.

On the way out, after they had completed the attack, the machine's gears suddenly stripped, and Smith was left with no means of varying the speed and none of going astern. He could have surfaced along-side the net, where he knew there to be a launch from *Wolfe*, but he decided to carry on out to sea to pick up *Trenchant* in spite of the defect. But before they could get back to the rendezvous, and because of the many extra obstacles they had had to surmount, the machine was completely out of compressed air and Smith and Brown were completely out of oxygen. They were accordingly running on the surface with visors open when they sighted the submarine. There was only the problem of stopping. Round and round they went, again and again, until they could reach a line thrown from the big boat's casing, which eventually halted them. When they climbed out of the water it was twenty past four. It had been a long night.

Trenchant sailed on October 22. As the submarine stood out to sea the silhouette of the two machines could be seen, snugly resting on the port and starboard saddle-tanks. Down below in the control-room the four charioteers were quietly observing all that was going on round them. They had checked their escape-equipment just before leaving. Each of them had been issued with a ·38 revolver and ammunition, local currency, a small bag of twenty-five gold sovereigns, a silk map, a small dagger, needle and thread for sewing up wounds, compasses, hacksaw blades, a watch, and a tablet of poison. All of this had to be concealed among their clothes and carried inside the diving-dress.

There was also the "Siamese Blood Chit," a small square of white silk. On this, in addition to a very garish Union Jack, was a message inscribed in several Oriental languages, to the following effect: "I am a British Naval Officer who has been engaged in operations against the Japanese. If I am captured I cannot continue to fight against the Japanese, so I appeal to you to hide me and provide me with food until I can rejoin our forces. If you will help me by giving me food and hiding me in safety until our armies arrive in Malaya, you will earn the gratitude of my Government, who will give you a big reward, and I am authorized to give you a chit to this effect."

The sea-trip to Salanga Island, on the coast of which lay Phuket Harbour, occupied five completely uneventful days and nights, and on the morning of the attack *Trenchant* was in position six and a half miles to seaward from the target-area, with her periscope occasionally breaking a flat, calm sea. Hezlet gave the four charioteers every opportunity of looking at the targets, and by nightfall each man clearly understood what was required to be done. Eldridge's target was just inside the harbour entrance. She was the 5000-ton merchantman *Sumatra*, which had recently been salved and was awaiting towing to Singapore. The other merchantman, the *Volpi*, of 5272 tons, was not so easy to distinguish as she was lying farther in, right at the extreme end of the waterway. To reach her Smith and Brown would have a considerably longer trip. She too was out of commission, being partly submerged and in the process of being salved by the same team as had refloated the *Sumatra*.

The day seemed to pass terribly slowly, and nightfall brought a great sense of relief. Dressing took less time than had been expected, and the four men had to sit about in a sweltering control-room, clad in thick rubber suits, with the sweat literally pouring off them. They were intensely glad when they were able to man the machines at ten o'clock. The sea was perfectly flat as the submarine submerged and left her two offspring afloat. The night was lit by a brilliant moon, which had its advantages as well as its disadvantages, and for the four charioteers life was just grand. This was what they had joined for.

Sitting astern of Smith, Brown was happily connecting himself to the machine's oxygen-supply. Then came the trim-dive, which went well enough as far as Smith and the chariot were concerned. But for Brown things were not plain sailing. As soon as they submerged he felt the water coming in through the vent in the headpiece, and within a few minutes he was flooded from feet to neck. This did not worry him very much until he had to dismount to secure the warhead, which Smith had noticed working loose. He had to keep a very firm grip on the securing-gear to prevent himself plummeting to the bottom.

The two men felt very, very confident about the whole job. It was quite straightforward, there being no nets across the harbour to worry them, and probably no other defences either. Both of them were old hands at the actual business of handling a machine below

the water, so the night should be a 'quiet number.' They had had
several 'natters' together to formulate a plan of campaign and had
decided simply to ride in on the surface for the first four and a half
miles and to keep dived for the last two. Fortunately nothing happened to prevent their adhering to this programme, and after having
gone about three miles they were able to distinguish first of all
Eldridge's target and then their own. There was no sign of life from
the harbour.

Smith was a little worried about the phosphorescence that the
propeller was churning up. This was a feature of tropical waters to
which none of them had become fully accustomed. When the time
came for diving they remained below for 400 yards at a stretch, surfacing slowly every time to check course and to take in the situation
as a whole. This part of the trip seemed slow going, and, indeed,
they were being forced off course considerably by the strong cross-
currents. However, by trial and error they eventually got into
position some 300 yards away from the target and dived for the
attack. Soon they could see the dark shape of the hull appear, and
with motor stopped they glided smoothly alongside, the depth-
gauge registering twenty feet.

The intention was to place the charge vertically under the centre-
line of the ship, as nearly as possible on the engine-room plates, but
on sinking slowly to forty feet they both realized that with the position in which the ship was wedged they would never manage to get
themselves or a charge underneath her. Partly to think again, partly
to try another run-in for luck, they withdrew.

They kept deep on the next attempt, but their luck was no better.
Brown dismounted and went for'ard to have a look at the ship's side,
moving slowly past Smith and past the warhead. The water was so
dark that before he had gone four feet from the nose of the chariot he
was completely out of sight from Smith. In a few minutes' time he
was back, to indicate by signs that there was no hope of securing the
charge on the ship's side, owing to the barnacles being so numerous
and so firmly stuck. This was disappointing, but there was nothing
to be gained by stopping where they were, so with the main ballast
slowly blowing they crept up the side of the ship towards the surface.
At fifteen feet they came to a deck, where Smith stopped the ascent
for Brown to dismount for the third time on the trip. This time he
took the charge with him and soon had it lashed to one of the deck-
fittings and the pin out of the time-setting clock. But before he could
turn away the lashing parted and he had to grab the charge again and
struggle with it across the deck. The fuse-clock was ticking away as

he negotiated a series of steps down into an engine-room and placed the charge where it could not move.

If it was eerie in that lonely, submerged engine-room Brown never mentioned it in his subsequent report. Perhaps he was too pre-occupied with his several personal discomforts. To start with, his suit was full of water and one of his hands was bleeding badly from a cut sustained when he half stumbled with the charge. A further fall had torn open his headpiece and gashed the top of his skull. He could feel his hair, sticky with blood, through the hole in the rubber. However, as he made his way up the engine-room ladder and across the deck to where he knew Smith to be waiting he was able to reflect on the big bang he had left behind him.

By the time he rejoined Smith he had been inboard for some twenty minutes—long minutes they had been too. He let Smith feel the split pin that meant the charge had been set, they shook hands, and were away. The usual routine for departure was a long dive, for about a mile, at about ten or fifteen feet, course to be as estimated by the Number One. This was Smith's intention as the chariot surged slowly forward and away from her target, but they had barely gone ten yards before he felt his breathing coming with difficulty, and before they had gone very much farther he knew for certain that his equipment had a defect. In a hurry he brought the machine to the surface, ripping open his visor and disengaging his mouthpiece. His mouth was badly burnt by the soda-lime that had worked loose from the canister. Luck had changed, and they were in a not very promising situation. All they could do was to carry on at full speed on the surface and hope that the journey out would be as quiet as the journey in. Fortunately it was.

They had been proceeding in this fashion for about ninety minutes, and the time was between 2 and 3 A.M., when they sighted *Trenchant* some forty yards away. They had been dead on course. The next moment a dark shape appeared to port and proved to be Lofty Eldridge's machine. Things could not have been better timed.

Hezlet quietly ordered them to scuttle the chariots close to the saddle-tanks and then swim the remaining few yards to come aboard. Obediently, Smith opened everything up and they could feel "Slasher"—named in memory of Sladen—sinking beneath them. Smith let himself float clear, and then felt Brown grab one of his legs and hang on for dear life. This hampered Smith's swimming—especially as, with his visor open, he was not in a condition to sub-merge—and he was glad of the line thrown to him from the sub's casing. As soon as they were aboard they were hustled below, and Hezlet had the 'plugs pulled out' in double quick time.

Brown's suit was almost bursting open with the weight of water inside it, but his wounds proved superficial and he soon recovered. Over a cup of coffee he explained to Smith the reason for the frantic grab at one of his legs. Brown was a non-swimmer. The mystery was that he had managed to conceal the fact through the best part of three years of diving. When McCarter heard of this he was highly amused, but nevertheless took the opportunity of having Brown taught to swim at the earliest possible moment. Back in *Trenchant* there was an air of satisfaction, and the four divers, after a brief comparison of notes, were packed off to get a few hours' sleep.

They were called again at 5.30, half an hour before the charges were due to go up. Punctually Eldridge's and Woolcott's target disintegrated, to be followed five minutes later by Smith's and Brown's. They were all allowed frequent peeps through the periscope to see the effects of their handiwork. The two explosions were quite different. The first was a sharp crack, and the vessel seemed to move upward. The second was considerably duller, and seemed to expend its energy horizontally outward.

There the story virtually ended. *Trenchant* continued on patrol for a further three weeks, much to the delight and interest of the charioteers. During this time Hezlet was able to make a successful attack on a convoy and the boat was subjected to some depth-charging. On return to Trinco reports were submitted, and the four men went on leave to a rest-camp in the hills. When they returned to join the other teams they found them packing for home. Authority had decided against any further chariot operations in the Far East.

The Commander-in-Chief had said that he would not be responsible for sending men on operations where return might not be possible and when it was known that all men captured would immediately lose both eyes and testicles. As a result everything was being wound up as far as this mode of warfare was concerned. All those now 'out of work' would be given a comprehensive choice of jobs, and every effort would be made to see them placed in the appointment of their choice.

Charioteering had come to an end.

CHAPTER TWENTY-FOUR

Preparations at Home

CHARIOTEERING had come to an end by the time 1944 became 1945. But *X*-craft were still flourishing. There were twelve *XE*-craft either delivered or still on order at the turn of the year. The first six of these were to comprise the senior division of a new flotilla to be dispatched to the Far East in *Bonaventure*. The second division were to follow in penny numbers—the first two in a liberty-ship, the next two in another merchantman, and so on—as soon as they were delivered and fully worked up to operational standard.

The new craft were not very different from their predecessors. The continuous upper-deck line that curved gently away to a rounded, bull-nosed stem afforded much-needed stowage space between casing and pressure-hull for ropes, mooring-gear, net-cutters, and limpet-mines. The only other noticeable external modification was the provision of three antennæ, two for'ard and one port side aft. These were spring-loaded 'legs,' fitted to enable a craft to come up and rest, slightly positively buoyant, underneath the hull of a target. In their housed position these were visible against the dark-grey casing on account of the white 'non-flotus' grease which covered all their moving parts.

Internally the most important addition was the air-conditioning system, which had been designed to cope with the heat and humidity that would be encountered in the tropics. It was estimated that under actual tropical conditions this apparatus would extract enough moisture from the air to provide an ample supply of water for washing-up and cooking, thus relieving demands on the freshwater supplies. Also the water in the engine-cooling system would be able to pass through a refrigerating plant, adding to its efficiency and avoiding any risk of engine overheating. Finally, the system included a small domestic refrigerator for the storage of perishable food and drink. The whole apparatus was a great boon, and, after a few initial snags, worked well.

The process of standing by a new craft at the builders was an

o

experience never to be missed. For the First Lieutenant and E.R.A. it meant joining the craft's commanding-officer-designate some three weeks before the date of completion. The C.O. would by this time already have been in attendance for anything from a few days up to a few weeks. Many of the craft were built inland, the departure from having them all constructed exclusively by Vickers at Barrow dating from the first deliveries of the "20-class" boats. The three new firms, brought together so successfully by Commander H. L. Rendel, R.N. (retired), who had taken over from Commander Varley in the early days, were Broadbent's of Huddersfield, Markham's of Chesterfield, and Marshall's of Gainsborough. None of these had had any previous connexion with shipbuilding, being agricultural, colliery, or general engineers, and it was the more remarkable, therefore, that an absolutely first-rate job was produced in each and every case, with no possible cause for even the slightest complaint, and with every degree of mechanical and imaginative helpfulness forthcoming.

At *Varbel* there had been one major change during the winter. Captain P. Q. Roberts returned to the flotilla in November 1944, to take the place of Captain W. E. Banks as S/M 12. Willie was to get a cruiser, and, though every one was sorry to see him go, it was good to know that he had been given a sea-going appointment and that his successor was not a stranger. "P.Q." indeed, was to continue the enlightened and inspired leadership that the flotilla had hitherto enjoyed. There could be no higher compliment.

One of the second six craft to be delivered was *XE.11*. Under the command of Lieutenant Aubrey Staples S.A.N.F.(V), and with her First Lieutenant, Sub-Lieutenant Bill Morrison, R.N.V.R., at the controls, she left *Varbel I* on March 6, 1945, to exercise in Loch Striven. That morning she was calibrating instruments, and Staples had been glad of the chance to take the E.R.A. and two of the junior ratings from the passage-crews out to gain experience.

They had safely settled and found a trim at 100 feet. Then they had moved up to ninety feet and stopped, then to eighty feet, to seventy, to sixty, and up by intervals of ten feet to thirty.

"Permission to use the heads, sir?" asked Morrison at this point.

So he went for'ard, having first handed over the main controls to Stoker Higgins, one of the passage-crew ratings. Squatting in the "W and D" he relieved himself, and then sat waiting while another calibration was carried out.

"Just wait there, will you, Bill?" asked Staples. "Don't spoil the trim until we've finished at ten feet."

A gentle touch on the hydroplane controls and up came the craft from twenty feet to ten. At what exact depth she was when the first crash occurred it is impossible to say. In seconds two great holes had been rent in her pressure-hull, high on the port side just aft of where the 'planesman was sitting under the after-hatch. Water was pouring in—a continuous stream that became a fierce jet that became an imperious torrent, and in spite of all that main air motor, pumps, and 'planes could do the craft was going deeper, deeper, deeper. In no time it was pitch-dark. The fuses had blown.

From the very moment of the impact Staples made an effort that was absolutely superb. "Blow main ballast!" came his command. "Hydroplanes hard to rise. Full ahead. Group up." At no time was there any hint of panic in his voice, in spite of the almost immediate stern-down angle of fifty to sixty degrees that the craft assumed.

Bill Morrison was still for'ard. In the darkness he had little time to think. He knew they had been hit by a ship. 'How' and 'Why' would have been beyond him at that instant, even had his mind got round to them. Instead he was straining every muscle.

"Try and open the hatch, Bill," Staples had said. Calmly, coolly he had said it, as though it were just another order on an ordinary day.

Bill was trying, but with no success. The clip was off, but the external pressure was too great. As he continued straining he could hear Staples talking to the ratings in the control-room, talking as he passed the D.S.E.A. sets round, talking and telling them all that everything "will be all right."

How difficult it is to rechart the happenings of crowded moments such as those, even in one's own mind, without having to rediscover them out of a half-forgotten wilderness and communicate them to an inquiring would-be historian, can perhaps be imagined. What the exact sequence of events was when the craft eventually hit the bottom of the Loch (at slightly over 180 feet) is, therefore, not surprisingly difficult to reconstruct. There must have been a not-inconsiderable thump. The stern-down angle must have been taken off. The water-level must have improved for those aft and worsened suddenly for those for'ard. But what is known to have happened is that the hatch yielded.

The pressure inside had more than equalized with that above the hatch the moment the submarine's descent ceased. The control-room's air had been squeezed up into a small cubic capacity and with a rush it was finding its way up to the surface via the loosened fore-hatch. Its urgent upward movement started to take Bill Morrison with it. He could feel the upward compulsion lifting him clear of the "W and D." But he wasn't quite satisfied. Able Seaman Carroll was at the helm and E.R.A. Swatton was beside him, having been ordered to give Morrison a hand with the hatch if he could. Surely, Bill thought, he could do something about one of these two at least.

It was with great difficulty that for yet another critical fraction of time he managed to resist the surge and reach inside the control-room door. He managed to get hold of Swatton's battledress tunic and force himself down and away when the two of them got stuck in the narrow hatchway, letting the "tiffy" precede him upward. Too many difficulties had already been surmounted by this time, and when he tried to reach back into the craft in the hope of grasping another shoulder, that would be Carroll's, he could manage no more than a despairing wave of the hand that, had it been visible in the dark and swirling water, could have been construed as a sad farewell. Then all thought stopped.

It started again on the deck of one His Majesty's boom-defence vessels. After the inevitable "Where am I?" he saw Swatton, and then memory came flooding back. In a way that was the end of the story.

There were just a few details that had to be filled in for him as soon as he felt more or less recovered. The boom-defence vessel had seen the beginning as well as the end of the tragedy. XE.11 had drifted out of her exercise area to where a new line of buoys was being laid. In coming up to ten feet she had met the bows of the boom vessel just as the latter was starting her engines after having laid a buoy. Therefore, as she had been lying with engines stopped, there had been no warning water-noises to be heard by the craft. The dice had been fiercely loaded.

The one head surfacing and then the other a second or two later were both seen from the boom vessel too. Swatton had miraculously remained conscious all the way up and had been able to grab hold of his First Lieutenant when he surfaced unconscious, almost along-side him. One good turn had received its reward.

The three others—Lieutenant Staples, Able Seaman Carroll, and Stoker Higgins—were dead. The craft was raised some two or three days later. Each of the dead men was wearing his D.S.E.A. set, but presumably they had all died from oxygen poisoning before they could complete the orthodox escape-routine.

For Morrison and Swatton began a nerve-wracking few days. First there was the funeral, then the court of inquiry, then Bill's twenty-first birthday party—which every one at *Varbel* made into perhaps the most hectic ever, with a view to helping him to forget.

XE.11 had been named *Lucifer*. It had been the semi-official practice in the flotilla for each *X*-craft to carry a name as well as a number. The practice was sufficiently recognized—even though the names of the craft never appeared in the Navy List—for Captain S/M 12 to organize launching ceremonies with ladies present. The general run of names began with 'Ex' or with 'X.' For instance, *X.23* was *Xiphias*, the swordfish; *XE.9* was *Unexpected*; *XT.5* was *Extended*; and so on. Staples had challenged the unwritten tradition in his choice and had moreover offended against the old seamen's custom that no ship or boat should ever be named after the Devil.

"No good will come of it," he had been told by a grizzled old Warrant Officer in *Varbel*'s wardroom when he announced his intention. No good had come of it, and it took the wardroom a long time to forget the sad warning that had come so horribly true.

The other craft had no comparable incidents in their working-up programmes. The techniques employed by C.O.'s and base Staff Officers in the early weeks of each new craft were much the same as those that had been developed with the *Tirpitz* boats and perfected with the "20-class." An early routine was the deep dive, for which the craft was lowered on a stout hawser from the bows of a diving-vessel to a depth of 300 feet. This was followed by routine tests of all the main items of the craft's equipment, and finally the crews were allowed to test themselves, as well as the craft, on all the multitudinous exercises with which they had already become familiar.

During that winter as many as twenty-four *X*-craft were operating from one or other of the shore bases or depot-ships that comprised the Twelfth Submarine Flotilla. From such a profusion of activity it is difficult to select isolated incidents, but, naming no names, it is possible to report, for instance, that on a four-day navigational and endurance exercise a craft went aground, not long before dawn, on the eastern shore of Loch Fyne. Everything was blown and pumped dry for'ard. Everything was flooded and pumped full aft. But still the bows would not shift. Happily the C.O. and First Lieutenant, while reviewing the position from the casing, caught sight and attracted the attention of a fishing-boat in the near distance. With a bit of luck, they thought, they might get off before any inquisitive naval vessel stuck its nose round the corner. So a line was rigged from a deck-bolt aft to the stern of the fishing-vessel. The latter went slowly ahead, and the nose of the craft wriggled gently off the ledge on which it had been resting. Suddenly she was free. It was then, and only then, that the two exulting officers on the craft's upper deck remembered that all the weight was aft!

Sure enough, she dived astern. There was just time to kick the main hatch shut and thus prevent a tragedy. The next moment they were both treading water. In that January of 1945 it had seemed only sensible to wear sheepskin flying-boots and zip-jackets to match. But these were a sad liability when it came to keeping oneself afloat. Luckily the two characters who had been left inside the craft were soon able to bring her to the surface on a more or less even keel, and a rescue was immediately effected.

The small rum-store was speedily drained, and the fishermen, who appeared to think that this was all part of the normal routine, were warmly thanked. Then the exercise was continued. A few days later the incident was to be laughingly retold in the wardroom, to the Wrens in the signal-tower, or quietly in the lounge of the Victoria Hotel in Rothesay.

CHAPTER TWENTY-FIVE

America and Australia

F INALLY, *XE.1* to *XE.6* were ready to sail in *Bonaventure*. They had been formed into the Fourteenth Submarine Flotilla, as an offshoot of the Twelfth. Captain Fell became S/M 14. 'Unlucky 13' had been avoided.

When they left Port Bannatyne on February 21, 1945, the Pacific war was at its height. All the crews were entertaining great hopes of frequent operations and *XE.7* to *XE.12* were by no means less sanguine. Things looked rosy. The craft were undoubtedly coming into their own.

The passage across the Atlantic to Trinidad, in the West Indies, was calm, clear, and uneventful the whole way, apart from the occasional *U*-boat scare. Two swimming-baths were rigged, and as much upper-deck exercise as possible was organized. But the predominant interest was in the approaching contact with the American continent.

As things turned out, everybody was considerably disappointed. The demand for security concerning *Bonaventure* and her cargo made life almost unbearable. In Trinidad they were forced to anchor out of sight of land in an uncomfortable seaway. No leave was allowed.

The leave embargo was repeated at both ends of the Panama Canal, and as this was the first time such a prohibition had been applied to any British ship considerable curiosity was evident as to the reason for the edict. It was even rumoured that the ship's company were being kept on board because there had been a mutiny.

From Panama course was set to San Diego, California. The ship was berthed alongside the dockyard for part of her stay, and much good-humoured badinage was exchanged between the "Waves" and the ship's company, although this sight of American womanhood presumably made the continuing ban on leave even more difficult to endure.

To make matters worse, invitations were received for parties to visit Hollywood, Los Angeles, and Beverley Hills, but the official decision was unbending, and no shore leave was sanctioned. Official visits from shore were kept to a minimum, but various personages had to be received on board, and it was obvious on more than one occasion that these people knew pretty well what the ship's purpose in life was. Altogether the leave prohibition seemed a particularly bad one, especially with the tantalizing nearness of the bright lights and with the continual reminder of other ships' liberty-boats passing every few minutes.

The arrival at Pearl Harbour brought with it good news and bad. Leave was granted for organized parties for visiting U.S. rest-camps, and the generosity exhibited by the American authorities was remarkable, no British ratings being allowed to pay for anything to eat or drink throughout their stay.

The bad news, however, more than undid all the good of the leave. Tiny Fell was informed that Admiral Nimitz had changed his mind and no longer wanted to employ X-craft in the Pacific naval war. "Morale fell with a bang," wrote Tiny subsequently, "but some hope remained as we were told to proceed to Manus, in the Admiralty Islands. Before we got there we were diverted south to Brisbane and arrived with our tails right down, in black despair."

All the opposition that had been personified in earlier days by the unreasoning attitude of Admiral King at the time of the first human-torpedo demonstration had welled up as strong as ever. It was not solely that the American naval high-ups wanted to win the war with orthodox weapons only, as far as could be learnt, but rather that the suicidal methods employed by the German, Italian, and Japanese navies had clouded the general picture of small underwater craft and caused them to be condemned without a hearing. The American authorities were convinced that the craft were similar in type to the Japanese midget submarines that had attacked Pearl Harbour and that the two shared the same limited range. This conviction was so strong that it prevented any information to the contrary ever permeating through.

The general depression in the flotilla was partly alleviated by the magnificent Australian hospitality and the sincere and warm welcome extended to all and sundry. After the second night in Brisbane the majority of the ship's company had found good homes to go to, and the most liberal generosity had been showered on them from all sides. Two weeks later they moved north to Townsville, farther up the Queensland coast. There, and in other smaller towns that they visited, it was common to find prospective hosts fighting over who was to have Stoker X or Steward Y to stay.

From Townsville Tiny Fell flew to the headquarters of the British Pacific Fleet, at Sydney, to have a last crack at getting an operation for the craft, failing which, he told the ship's company, he would ask for permission to pay off.

He succeeded in seeing Admiral Fraser, who, in spite of the great friendliness he felt towards the flotilla, could only give orders for Fell to proceed to Melbourne to discuss a possible use for *Bonaventure* in the "Fleet Train." To have finished the war running stores would have been the supreme indignity. Clutching at a straw, Tiny asked to be allowed to make one final appeal to the Americans for at least one last operation, and grudgingly, believing it to be a waste of time, Admiral Fraser said, "Yes."

Shortly afterwards, therefore, Fell flew north to the Phillipines. It was an amazing journey in many ways. He was unable, lacking sufficient priority, to arrange all the legs of his trip beforehand and had to resort to a technique that was nothing less than hitch-hiking. Everywhere he landed there were movies, ice-cream, doughnuts, and Spam. American Red Cross girls met each incoming plane at most of the air-strips with cartons of sweet, tepid syrup and packets of dry biscuits.

There was plenty of evidence of the severity of the War in that theatre. Air-strips were scarred and battered. Smashed planes, shorn-off trees, and the natural havoc of swamps and jungle were constant surroundings. And then there were the Americans. Fell found their kindness continually exceeding his comprehension, and he was even more at a loss to understand their ignorance of all things British. "Are any of your ships in the Pacific yet?" he was asked by a senior general. He learned that no news of the British Pacific Fleet or of Australian activities ever appeared in the American Press or in the official communiqués.

Eventually he reached Subic Bay, and found himself before the American submarine 'chief,' Admiral James Fife. Of this meeting Tiny was later to write:

> We sat on his veranda drinking cups of coffee, and he listened for hours while I used every argument I could think of for making use of us. At the end he showed the most astonishing grasp of what I had said and in words that somehow softened the blow, and making his reasons seem so sane, he explained that we were too late. Two months earlier he could have used us and two years earlier he needed desperately something just like us, but now we were 'stale.' In these unhappy circumstances our friendship began, and the more I saw of this man in the next few months the more my feelings were strengthened that I had met the most sincere, the straightest, and the ablest of men.

At least the flotilla had made a much-needed friend, so perhaps the visit had not been completely in vain, Fell thought. The little forage-capped Admiral had made him feel happier about the sad trip back to *Bonaventure* and the report to Admiral Fraser, but it was a very dismal picture. At Sydney, Fell reckoned that things had reached their lowest ebb. The disbandment of the flotilla was being taken as a foregone conclusion. Then, at the eleventh hour, the luck began to change.

By the purest chance, and through the most roundabout and unofficial channels, news came to Fell of the urgent operational need for cutting the underwater telephone cables from Singapore to Tokio via Indo-China and Hong Kong. The problem was to discover a means of doing the cutting. There had been no bright ideas at all, and when Tiny said that his flotilla would and could undertake the task he was immediately hauled before the C.-in-C., who accepted his offer, telling him to go and prove the ability as well as the will.

Bonaventure was therefore taken to a hidden anchorage in the Great Barrier Reef to prove that a submarine cable could be located and cut by an *X*-craft. Intensive training started for all the crews forthwith. There were two problems to be solved: to discover a technique for finding a submerged cable, and to perfect a means of cutting the cable when found. There was already in existence the net-cutter with which all the craft were equipped, and in the use of which all the divers were experienced. The jaws of this weapon had to be slightly enlarged—a simple process—and then it was immediately capable of cutting any submarine cable anywhere.

Finding the cable presented more difficulty, as so much depended on the nature of the sea-bed and at what depth the cable was lying. And while the charted position of the cable would doubtless be of great use in defining the general area of operations, it could not be accurate enough to obviate the need for a comprehensive method of underwater searching. It was not long before a satisfactory grapnel and the method of towing were unanimously agreed upon.

In a very short time crews and craft had proved the bold assertion that Fell had made in Sydney. Unhappily this had to cost the lives of two officers—Bruce Enzer, the C.O. of *XE.6*, and Dave Carey[1], the First Lieutenant of *XE.3*, both of whom had insisted on gaining first-hand experience of what their respective divers would be required to do.

The craft had been experimenting under conditions as near as possible to those of the 'real thing.' They had been cruising about to

[1] Lieutenant D. Carey, R.N.

find the best type and shape of grapnel to tow easily and yet to penetrate well into the mud. In the course of these experiments divers were working at depths of between forty and forty-five feet, where there was a certain risk of oxygen poisoning. The tragedies occurred within two days of each other. No trace was ever found of either of the casualties. All kinds of theories were advanced, including octopuses, cuttlefish, and sea-snakes. But as none of the other divers ever saw anything of this queer nature the matter had to be regarded as an unsolved tragedy, which cast a gloom over *Bonaventure* for some time.

As soon as the method had been established Tiny flew north again to revisit Admiral Fife, whose staff were soon put to work on plans for a number of operations. These included, in addition to cable-cutting off Saigon and Hong Kong, an attack on two Japanese cruisers in the Singapore Strait. The oracle seemed to have been worked.

On Tiny's return *Bonaventure* moved south, to anchor off Bundaberg, still on the coast of Queensland. An old disused cable lay close inshore. This was to be the final practice-ground. Only one week was available for the last stage of the working-up, and then "B.V." sailed for the Phillipines. The first part of the cable-cutting operation was to start from Subic Bay. The craft chosen was *XE.5* (Lieutenant H. P. Westmacott, D.S.O., D.S.C., R.N.). She was to tackle the cable outside Hong Kong.

The other three craft to be awarded operations were *XE.4* (Lieutenant M. H. Shean, D.S.O., R.A.N.V.R.), who was to be concerned with the cable outside Saigon ; and *XE.1* (Lieutenant J. E. Smart, M.B.E., R.N.V.R., and *XE.3* (Lieutenant I. E. Fraser, D.S.C., R.N.R.), who were to attack the two heavy cruisers lying at Singapore.

CHAPTER TWENTY-SIX

"Little Guys with a Lotta Guts"

W ITH Westmacott and *XE.5* left behind in Subic Bay, *Bonaventure* sailed for Borneo, wearing the flag of Admiral Fife. The new base—Labuan Island—had just been cleared of Japanese by a very tough consignment of Australian troops and was an obviously suitable starting-point for a two-pronged attack on Saigon and Singapore. In any case, it was one of the most delightful spots the flotilla had come across. During off-duty hours the crew would go ashore in Labuan or else bathe from one of the many small nameless islands near by, where the water, as well as being gloriously warm, seemed free from all the more evil types of tropical fish.

XE.1 and *XE.3* were due to leave for their attack in Singapore Strait on July 26 at about noon. Shortly before manning their craft the crews were addressed by Admiral Fife. His lavish compliments, in which the crew of *XE.4*, due to leave for Saigon a day later, were not forgotten, were a cause of much embarrassment to all concerned, except the Admiral himself.

The speech was brought to a close with the words, "You're the little guys with a lotta guts. Good luck!"

The targets for the Singapore operation were the 10,000-ton Japanese heavy cruisers *Nachi* and *Takao*, lying in the Johore Strait on the north and east side of Singapore Island. They had not been to sea for some considerable time, but their presence was a potential menace to Allied shipping. Furthermore, they were in a position to shell the Singapore Causeway and could have been of great danger to any Allied troops wanting to use that approach to the island. *Nachi* was allocated to *XE.1* and *Takao* to *XE.3*.

From Brunei Bay the two craft were towed by operational submarines, *XE.3*'s guide and mentor being H.M.S. *Stygian* (Lieutenant G. C. Clarabut, D.S.O., D.S.C., R.N.). Telephonic communication between *Stygian* and the craft broke down at a very early stage, but fortunately the passage-crew were able to keep in touch each time the two submarines surfaced by means of walkie-talkie sets.

The passage C.O., Sub-Lieutenant Frank Ogden, R.N.V.R., had earlier been Max Shean's third officer in the attack on Bergen. With him were E.R.A. Albert Nairn, Able Seaman Ernest Dee, and Stoker "Spike" Hughes. Their work during the four days of the outward tow consisted of the usual fixed routines plus the rectifying of certain small defects that occurred. The concensus of opinion was that monotony was the greatest enemy.

In his report to the Commander-in-Chief, British Pacific Fleet, Tiny Fell commented on the passage out:

> This was carried out in good weather, and both craft were taken to the scene of operations without a hitch. The passage-crews did their jobs splendidly. It is not often realized how big a part these men play in the success of an operation. Towing at high speed (it was sometimes as much as eleven knots) is far from being an easy or even a particularly safe job and it is very far from being a comfortable one. It calls for a high degree of alertness under trying conditions for several days at a time. In addition it calls for constant attention to the vital routine duties of mopping up moisture, testing, and, if necessary, repairing every item of equipment in the craft. To a considerable extent the success of an operation depends upon the condition in which the craft is turned over to the operational crew. In no sense of the word are the X-craft passage-crews 'maintenance crews.'
>
> The best analogy that can be given is that they correspond to a diving-watch in a large submarine (except for the fact that they are continuously on watch for days, without a break), and like the diving-watch of a big submarine they are relieved when the crew goes to action stations. That both craft were turned over to the operational crews in perfect condition reflects the highest credit on the passage commanding officers and their crews.

The change-over of crews, as far as *XE.3* was concerned, took place at 6 o'clock on the morning of July 30, and by 11 o'clock the same night the tow had been slipped in a position forty miles from where the *Takao* was lying. The operational crew were on their lonely way. The final stage of Operation "Struggle" had begun.

After the adjustment caused by the loss of Dave Carey, Fraser had with him Bruce Enzer's former First Lieutenant, Sub-Lieutenant W. J. L. ("Kiwi") Smith, R.N.Z.N.V.R., as well as E.R.A. Charles Reed, and Leading Seaman J. J. ("Mick") Magennis, the craft's diver. Fraser had entered X-craft early in 1944 under a special entry scheme for trained submariners and at the same time as Westmacott and Carey. He was of an ideal build for submarines of any description and for X-craft in particular, standing five feet four inches in his stockinged feet. He had brought with him an element of extreme liveliness in all that he did, and this extended to the suggestion of novel experiments to improve the efficiency of the craft. On one occasion he tried very hard to be allowed to have the Manilla tow-rope (this was before the arrival of nylon) cast off from the stern of the submarine while they were both under way. The purpose of this was to further research into what was probably the greatest danger in the operation of X-craft—the loss of a craft due to the tow-rope parting near the parent submarine and proving to be too much of a bow-heavy weight.

Fraser's contention was that the risk of being crushed to death several hundreds of fathoms deep was a very real danger, and that if the welfare of X-craft depended upon a craft diving with, and analysing the effect of, the full weight of a tow-rope, it had better do so on exercises, in water of a given depth, over a given type of bottom, and with a diving-vessel in close attendance to unshackle the tow in case of need. His suggestion, however, was not approved. Fortunately, there were no subsequent tow-parting incidents.

It was not surprising that a man of such ideas should act coolly and brilliantly in his first X-craft operation. During what remained of the night and through the early hours of the morning he spent most of the time seated on the casing with a pair of binoculars. He had deliberately left the safe channel and entered a known minefield in order to avoid enemy listening posts. Once he sighted a tanker with an armed escort coming down the entrance to the Singapore Straits and had to dive. He decided that the safest thing to do was to sit quietly on the bottom for about an hour until the procession had passed. It was not until coming to periscope-depth some thirty minutes later that he discovered that XE.3 had been actually resting on a mine which, for reasons best known to itself, had decided not to explode.

By 1030 he had sighted and closed the trawler that was acting as guard-vessel at the submarine net-boom. Magennis was prepared to leave the craft at short notice and cut a way through the net, but Fraser was both surprised and pleased to find that the 'gate' was open. This made things considerably easier, even though to pass through meant travelling dead slow along the side of the guard-vessel in water that was comparatively shallow and very translucent. A chance observation could have ruined the whole show. But the Japs could not have been looking!

After leaving the boom XE.3 had to be taken through several miles of narrow waterway and a certain amount of traffic. This called for accurate pilotage from Fraser, for steady depth-keeping and great

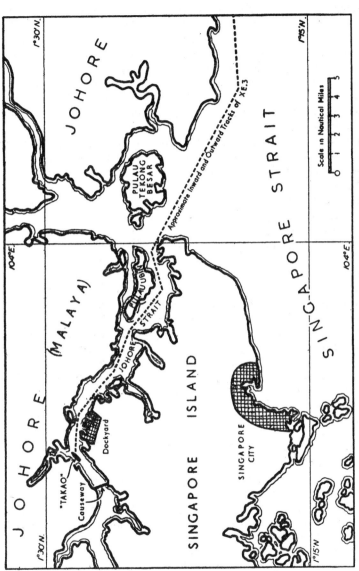

ATTACK OF XE.3 ON "TAKAO" (OPERATION "STRUGGLE")

concentration from Smith, and for watchful steering from Reed. There were no snags and no major incidents, and just after noon Fraser sighted the *Takao*. She was a heavy cruiser in name— carrying eight guns of approximately 8-inch calibre as main arma- ment and displacing 10,000 tons—and she was a heavyweight in appearance too. The typically Japanese pagoda-like bridge super- structure gave her an almost top-heavy appearance, which was not materially diminished by the distinctly inclined fo'c'sle running up to a high fore-peak.

Around 2 P.M. Fraser commenced the attack proper. He ventured a hasty periscope observation, only to see a motor-cutter full of Japanese liberty-men less than thirty yards away from the lens. So he continued without looking. The cruiser was lying in uncommonly shallow water, and *XE.3* had to approach with her own keel just scraping the sea-bed. Even so she was not able to find sufficient water under 'A' turret, and came up hard against the cruiser's plating with a resounding bang. Surely that must have given due warning of their presence, they thought. If such had been the case there was nothing they could do about it, so Fraser cheerfully gave orders for the craft to come out astern. Further investigation, principally by trial and error, showed the cruiser to be nearly aground fore and aft with sufficient water only under the midships section.

After another forty minutes of pushing and prodding her way along the sea-bed and against the hull of the *Takao*, *XE.3* finally found herself more or less satisfactorily in position half under the cruiser. By driving the craft in between the hull and the sea-bed Fraser had wedged them in a position from which Magennis should be able to carry out an attack, even if the conditions were not exactly as per text-book.

Magennis's job was not to be easy, however. Owing to the craft being so tightly wedged it was not possible for the antennæ to come fully into play. The spring-loaded legs should have pivoted until they stood vertically and provided some three feet of space for the diver to operate between craft and target. As it was, the for'ard antennæ had no freedom of movement at all, and the small 39-ton *X*-craft was wedged rather frighteningly between a 10,000-ton cruiser and a hard sea-bed, with the prospect of being squeezed even tighter on the falling tide. In this complicated state of affairs Magennis was probably not surprised to find that the craft's external hatch would open only a quarter of its normal distance.

Many another man might have given up, but Magennis quickly

deflated his breathing-apparatus and exhaled until his chest shrunk to its smallest possible dimension. Then he managed to squeeze through the small gap. His troubles had only started. As he began to unload the limpet charges from the port container he saw that there was a steady stream of oxygen-bubbles emerging from his equipment, which had doubtless been damaged in his struggles to extricate himself when caught in the hatchway. These were speeding up to the surface, a sure signal to any observant Japanese who might be watching above. He could only hope.

XE.3 was carrying only one side-cargo, on her starboard side. To port she was equipped with a similarly shaped limpet-container, in which there were a number of small limpet-mines. These it was Magennis's job to place. He experienced great difficulty with the first of them, and it was soon apparent that the story was going to be the same throughout. This was partly owing to the hull of the cruiser being so befouled with barnacles that the magnets would not stick, but also the pronounced slope of the base of the hull, so different from that of a European-built ship, seemed almost too much for the magnetic attraction to overcome. Before the placing of each charge, therefore, Magennis had to scrape the area thoroughly clean of barnacles and then secure the charges in pairs with a line running under the cruiser's keel. This called for a good half-an-hour of swimming, carrying, scraping, and tieing—a tiring job for any diver, but especially for one handicapped by a steady leakage from his precious oxygen-supply.

Magennis might well have been content to secure one or two of his limpets and then return to the craft, and no one would have blamed him; but he carried on until the complete outfit of six was finally on the cruiser's hull, firmly and safely, spread over a total distance of forty-five feet. Then he returned to the "W and D," repeating the antics necessary for squeezing through the slowly narrowing space, in a completely exhausted condition. It was wonderful that he managed the difficult job of shutting the hatch, for his hands were so badly lacerated from the barnacles, and he himself was generally in such a state of near collapse, that he could only just operate the valves for draining the compartment.

So the job was done, and *XE.3* could withdraw. She just had to release the starboard side-cargo and the port limpet-container and then go out astern. But it was not to be as simple as that. *Takao*, it seemed, did not want *XE.3* to be extricated from under her. For fifty minutes—how much longer must this have seemed—the craft, under Fraser's instructions, went full astern and full ahead, pumped into tanks and blew out of them, and used every means that the collective ingenuity of four experienced X-craft crew could call to mind. Then, just as they were really beginning to think that they would still be there when all the bangs went off, they suddenly shot out astern, without any semblance of warning and completely out of control. Inevitably, they almost broke surface and caused a considerable upheaval of water not more than fifty yards away from *Takao*. Miraculously they were not seen. Within seconds they were back on the bottom again with everything flooded and rather fast-beating hearts.

Only then was it realized that the port limpet-container was damaged and had not released itself. This was making the craft very difficult to manœuvre, and for any hope of successful escape to be entertained it was essential that the container should be cleared. Despite his exhaustion, the oxygen-leak which he knew to be in his set, and the fact of their being very open to observation as they lay in only fifteen feet of water, Magennis immediately volunteered to leave the craft and free the container rather than let a less experienced diver undertake the task. So, armed with a large spanner, out he went. It took seven long minutes of nerve-racking and back-breaking work before he could release the container from the attachment bolts and then return inboard. Fraser himself had wanted to venture out, but Magennis had refused to allow this.

So at last they were on their way home. The return journey was comparatively uneventful, if the minefields, hydrophone positions, loop-detector gear, and the net-boom be discounted, and the rendezvous with *Stygian* was successfully achieved. They all could enjoy intense satisfaction during the long way out of the Singapore Strait. They were glad Fraser had been determined to pursue his objective without any hesitation. They were glad that, regardless of all consequences, he had persisted in forcing the craft underneath the cruiser instead of merely dropping his side-cargo alongside the target's hull.

Fraser's and Magennis's actions had been superb in every way. Scarcely less so had been the performances of Smith on the craft's controls and Reed at the steering position. They had all been on duty without sleep for fifty-two hours before they rejoined *Stygian*, and Reed had been at the helm constantly for thirty hours, during which they had been submerged for one period of sixteen and a half hours at a stretch. In his final report on the operation Fraser paid tribute, as many X-craft C.O.'s had done before him, to the high standard of the men produced by the Navy's training schemes for

Engine Room Artificers, of whom Reed was such an outstanding example.

It was learned subsequently that the charges had exploded at about 9.30 P.M. on the evening of the attack, tearing a sixty-foot by thirty-foot hole in the hull of the *Takao*, putting her turrets out of action, damaging her range-finders, flooding several compartments, and successfully immobilizing her for a considerable time. This was welcome news for all eight members of *XE.3*'s two crews who had taken part in the gallant operation.

Meanwhile *XE.1* had also been operating in the same waters. Jack Smart had with him Sub-Lieutenant Harold Harper, E.R.A. Fishleigh, and, as diver, Leading Seaman Pomeroy. The last of these was thus taking part in the last *X*-craft operation of the War after having been associated with *X.3* in the early days at Hamble and a member of Smart's passage-crew in *X.8* on the *Tirpitz* operation.

Like *XE.3*, Smart had also left the believed safe channel during the long approach up the Singapore Strait and entered mined waters to avoid suspected hydrophone posts. His target was lying some two miles beyond the *Takao* and he was therefore planned to pass through the boom some time before *XE.3*. However, he was much delayed by several encounters with surface craft and ended by passing through the net-gate approximately ninety minutes after Fraser. This delay robbed him of the necessary margin of time to reach his target and withdraw before dark, and he accordingly decided to attack Fraser's cruiser rather than waste his side-cargo. Unable, as Fraser had been, to get his craft under the cruiser—the position being even more difficult owing to the continuing fall of the tide—he dropped his main charge close alongside the target and withdrew. In this he was also unfortunate, as the delay that had ruined his attack also made him too late to achieve his rendezvous with the submarine *Spark*,[1] and much wandering about the ocean was necessary before he and his craft could start the final stage of their journey back to Borneo.

Decorations eventually announced for these attacks included the Victoria Cross for both Fraser and Magennis, the D.S.O. for Jack Smart and Kiwi Smith, the C.G.M. for Reed, one D.S.C., two D.S.M.'s, two M.B.E.'s, and three Mentions in Dispatches.

[1] Lieutenant D. G. Kent, R.N., in command.

CHAPTER TWENTY-SEVEN

Hong Kong: Saigon

MEMORIES of Bergen were in many people's minds as *XE.4* left *Bonaventure*, anchored in Brunei Bay, at noon on July 27. The passage-crew was under the command of Sub-Lieutenant John Britnell, R.N.V.R., who had filled the same position in *X.24* during her first Bergen escapade. And of the operational crew both Max Shean (in command) and E.R.A. "Ginger" Coles[1] were repeating the partnership that had led to the sinking of the *Barenfels*.

In no time they were in tow of the submarine *Spearhead*[2] and were headed north-west for a three-day passage of some 650 miles to a point just off the entrance to the French Indo-Chinese harbour of Saigon. There they were to attempt to cut two telephone cables, and Westmacott would be on a similar errand at Hong Kong at the same time.

The towing-crew of Britnell, E.R.A. Sheppard, Petty Officer Rhodes, and Stoker Butters were all, by this time, very experienced in the business of being towed astern of a big submarine and of Far Eastern conditions in particular. But Britnell could not help harking back, in memory, to his trip to Bergen of a year or more previously. Present conditions were so infinitely better. The craft was actually called to the surface for a longish period every afternoon, and the passage-crew took turns in going over the side for a swim. This was luxury indeed. But, apart from the weather, there was much more in favour of operating against the Japanese. The Germans had still possessed a strong and numerous fleet of *U*-boats when the Bergen attack had been made, and any time spent on the surface during daylight, other than the minimum necessary for ventilation, was asking for trouble and could easily have prejudiced the whole operation. Here there was no such risk, so the glorious sunshine and the luxuriant water could be enjoyed almost at leisure. It all made the hours below so very much more bearable.

[1] E.R.A. V. Coles, D.S.M.
[2] Lieutenant-Commander R. E. Youngman, D.S.C., R.N.R., in command.

Only one enemy vessel was sighted in the whole of the 650 miles, and that was a junk. *Spearhead* was on the surface when the square sail was sighted and was forced to dive until the periscope once again showed that they had the waters of the Nan Hai (or China Sea) to themselves.

During the night of the 30th they changed crews. This was also very much easier and more pleasant than it had been in Norwegian waters. The sea was so flat that the craft was able to come right alongside the parent submarine, and 'wet shirts' were accordingly a thing of the past.

The change-over took place between twenty-five and thirty miles off shore. The night was good and dark, which pleased the operational crew. There were five of them. In addition to Shean and Coles *XE.4* carried Sub-Lieutenant Ben Kelly, R.N.V.R., as First Lieutenant, and Sub-Lieutenants "Jock" Bergius[1] and Ken Briggs[2] as divers.

During the run-in the weather blew up considerably—just for spite, it seemed. Indeed, there was almost a grave tragedy, due to the changed sea-conditions. Max Shean was nearly lost overboard. The 'moderate-to-fresh' swell was breaking heavily over the for'ard casing while Max was conning the craft from further aft. Ever conscientious, he thought he could see one of the casing bolts—for'ard where the waves were buffeting worst—working loose. Leaving the induction trunk to investigate, he slipped, and in one movement went clean over the side into the water. No sound, and no one below was any the wiser. Perhaps it was luck, perhaps it was supreme exertion, but as the after-end of the casing was slipping past him through the water, he just managed to obtain a hand-hold on a projection and pull himself back on board. He looked a very watery apparition seen through the control-room hatch.

If any of the other four had been asked they would probably have said that it seemed unthinkable that anything should ever happen to Max or that anything should ever happen to the craft while Max was in command. He was the ideal C.O. He had a very highly developed mechanical brain and thoroughly understood all the technical side of the craft. Then, his coolness in difficulties and his extreme quickness of thought made him the perfect submarine skipper. Whatever went wrong, one felt sure that Max would think of a remedy before things became too serious. In this he was particularly assisted by Ginger Coles. For a Continuous Service rating Coles had few 'pusser'

[1] Sub-Lieutenant A. K. Bergius, R.N.V.R.
[2] Sub-Lieutenant K. M. Briggs, R.A.N.V.R.

habits, but was distinguished rather for combining his first-rate
technical knowledge with an astounding facility for finding the
humorous side of mishaps that would have completely upset most
people. He was yet another proof of the soundness and the capability
of the products of the Navy's training schemes for apprentices.

Nearer dawn the craft dived, and the two divers went for'ard to
squeeze themselves into the battery compartment for a last sleep to
replenish their strength. They had not been asleep long before they
were shaken back into consciousness with a terrific bump. It was a
relief for them to see Max roar with laughter at the sight of their white
faces peering round the watertight door. By this time it was quite
light, and through the periscope enough could be seen to learn that
the craft had run into a submerged wreck. Once it could be decided
which of the several such wrecks in the area they had actually
stumbled upon they were able to convert this slight contretemps into
an accurate navigational fix. They found themselves well inside the
reputed American-laid minefield, so it was as well to know.

Not long after this the grapnel was streamed, and the business of
keeping a good and steady trim began to be very difficult. This was
partly due to the trying effect of dragging a heavy grapnel over the
bed of the ocean, but the whole thing was complicated by the varying
water-densities caused by the discharge of fresh water from the many
mouths of the hundred-mile-wide delta of the Mekong river.

Through the periscope Max kept a regular look-out for surface
vessels that might unwittingly hinder the search. But they seemed to
have the sea to themselves, with only an odd junk here and there.
There was one steamer that came out of Saigon harbour during the
day, but that was all. It passed a good way away from them, but a
couple of hours or so later it was very definitely within range of
Spearhead's torpedo-tubes. This caused much wailing and gnashing
of teeth aboard the submarine, but the orders were very explicit, and
no attack was carried out.

Back in the craft the grapnel suddenly took the strain. It was into
something. The "W and D" was flooded up with Ken Briggs inside.
But in a few minutes he was back. It was a false alarm, and the flukes
of the grapnel were embedded in some projection of the sea-bed. So
they recommenced the sweep.

There it was again. On face-piece! Off air, and on oxygen! Shut
the "W and D" hatch, flood up, and out again into the warm sea!
Luck was with them this time, for *there* was the cable, lying on the
sea-bed with practically no mud at all to hinder the work, and the
amount of light filtering down from the surface was extremely good.

Ken was delighted, and in no time re-entered the craft with a twelve-inch length of the Saigon-Singapore telephone cable.

"There's my paper-weight," he said, as they joyously relieved him of his breathing-apparatus and suit.

The first cut had been surprisingly easy, and now they only needed to find the Saigon-Hong Kong cable with as little difficulty and in equally good conditions. It was not long before they caught up again, and this time it was Jock Bergius's turn to venture out into the lonely water. They were even luckier with the second cable, for they had hooked the right object on the first attempt. Conditions were much the same, as far as he could judge from Ken Briggs's description, except that he knew from the depth-gauge reading before leaving the craft that they were a little deeper on this occasion—between fifty and fifty-five feet.

Bergius took the first cutter from out of the for'ard casing and made his way along to where the cable was lying, only to find that the cutter would not work—presumably its air-supply had finished. Back he went to the craft to re-stow the first cutter and prepare to take the second. Before he made a second attempt, however, he decided to re-enter the craft, have a short respite, and breathe some air. With the depth being what it was, and knowing that he would need to exert himself considerably while breathing oxygen, he had no wish to run any unnecessary risks.

After a short spell inside he went out again and took the other cutter. There were no snags, and he had soon followed Briggs's example and was back in the craft with a short length of cable, duly decorated—before it was cut—with two lengths of ribbon that had been specially prepared.

The operation was over, and in little over a day—thirty hours, to be precise—a rendezvous with *Spearhead* had been successfully made, the crews had been changed, and the return journey had begun. This was also made without major incident. More self-restraint had to be practised by *Spearhead*'s C.O., this time some Japanese seaplanes moored not far off shore being the potential targets. But as well as not being allowed to attack anything while the *X*-craft was away, the submarine's orders also precluded any attacks being made even with the *X*-craft in company, except in the unlikely event of any enemy capital units being encountered.

During the passage back the news was received that the atom-bomb had been dropped, and all thought that peace might well be declared before they reached Borneo. This seemed to make a speedy return a matter of greater urgency, so, as the craft was behaving herself perfectly in every way, the tow was conducted with the greatest possible dispatch, and "B.V." was reached—with mixed feelings about the possibility of the War being over—in the early evening after a three-day trip.

Westmacott and *XE.5* had not been so fortunate in their attempt to cut the cables into and out of Hong Kong. Conditions had in his case, as well as in Max Shean's, been the very reverse of what had been expected. Saigon was supposed to be muddy inshore and Hong Kong was supposed to be blessed with clear water. It was most galling, therefore, for the crew of *XE.5* to arrive in the defended waters of Hong Kong after a very rough trip, and then to have to spend three-and-a-half fruitless days and nights in the dangerous area west of Lamma Island and to have to make the passage between these waters and the open sea on four separate occasions, all to no avail. For the best part of four days they were dragging the bottom, and for much of the time the two divers, Clarke[1] and Jarvis,[2] were working up to their waists in mud—but not the merest trace of a cable was to be found. For Westmacott, his First Lieutenant, Beadon Dening, and his E.R.A., Clifford Greenwood, this meant hours and hours of intense concentration, practically no sleep, and, for all of them, considerable disappointment.

Harking back to the happier story of *XE.4*, her crew were to find, on coming aboard *Bonaventure*, that they were the first craft back. Jimmy Fife was still flying his flag in the depot-ship, and they were immediately paraded before him to be welcomed in very stirring tones. *XE.1* and *XE.3* returned within the next two days and were treated to even greater heights of oratory. The operations had, by and large, been successful, and everybody was pleased.

But, in spite of the first atom-bomb, the Japanese still seemed to be carrying on, and the invasion of Malaya was still a possibility from our point of view. So orders were given for the return-trip to Singapore. The two cruisers that had been the targets for Fraser and Smart still constituted a potential menace to troops advancing into Singapore Island. The *Takao*, although she had been successfully attacked, was lying in such shallow water that her guns—or, at least, some of them—could still be brought to bear. Within a week of their return to Labuan Island *XE.3* (Fraser) and *XE.4* (Shean) were storing ship again for another visit to the Johore Strait to try to finish off the cruisers. The willingness to undertake this was particularly remarkable in the case of Fraser and his operational crew, and, apart

---

[1] Lieutenant B. G. Clarke, R.N.V.R.
[2] Sub-Lieutenant D. V. M. Jarvis, R.N.V.R.

from their efforts on the first trip, the fact that they were all prepared to go again and face the same things was highly commendable.

Meantime another atom-bomb had been dropped, and rumours of peace were stronger, but every indication was that the craft would still sail. Indeed, both craft were actually in the water and had passed and secured their tows before the cancellation came through, about half an hour before sailing-time. The end of the War had come, and *Bonaventure* was soon on her way to the Phillipines to pick up *XE.5* after celebrating VJ Day in no uncertain manner.

The awards for the Saigon and Hong Kong trips included a bar to his D.S.O. for Shean, a bar to his D.S.C. for Westmacott, D.S.C.'s for Bergius, Briggs, Clarke, and Jarvis, and eight Mentions in Dispatches.

CHAPTER TWENTY-EIGHT

Paying Off

WITH the end of the War in the Far East came the dissolution of the Fourteenth Submarine Flotilla. This took place in Sydney, and a better place for the celebrations that ensued could not be imagined by any of the crews. There were Victory Parades and end-of-war parties; there were spells of leave to be spent among hospitable Australian families in the interior; there was Bondi Beach.

And yet all the merrymaking was tinged with unhappiness. It would have been madness to wish for the War to continue merely to indulge in the pleasure of operating the fascinating little craft. But it was perhaps not unreasonable to want a less speedy upsetting of the comfortable and happy way of life that had grown up in *Bonaventure*. In actual fact the depot-ship was stripped of her craft and all the equipment pertaining to them within the shortest possible time. She was transferred to 'trooping' and running stores between Sydney and Hong Kong. A small number of the X-craft personnel remained with her as ship's company, but the majority were either sent home or appointed to other jobs. Later *Bonaventure* was returned to her owners, with whom she resumed her original name, *Clan Davidson*.

There were brighter moments. There was, for example, the day on which the award of the Victoria Cross to Fraser and Magennis was announced. The radio message was received in *Bonaventure* in the early hours of the morning. Within minutes the news was round the ship and the party had started. It was still in full swing when the next day dawned.

Then there were several pleasant reunions with old friends. Derek Simonds[1] had given up command of *XE.12* in Home Waters at the end of the War in Europe and had transferred to an Australian transit camp to await appointment. By purest chance his posting as watch-keeping officer was—to *Bonaventure*. Another chance meeting was on *Bonaventure*'s second or third arrival in Hong Kong.

---

[1] Now Lieutenant-Commander W. D. C. Simonds, R.N.V.R.

There she was greeted by Alan Crouch,[1] who was employed as a Port Clearance diver after having driven the captured German midget submarine round the waters off Port Bannatyne in the heyday of the Flotilla.

It was sad to see the craft go away to Australian breakers' yards to be scrapped as so much metal. Admittedly, *XE.3* was kept behind for a while to go on exhibition. But she, too, eventually joined the other five in their sad destination.

The business of paying off the Twelfth Submarine Flotilla in Scotland had come a few months earlier. In some ways it was a less unpleasant affair, but for the crews of the second division of *XE.*'s there was none of the satisfaction of having done a final operation before coming to the end of their *X*-craft career.

It was possible during the last few weeks of the War in Europe, before H.M.S. *Varbel* finally closed down, to contemplate the part played in the story of human torpedoes and midget submarines by some very special people. This account has concerned itself principally with the conglomerations of metal and machinery that were the two weapons of the Twelfth Flotilla and with the men who operated them either offensively or solely in the equally testing atmosphere of training, trials, and working-up. Mention has also been made of the men who designed, built, directed, and maintained these craft, and it is hoped that the debt of operational members of the Flotilla to these scores upon scores of unseen and, largely, unsung heroes has been acknowledged herein. But there still remains one glaring omission—the women of the W.R.N.S.

It would take another book to tell of the work of this branch of the Flotilla, and this narrative can only hope to include a brief and inadequate note of tribute. The Wrens at *Varbel I* and *Varbel II* served as signal staff, telegraphists, coders, cooks and stewards, drivers, stores personnel, boats' crews, writers, technical maintenance mechanics, and in many other jobs besides. Their contribution to the smooth working of the administrative side of the Flotilla was enormous.

They had a large part to play too in the social life of the two bases. Not only in the obvious sphere of romance was this true—although many a warm friendship and several happy marriages resulted from meetings within the perimeter of the base—but also in the less apparent aspect of their civilizing influence. It may well have been that a certain exposure to danger and to hard living conditions had tended to rub more of the corners off the much-maligned younger

[1] Sub-Lieutenant A. Crouch, R.N.V.R.

generation of civilian males than was really desirable. If this *was* the case, then the presence of a number of charming ladies was more than sufficient to offset any such unpleasant tendency.

So, by the middle of April 1945, H.M.S. *Varbel* was approaching the end of her career as a naval base. The last two *X*-craft remaining with her were *XE.8* and *XE.12*. *XE.* 7 and *XE.*9 had completed their trials and preliminary working-up and had returned to a condition of reserve at Blockhouse. The other two members of the second six were *XE.11*, which had been salvaged from the bottom of Loch Striven and returned to the original builders, and *XE.10*, the final delivery of which had been cancelled in the light of the knowledge that the second division of craft would never go on operations.

At the beginning of May *XE.12* steamed away under the command of Lieutenant W. D. C. Simonds, R.N.V.R., to join her fellows in reserve. That left *XE.8*. The original C.O. of this craft had been a Canadian reserve lieutenant, "Johnny" Ruse.[1] When he left the Flotilla the honour finally passed to Sub-Lieutenant J. Benson, R.N.V.R.

Under this last commanding officer the last of *Varbel*'s *X*-craft spent the weeks before the base paid off on May 14. During this period she completed the final trials that were necessary before she could be accepted as fit for service, and, into the bargain, embarked on a few semi-official working-up exercises. There was still satisfaction to be gained from successful deep-diving trials, submerged speed tests, periscope exercises, and the like, although one had to try to forget that it was all really a waste of time. However, all the members of the crew were delighted at being able to make several submerged entrances into a near-by Combined Operations base for the purpose of bringing back stores of various foodstuffs, principally cheese, of which the wardroom pantry at *Varbel* seemed to be running short.

Owing to VE Day coinciding with the business of paying off the base, life seemed to consist of one long series of parties. Sleep tended to become rather precious. It was typical that *XE.8* should arrive alongside the pier at Port Bannatyne just in time to hear the Prime Minister's end-of-the-war speech, and then set about charging her depleted batteries. The latter part of the evening and the whole of the night, right through until breakfast-time, was then spent in dancing and jollification, and there was another day with the craft to follow.

On the morning of May 14 *XE.8* cast off from the moorings at

[1] Now Lieutenant-Commander J. C. Ruse, R.C.N.V.R.

Port Bannatyne for the last time. H.M.S. *Varbel* had been paid off. By some mischance the special railway truck that carried all the *X*-craft on their landward journeys had not returned from taking *XE.12* down to Portsmouth. It was necessary to find accommodation for craft and crew for a few more days. Happily she was instructed to join the Seventh Submarine Flotilla for the necessary period, and to lie alongside one of the depot-ships in Rothesay Bay.

This meant a renewal of old acquaintances. The subsidiary depot-ship to whose care the craft was entrusted was H.M.S. *Alecto*. And Captain S/M 7 was a very special personality, none other than the David Ingram, by this time a Captain, who had worked so hard to mould the original *X*-craft into a fighting force.

XE.8 stayed with the Seventh Flotilla for just over a week. Her last night was not a very comfortable one, for a full gale made her position alongside a far from ideally fendered *Alecto* almost untenable. Hawsers kept on parting, and one of the crew had eventually to go over the side and into the water wearing an inflated watch-keeping suit before a satisfactory securing could be made.

Delivery to the railhead at Faslane Docks was made on May 22. It was a sad parting.

It may well be that this book calls for a summing-up. This is no easy matter. Chariots are admittedly—and unfortunately—only a matter of history now; but the Navy is still operating three or four of the second division of *XE*-craft, and the strategy behind them is almost certainly on the secret list.

Nor is it possibly the authors' place to attempt an authoritative summing-up of what was achieved and what might have been. All those who participated in the operating of these two weapons are almost certainly biased in their favour and of the opinion that they should have been much more extensively used in the recent War. And they were by no means the worst judges. The future, with atomic warheads and side-cargoes by no means impossibilities, seems no less favourable.

There seems to be little room for doubt, for instance, that the craft proved themselves to be an efficient and economical striking-force. Similarly it appears obvious that they were comparatively infrequently employed. Looking back, it seems that it can only have been the failure fully to appreciate their potentialities that caused their use to be so restricted. It has been admitted in this country that if the Italians had realized the effectiveness of their human-torpedo attack on Alexandria they could probably have finished the naval war in the

Mediterranean, to their own advantage, in a very short time. Surely the converse must have been true to a certain degree, or should one assume that the Italian system of harbour defence was markedly superior to our own?

If the considerable under-employment of the two types of craft was not due to a failure to appreciate, the question of why they were not more used becomes increasingly difficult to answer. It would be ungracious to ascribe to our own senior officers in command of battle-fleets the same 'we want to do it ourselves' attitude that seemed to be held by the naval authorities in the U.S.A. But is there a third possible reason?

Perhaps the authorities deprecated the use of any 'suicide' methods. If this was the reason it can only be described, in the light of there having been no more than thirteen lives lost on X-craft and chariot operations during the whole three years of their existence, as ill-founded. Even admitting an increased risk to be present in the handling of these craft, was it not surely at least equally as desirable to expose two or four men to a given danger as to send a submarine's crew of sixty into conditions only slightly less arduous.

It does appear too that there was a definite objection to operating these weapons for purposes of planned strategy as opposed to those of defined offensive action. For instance, it would seem that both types of craft were eminently suitable for laying mines in narrowly enclosed waterways—for example, the entrances to Singapore Harbour, the Corinth Canal, Kiel, etc. There were, admittedly, the Normandy and Hong Kong/Saigon operations, which fall into the category of strategic employment, but as the latter were the result of a casual overhearing rather than of any long-planned strategy, the exception is limited to one, and possibly proves the rule.

In total, the craft had accounted for a weight of enemy war- and merchant-shipping approaching very nearly to 100,000-tons' displacement, in a matter of half-a-dozen offensive operations. But figures give only the very least part of the picture. Between them X-craft and chariots had achieved a large number of important contributions towards the winning of the War.

They had helped to ensure the safety of the Arctic convoys; enabled British capital ships to be freed from Home Fleet duties by the removal of the *Tirpitz* from the active list; restricted U-boat repairs in Bergen, and thereby lessened the amount of German submarine activity off the west coast of Norway; assisted in the success of the invasion of Europe, as well as in that of Sicily; forced the German and Italian naval authorities in the Mediterranean to devote more men and greater quantities of material to harbour defence, as well as destroying two important units of the enemy fleet and easing the strained balance of sea-power in this theatre at the same time; destroyed two potential reinforcements for the depleted Japanese merchant fleet; ensured a somewhat safer entry for any troops who had been obliged to invade Singapore Island from the north; deprived the Japanese of one of their principal channels of communication during the vital last weeks of the War in the Far East; and generally worried, damaged, and destroyed the enemy in all corners of the world.

All this was accomplished for the loss of thirteen lives on operations—out of a total of some 180 officers and men who were sent against the enemy. Nor was the cost made appreciably greater by the addition of the sixteen who died in training and the ten lost on passage in a 'big' submarine, making a total of thirty-nine out of approximately three hundred operational personnel. The losses were in no way expensive.

Perhaps it is fitting to close with the words of the world's greatest-ever submariner, Admiral Sir Max K. Horton, G.C.B., D.S.O., spoken in reply to the toast of "The Guests" at the First Reunion Dinner of the Twelfth Submarine Flotilla Association:

I can only say that the one object these people set out to achieve in the first place was to see that the *Tirpitz* would never endanger us at sea again, particularly up there where the Russian convoys had to go. She never did. She was immobilized. And these people were responsible. Similarly, their other operations showed the same singleness of purpose, were almost equally ambitious of concept, and achieved the same outstanding success. One can only say: Well done!

Appendix

I. HISTORICAL BACKGROUND

The prototype of the human torpedo (or, for that matter, of the midget submarine) was conceived by an Englishman, Commander Godfrey Herbert, R.N. (retired), as early as 1909. The design of the "Devastator" was for a one-man torpedo, which was to be fitted with a detachable buoyant compartment for the vessel's navigator. In the words of the patent: "... it had for its object to provide means for propelling against an enemy ship or other target a large quantity of high explosive, and of effecting this with great economy of material and personnel."

This was the idea that Herbert suggested to the Admiralty before and during the First World War, only for it to be turned down by, among others, the pre-1914 First Lord and First Sea Lord, Mr Winston Churchill and Prince Louis of Battenberg respectively. They described it as being too dangerous for the operator and the weapon of a weaker Power. The idea was modified and resubmitted by Max Horton later in the War, but to no avail. Perhaps, as Horton was proposing to operate the "Devastator" himself, the Lords Commissioners were thinking, too, that he was more valuable to his country as a senior submarine officer.

Another design, this time for a three-man submarine, was incorporated in his Diving Manual and patented in 1915 by Robert H. Davis of Siebe, Gorman and Co., Ltd. (now Sir Robert Davis and Chairman of that company). This project included an escape compartment such as was adopted more than twenty-five years later in all the *X*-class submarines.

The next development came from Max Horton again, who produced a threefold suggestion for the construction of very small submarines in 1924. He was then Captain (S) at Fort Blockhouse. His idea consisted, first of all, of the Type "A" submarine, of between 30 and 40 tons' displacement. This craft would have had a detachable conning-tower—a development of Herbert's buoyant compartment—and would have been carried to the area of operations by a surface vessel. Type "B" was to consist of a "miniature submarine, to contain a crew of two, and to be fixed to but detachable from a bi-lobular main hull in which would be situated the main engines and the explosive head." This suggestion would again have been of about 40 tons' combined displacement.

The design which most nearly succeeded in winning official approval was Type "C." This was for a small submarine, of the same approximate displacement as Types "A" and "B," which would carry a large, short-range, heavy-headed torpedo slung outside and underneath the hull in a recess. This design had the supreme advantage of being the only one of the three in which the main hull, containing the crew, would remain under mechanical power after the attack had been made. As has been said, this type was the one most preferred by the authorities, almost entirely because of the advantage of possible recovery. But the major serious objection to the adoption even of Type "C" was that, in addition to the admitted risk to the operators, the employment of the craft would necessitate the use of a special carrier vessel which would have to proceed unwarrantably close inshore.

A fourth idea was that conceived by Commander Cromwell Varley, D.S.O., R.N. (retired), in the inter-War years. At the end of the First World War Commander Varley was in command of the submarine *L.1.* In the 1920's he was retired under one of the several schemes for cutting naval personnel, which event caused him to adapt his talent for marine engineering to the commercial field. It was during the 1930's that his ideas for a midget submarine first took shape in his mind. His initial plan was for a craft some 26 feet in length, to carry a crew of two. Nearer the crucial year of 1940 he modified his early ideas, extending the overall length to 50 feet, increasing the crew to three, and embodying Sir Robert Davis's escape compartment.

Varley's idea was accepted by the Admiralty, largely in the person of Max Horton, in 1940. This was partly due to Sir Max's own enthusiasm for Varley's suggestions; partly to Varley's own selling efforts; partly to the representations of Colonel Jefferis (a pre-War associate of Varley's), some of which reached Mr Churchill; and partly—very largely, indeed—owing to the fact that Max Horton and Godfrey Herbert were already investigating ways of carrying out submarine attacks against enemy capital units in Norwegian harbours.

The strategical reasoning behind the final acceptance of the idea was doubtless based upon Max Horton's own views upon the subject as expressed in some of his written notes:

> The need calling for this type of submarine is due to the less effective potential hurt that the ordinary modern submarine and torpedo are capable of inflicting on a modern capital ship, together with the increasingly effective defensive measures against submarines endeavouring to bring off a close attack. A weapon for such a purpose (to attack the enemy battle fleet when in harbour) has been looked for without real success for many years. Equipped with cutters and a stout hull, this small submarine could choose its depth to penetrate harbour defences.

This, therefore, was the history that led up to the development of the first human torpedo and the first *X*-craft, as told in the foregoing chapters. Incidentally, it was necessary that the first *X*-craft should be numbered *X.3*. *X.1* had been an experimental giant submarine with twin gun-turrets that had been scrapped by the Navy as being impracticable; and *X.2* had been a captured enemy vessel.

Even after *X.3* had been approved her development was full of anomalies. For instance, it was typical of the whole set of circumstances in which she came into being that she should have been built by a private company, Varley Marine Limited, and not by a naval dockyard. It was typical, too, that Commander Varley should never re-enter the Navy, but should design and build the Navy's most secret project, be called Commander by all who met him, and yet wear a thick tweed suit among all the uniform.

Parallel to the early development of the first *X*-craft, the "W and D" escape compartment had been rigorously tested. A steel 'mock-up'—consisting of escape chamber and adjoining watertight compartment—had been constructed as early as 1940 and had been put through its paces in the 60-foot deep torpedo-testing tank at Portsmouth, where Captain Herbert, Commander Varley, Professor Haldane (of the Experimental Diving Unit), and Colonel Jefferis had gone down, two at a time, to conduct various experiments.

II. AWARDS

The following officers and men were decorated while serving in or attached to *X*-craft and Chariots. The four columns show name and previous decorations; rank at time of award; decoration; and operation or duties concerned.

R. AITKEN	Sub-Lt. R.N.V.R.	D.S.O.	Altenfjord
W. E. BANKS, D.S.C.	Captain R.N.	C.B.E.	Flotilla Duties
C. L. BEREY	Petty Officer Cook	D.S.M.	La Spezia
A. K. BERGIUS	Sub-Lt. R.N.V.R.	D.S.C.	Saigon
F. W. BRAMWELL	Lt. R.N.V.R.	D.S.C.	Askvoll
W. R. BREWSTER	Lt. R.N.V.R.	D.S.C.	Trondhjemsfjord
K. M. BRIGGS	Sub-Lt. R.A.N.V.R.	D.S.C.	Saigon
J. BROOKS	Sub-Lt. R.N.	D.S.C.	Bergen
A. BROWN	Steward	D.S.M.	Phuket Harbour
J. F. B. BROWN, D.S.C.	Lt.-Cdr. R.N.	O.B.E.	Flotilla Duties
D. CAMERON	Lt. R.N.R.	V.C.	Altenfjord
M. R. CAUSER	Sub-Lt. R.N.V.R.	D.S.O.	La Spezia
B. G. CLARKE	Lt. R.N.V.R.	D.S.C.	Hong Kong
V. COLES	E.R.A.	D.S.M.	Bergen
B. DAVISON	E.R.A.	D.S.M.	Bergen
B. H. DENING	Sub-Lt. R.N.V.R.	D.S.C.	Bergen
R. G. DOVE	Sub-Lt. R.N.V.R.	D.S.O.	Palermo
A. A. DUFF	Lt. R.N.	D.S.C.	Altenfjord
A. ELDRIDGE	Sub-Lt. R.N.V.R.	D.S.C.	Phuket Harbour

W. R. Fell, D.S.C.	Captain R.N.	C.B.E.	Flotilla Duties
A. Ferrier, V.M.[1]	Ldg. Signalman	C.G.M.	Palermo
R. E. Fisher	Chief E.R.A.	B.E.M.	Flotilla Duties
H. J. Fishleigh	E.R.A.	D.S.M.	Singapore
I. E. Fraser, D.S.C.	Lt. R.N.R.	V.C.	Singapore
J. Freel	Ldg. Seaman	C.G.M.	Palermo
E. Goddard	E.R.A.	C.G.M.	Altenfjord
R. T. G. Greenland	Lt. R.N.V.R.	D.S.O.	Palermo
H. E. Harper	Sub-Lt. R.N.V.R.	D.S.C.	Singapore
G. R. Harrison	Able Seaman	D.S.M.	Askvoll
G. B. Honour	Lt. R.N.V.R.	D.S.C.	Normandy
K. R. Hudspeth	Lt. R.A.N.V.R.	D.S.C.	Altenfjord
		Bar to	
		D.S.C.	Normandy
		Second	
		bar to	
		D.S.C.	Normandy
D. C. Ingram, D.S.C.	Commander R.N.	C.B.E.	Flotilla Duties
D. V. M. Jarvis	Sub-Lt. R.N.V.R.	D.S.C.	Hong Kong
C. E. J. Jenner	Senior Commissioned		
	Shipwright R.N.	M.B.E.	Flotilla Duties
R. H. Kendall	Sub-Lt. R.N.V.R.	D.S.O.	Altenfjord
D. W. Knowelden	Petty Officer Motor		
	Mechanic	D.S.M.	Askvoll
L. A. Larsen, D.S.M.	Quartermaster,		
	R. Norwegian Navy	C.G.M.	Trondhjemsfjord
W. K. Lawrence	Stoker	D.S.M.	La Spezia
J. T. Lorimer	Sub-Lt. R.N.V.R.	D.S.O.	Altenfjord
B. E. McNeill	Ordinary Seaman	D.S.M.	Askvoll
J. J. Magennis	Ldg. Seaman	V.C.	Singapore
W. G. Meeke, D.S.C.	Lt. R.N.	M.B.E.	X-craft Duties
E. H. Munday	Sub-Lt. R.N.V.R.	M.B.E.	Singapore
F. Ogden	Sub-Lt. R.N.V.R.	M.B.E.	Singapore
T. Otway	Chief Petty Officer	B.E.M.	Flotilla Duties
E. V. Page	Sub-Lt. R.N.V.R.	M.B.E.	Altenfjord
P. H. Philip	Lt. S.A.N.F. (V.)	M.B.E.	Altenfjord
B. C. G. Place, D.S.C., V.M.	Lt. R.N.	V.C.	Altenfjord
H. A. Pomery	Ldg. Seaman	D.S.M.	Singapore
C. A. Reed	E.R.A.	C.G.M.	Singapore
K. Richardson	Chief E.R.A.	B.E.M.	X-craft Duties
K. St. J. Robinson	Sub-Lt. R.N.V.R.	D.S.C.	Bergen
M. H. Shean	Lt. R.A.N.V.R.	D.S.O.	Bergen
		Bar to	
		D.S.O.	Saigon

[1] V.M., Virtuti Militari, the Polish V.C.

J. E. SMART	Lt. R.N.V.R.	M.B.E.	Altenfjord
		D.S.O.	Singapore
H. SMITH	Able Seaman	C.G.M.	Palermo
W. J. L. SMITH	Sub-Lt. R.N.Z.N.V.R.	D.S.O.	Singapore
W. S. SMITH	Petty Officer	D.S.M.	Phuket Harbour
J. V. TERRY-LLOYD	Lt. S.A.N.F. (V.)	M.B.E.	Altenfjord
C. E. T. WARREN	Sub-Lt. R.N.V.R.	M.B.E.	Chariot Duties
H. P. WESTMACOTT, D.S.C.	Lt. R.N.	D.S.O.	Bergen
		Bar to D.S.C.	Hong Kong
T. WILLIAMS	Chief Electrical Artificer	B.E.M.	Flotilla Duties
A. WILSON	Lt. R.N.V.R.	M.B.E.	Altenfjord
S. WOOLLCOTT	Petty Officer	D.S.M.	Phuket Harbour

TOTALS

VICTORIA CROSS	4
C.B.E.	3
D.S.O.	11
O.B.E.	1
M.B.E.	10
D.S.C.	17
C.G.M.	6
D.S.M.	12
B.E.M.	4
GRAND TOTAL	68

(In addition to the above there were approximately 100 Mentions in Dispatches.)

III. IN MEMORIAM

The following officers and men were killed in action or on active service while serving in X-craft and Chariots. The four columns show name, rank, whether in Chariots or X-craft, and month and year of death.

P. C. A. Browning	Lt. R.N.V.R.	Chariots	May 1942
J. E. Grogan	Sub-Lt. S.A.N.F. (V.)	Chariots	Oct. 1942
R. Evans	Able Seaman	Chariots	Nov. 1942
I. M. Thomas	Sub-Lt. R.N.V.R.	X-craft	Dec. 1942
C. E. Bonnell, D.S.C.	Lt. R.C.N.V.R.	Chariots	Dec. 1942
S. F. Stretton-Smith	Lt. R.N.V.R.	Chariots	Dec. 1942
J. Sargent	Sub-Lt. R.N.V.R.	Chariots	Dec. 1942
G. G. Goss	Sub-Lt. R.N.V.R.	Chariots	Dec. 1942
J. Kerr	2nd. Lt. H.L.I.	Chariots	Dec. 1942
B. Trevethian	Leading Seaman	Chariots	Dec. 1942
M. Rickwood	Leading Seaman	Chariots	Dec. 1942
R. Maplebeck	Able Seaman	Chariots	Dec. 1942
R. Anderson	Ordinary Seaman R.N.R.	Chariots	Dec. 1942
R. W. Pridham	Stoker	Chariots	Dec. 1942
H. F. Cook	Lt. R.N.V.R.	Chariots	Jan. 1943
W. Simpson	Able Seaman	Chariots	Jan. 1943
D. H. Locke	Sub-Lt. R.N.V.R.	X-craft	May 1943
H. Henty-Creer	Lt. R.N.V.R.	X-craft	Sep. 1943
L. B. Whittam	Lt. R.N.V.R.	X-craft	Sep. 1943
E. Kearon	Sub-Lt. R.N.V.R.	X-craft	Sep. 1943
A. D. Malcolm	Sub-Lt. R.N.V.R.	X-craft	Sep. 1943
T. J. Nelson	Sub-Lt. R.N.V.R.	X-craft	Sep. 1943
R. Mortiboys	E.R.A.	X-craft	Sep. 1943
W. M. Whitley	E.R.A.	X-craft	Sep. 1943
A. H. Harte	Ordinary Seaman	X-craft	Sep. 1943
G. H. Hollett	Stoker	X-craft	Sep. 1943
B. M. McFarlane	Lt. R.A.N.	X-craft	Feb. 1944
W. J. Marsden	Lt. R.A.N.V.R.	X-craft	Feb. 1944
C. Ludbrook	E.R.A.	X-craft	Feb. 1944
J. Pretty	Able Seaman	X-craft	Feb. 1944
P. J. Hunt	Sub-Lt. R.N.V.R.	X-craft	April 1944
K. V. F. Harris	Sub-Lt. R.N.V.R.	Chariots	July 1944
D. N. Purdy	Sub-Lt. R.N.Z.N.V.R.	X-craft	Sep. 1944
A. J. Brammer	Leading Stoker	X-craft	Sep. 1944
A. Staples	Lt. S.A.N.F.(V.)	X-craft	March 1945
J. J. Carroll	Able Seaman	X-craft	March 1945
E. W. Higgins	Stoker	X-craft	March 1945
D. Carey	Lt. R.N.	X-craft	July 1945
B. Enzer	Lt. R.N.V.R.	X-craft	July 1945

IV. GLOSSARY

A.E.D.U.: Admiralty Experimental Diving Unit.

A/S: Anti-submarine, especially of a type of large-mesh, deep net.

A/T: Anti-torpedo, especially of a type of small-mesh, shallow net.

Block-ship: Ship caused to sink in entrance to enemy dock, harbour, fairway, etc., to restrict or prevent enemy traffic.

Bottle: A sharp reprimand (*slang*). Also 'Blast.'

Cafuffle: A commotion (*slang*).

Captain S/M: Captain Submarines. The officer commanding a submarine flotilla.

Catamaran: Twin pontoons secured by a wood and metal framework over which tarpaulins could be stretched. The space between the pontoons was closed at one end and was just large enough to house an *X*-craft. The word comes from the Tamil, where it signifies two or more boats or logs secured together to form a raft. It was more generally used in this sense throughout the Navy.

Codline: Lightweight line of Italian hemp.

Compass button: Item of escape equipment consisting of a small magnetized button.

CQR: A type of light-weight quick-release anchor for small craft. Its initials punningly represent 'secure.'

Dan-buoy: Small buoy, used principally for marking the swept portions of a minefield, consisting of a buoyant can, a flagged pole, and a 3½-cwt. mooring sinker.

D.S.E.A.: Davis Submarine Escape Apparatus.

Duck (Or D.U.K.W.): Type of amphibious vehicle.

E.R.A.: Engine-Room Artificer.

Eyeties: Italians (*slang*). Also 'Ities.'

Fire-ship: Ship freighted with combustibles and set adrift to ignite enemy vessels and installations.

Heads: Lavatory.

H.M.T.: Her (or His) Majesty's Trawler.

Ities: Italians (*slang*).

Jag in: To give up (*slang*).

Jumping wire: Wire running for'ard and aft from a big submarine's periscope-standards, the highest point of the superstructure. Its object is to prevent the gun and bridge-unit fouling any underwater obstacle.

L.C.: Landing craft, the precise type being indicated by a third initial: A, Assault; F, Flak (anti-aircraft); G, Guns; I, Infantry; S, Support; T, Tanks.

L.S.T.: Landing ship, tanks.

M.L.: Motor-launch.

M.T.B.: Motor torpedo-boat.

M.T.S.M.: A special type of motor-boat used by Italian assault-swimmers. (*Italian initials.*)

N.O.: Naval officer.

N.O.I.C.: Naval officer in charge.

Oxylets: Small oxygen cylinders set inside breathing-bag of breathing-apparatus for emergency use.

Pellet buoys: Small circular buoys, approximately two feet in diameter by approximately nine inches deep.

Pongo: Soldier (*slang*).

Pusser: Strictly orthodox. In accordance with naval regulations and practice. From 'Purser.'

Repeater: An electrically operated dial which repeats the reading of a master-instrument. Principally in connexion with the gyro-compass.

Rhino-craft: Type of amphibious vehicle.

Schnorkel: Trunking, pivoted where it joins the pressure-hull, that can be raised to supply a submerged submarine with air, thus enabling the Diesel engines to be run beneath the surface. This process is sometimes known as 'Schnorkelling.' Also 'Snort' and 'Snorting' in anglicized form.

S/M: Submarine.

Spare Crew: Trained personnel (particularly Submarine Service) awaiting appointment. 'Spare crew' pay—somewhere between full submarine and ordinary general service rates—was invariably payable to prisoners-of-war.

Star sight: An observed altitude of a known heavenly body. Used in deep-sea navigation.

Stinker: Bad gale, particularly in the Clyde area.

Stooge-prisoner: Member of the enemy forces masquerading as an Allied prisoner-of-war for the purposes of eliciting information from genuine prisoners.

Stream: To pay out a rope or wire over the side of a vessel under way.

S.U.E.: Signal Underwater Exploding. Underwater signal charge, similar to a small hand-grenade.

Wind Force: Reckoned from Force 0 (Calm), through Force 4 (Moderate Breeze) and Force 8 (Gale), to Force 12 (Hurricane). Known as Beaufort's Notation.

Wiped: De-gaussed. Rendered safe from magnetic mines.

Index

256   ABOVE US THE WAVES

Warhead, human-torpedo, 41–43,
  202, 205 237; securing of, 34, 179–
  180; used on operations, 80, 179–
  180, 206–207
Warr, C. P. O., 106
Warren, Lt. C. E. T., 18–19, 26–34
  (*passim*), 106, 151–152
Washington, Lt. H. E. W., 46–48, 118
Water temperature, 39, 108
West Indies, 512
Westmacott, Lt. H. P., 167–170, 219–
  221, 228, 232–233
White, Stoker, 42
Whitley, E.R.A. W. M., 111–112, 128,
  134–135
Whittam, Lt. L. B., 116, 126, 133–135
Wilson, Lt. A., 126
Wolfe, H.M.S., 202, 204
Woollcott, Petty Officer S., 203–208
Worthy, Able Seaman, 44, 82–83, 88
Wraith, Lt. J. S., 75
W.R.N.S., 214, 235–236

X-CRAFT, production and building of,
  15, 45–46, 110, 210; general description, 15–16, 45–46, 112–113;
  discomfort in, 31, 113; first model,
  45–48, 109–111; size of, 45, 113,
  224; training in, 46–47, 109–119,
  140, 150, 151–157, 158–160; working-up programmes, 46, 152–153,
  195–196, 213, 236; recruitment for,
  47–48, 110, 118, 138, 167, 221;
  towing of, (in training) 115–116,
  119, 152–153, (on operations) 122–
  128, 147–149, 160, 165, 168–169,
  197, 220–222, 228, 231–232; part
  played by, 115; transfer of operational and passage crews of, 116,
  126, 141, 147–148, 160, 165, 168–
  169, 221, 229, 231; tow parting,
  123–125, 222; theory of operating,
  158, 166–167, 223, 231, 237–239;
  inspected by King George VI, 167;
  dissolution of, 234–237; summary
  of achievements of, 235, 237–239.
  See also Attacks, practice; Diesel
  engine; Diver; Main Motor; Passage-crews; Periscope; Side-cargoes; "W and D"; *XE*-craft; and
  individual *X*-craft by numbers
X-craft operations: against *Tirpitz*,
  122–149; in Bergen, 158–170; off
  Normandy beaches, 195–201; in
  Singapore, 220-227; off Saigon, 228-
  233; off Hong Kong, 228, 232–233

X.3, 113, 150, 227; launch of, 45, 46;
  general description of, 45–46; early
  development and trials of, 45–48;
  training with, 109–111
X.4, 111, 113, 150
X.5–10, 110, 113, 118, 154
X.5, 113, 116, 123, 154; operational
  crew transfers off Altenfjord, 126;
  sunk, 135
X.6, 111, 113, 116, 123; departs on
  Tirpitz operation, 122; takes part
  in *Tirpitz* attack, 126–139
X.7, 113, 116, 123; tow parts, 124;
  encounters mine, 127; takes part in
  Tirpitz attack, 126–139
X.8, 113, 116, 123, 227; tow parts,
  123–124; side-cargoes jettisoned,
  125–126; scuttled, 126
X.9, 113, 116, 123; tow parts and
  craft lost, 124–125
X.10, 113, 116, 123; commences
  entry of Altenfjord, 126, 128; is
  forced to retire and has adven-
  turous return journey, 139–148;
  scuttled, 148
X.20–25, 153, 210, 213
X.20, operates in English Channel,
  195, 197, 200
X.22, lost in collision, 158
X.23, 213; operates in English Chan-
  nel, 195–201
X.24, 228; operates in Bergen, 158–
  170
XT.1–6, 153
XT.5, 213
XE-craft, 209
XE.1–6, 215–219, 235
XE.1, 219, 220, 227, 232
XE.3, 218–219, 232, 235; takes part in
  attack on *Takao*, 220–227
XE.4, 219, 220; cuts cables off
  Saigon, 228–233
XE.5, 219, 220, 232–233
XE.6, 218
XE.7–12, 215, 235–236
XE.7, 236
XE.8, 236–237
XE.9, 213, 236
XE.10, 236
XE.11, 236; escape from, following
  sinking, 210–213
XE.12, 234, 236–237
Xiphias, 213

YOUNGMAN, LT.-CDR. R. E., 228
Ytre Reppafjord, 146